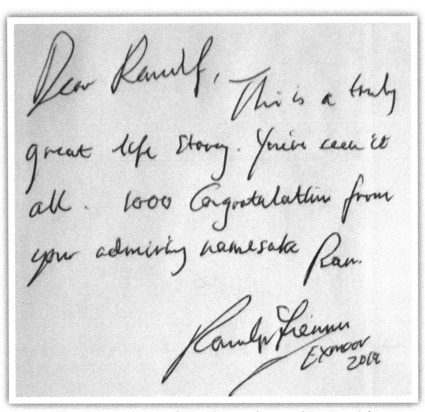

Dear Ranulf,

This is a truly great life Story. You've seen it all. 1000 Congratulations from your admiring namesake Ran.

Ranulph Fiennes

Exmoor 2008

The Guinness Book of World Records named Sir Ranulph
Fiennes as the world's greatest living explorer.

IS ANYONE OUT THERE?

Family group 1938

Robin and Rosie

IS ANYONE OUT THERE?

COMMENTS ON 100 LETTERS TO KEY PEOPLE IN MY LIFE
NOT ANSWERED

With all best wishes

THE MAJOR

November 2019

Rev. date: 10/11/2019

To order additional copies of this book, contact:
Xlibris
800-056-3182
www.Xlibrispublishing.co.uk
Orders@Xlibrispublishing.co.uk
787233

Contents

Letters shown in italics were answered by someone else, or months later.

My book is dedicated to my long suffering wife Annette

INTRODUCTION

My mother had written a letter to my father, who was both a Member of the British Parliament and a major in the British Army, from a mountain chalet high above Garmish Partenkirchen in Germany, just before the outbreak of WWII, saying:

> *We have been ordered to leave immediately before we are interned by Adolf Hitler.*
>
> *In fact it was too early to expect our irascible son to learn to ski or skate and a big mistake to bring him back to Bavaria at all, for, unlike his sister, he is far too difficult to control. This afternoon he covered me with shame and confusion when he biffed an Austrian grand duchess in the bosom. He is so fearfully wilful and determined that I feel quite worn out. Worse still he has a truly terrifying temper! I shall be glad to get home.*

On my return I only remember my father hugging my poor mother.

This letter, obviously, did not require a reply even if there had been time to receive one. But those that deserve a response but don't even get an acknowledgement infuriate me.

I may be getting old and bloody minded; but just as my mother preferred to write to my father rather than telephone him during those dangerous times, I have continued to write letters whatever the circumstances rather than resort to the insecurity of the social media, such as Facebook, texts and emails. Since the advent of word processors and their continuing threat to letter writing, I have always remained determined to put pen to paper while keeping photographs in a scrap book, thus recording for posterity most of the major milestones in my life.

Computers have ruined everything. Everyone now knows everybody and nobody is anybody or anybody nobody any more. I have always been a nobody but like everybody, I have never liked being anybody so letter writing, rather than electronic readouts will continue to come first.

We have all known people who have either transmitted or received messages sent through the ether to the wrong address. I have done so on many occasions and regretted doing so afterwards. On one of them I remember sending an email on behalf of my wife, asking some friends to dinner. Entirely the wrong couple, who my wife could not stand, turned up. A letter would have been better.

But letters are not as easy to delete as electronics and may also be dangerous and held against you later, particularly if you wish to live your life to the full and take a bite out of every chocolate in the box. It is natural, therefore, that all my chocolates are not sweet. Some were intended to leave a bitter taste in the mouths of those less likely to reply to them, so their names and addresses and others who may try and take me to the cleaners for scurrilous or revealing statements - are not always as stated.

My life has been an extraordinary one. As the eldest son of a well-to-do family, born on a beautiful agricultural estate in Devon I was never to own, my silver spoon became quickly tarnished.

After tipping over and escaping from my pram, I had been determined to try every venture and adventure I could dream up, good or bad, all of them at the least possible expense. This resulted in being expelled from five schools until, somehow, I reached public school, where I managed to cling on by my fingernails. Since then readers will notice that my life of adventure has not continued to be that much better.

'Join the army and see the world' was not just a slogan, it was irresistible to many young men after the war and on leaving school I was soon in it hook, line and sinker. The line was fine for a time, but the sinker was not. Since the war the military had remained 'sunk' in a rut of indecision and officer's personal initiatives were often frowned upon. Later, however, as I rose in rank, soon to become an instructor at Sandhurst and then to fly helicopters and command a squadron of armoured cars, 'towing the line' became often unbearable and every attempt I made to deviate from it landed me in trouble. As for seeing the world, if you joined the Royal Armoured Corps like me, forget it. The world was Europe.

So when I resigned, civvy street seemed to present me with more options than Her Majesty had given me although I was totally unemployable which would mean putting my hand in my pocket for a time, at least it enabled me to discover a clear path through the world and to enjoy far more adventures than I had been looking for.

The challenges that have followed, both in business and in pleasure, have been as varied as the chocolates in my box, only having one precious thing in common: the ability to make my own decisions. Since leaving the military I have started no less than thirteen totally different businesses, and written four books, some more successful than others but none making the return I was hoping for. All, however, were accomplished, as I intended, with minimal investment in both time and money. Some of that time, long before I left the army, has been spent writing letters but none of those I have chosen for this book, some to important people and others more important to myself, have ever received a direct answer. However, all of them would be meaningless if I did not include an explanation of why I had written them.

Unlike Henry Root - who in 1980, described in his book of letters, how he sent money to prompt certain people to reply - I have always preferred to use a question mark. In a very few cases my unanswered letters have been acknowledged by someone else, more recently by email, in which case, they are included. But rather than believing in today's world it is only letters that are always read, a few of them being kept for posterity, I have sadly come to the conclusion that most of our young are so immersed in the plethora of electronic perversions now available that they remain glued to their computers, iPhones or tablets for too many hours a day, no longer appreciating what they may see out of the window, or what the postman brings unless it is a refill of computer ink or a brown paper parcel. It is during such moments of deep depression that I feel like shouting to the rooftops **is anyone out there?**

You are and I hope you will enjoy my letters and my comments concerning them. Why none were answered is for you to decide.

Letter

1

Second in command of communications
HQ 21st Army Group
Germany

May 1945

Dear Papa

Thank you very much for the biscuits. A soldier took me on to the road and we saw an English carrier. We threw stones at it and it had to surrender.

Love from

Foxy

Are you coming home soon?

Comment: Why I was ever allowed by my mother to write this letter and that she then posted it to the British Army Headquarters in Germany is a mystery. On the back I had said I am longing to see your trophies.

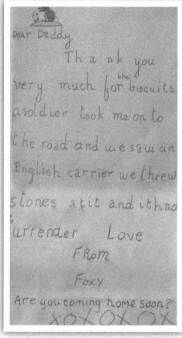

Letter to my father at the Front

First skiing lessons

If it had been opened by the censors it would have got my father into serious trouble. The souvenirs were so sensational, as described later in the book, that no wonder my father did not reply.

Three years previously I had built a tree house by the road at the end of our garden, which had a magnificent view far out over the English Channel, where I knew there were Huns lurking on the other side. One day I was sitting there when a German Heinkel flew past so close that I could see the pilot looking at me. So I ran back into the house as fast as I could to watch the flames light up the sky over Exeter like a firework display, probably unconcerned by all the people being killed there. It was from there that I had bombed the British Bren Gun Carrier with stones, which for me was as good as stopping any armoured vehicle German - or not, and I was proud of it. As a young boy I was fascinated by the war for in June 1940 my father had taken part in the evacuation from

Dunkirk. He told us that two boats had been sunk from under him, although he had never told us very much else except sleeping on a manure heap to keep warm at night. He was lucky to return alive.

After D-Day in June 1944, my father was promoted to become second in command of Field Marshall Montgomery's communications in 21st Army Group as they fought their way through France and Germany finally to reach Luneburg Heath, near Berlin, where Monty took the German surrender.

My father, who died in 1977, had previously enjoyed a remarkable military career, joining the Royal Flying Corps at the age of 16 to serve in WWI. Afterwards, and prior to fighting in the Spanish Civil War, he had then fought on the North West Frontier in India. Yet apart from the letters he sent to his mother, we have no other records of his early wartime experiences. Letters can mean everything and fortunately, we found two others, one sent while he was serving as-aide-de-camp to the governor general of Canada, and the other when he, the Earl of Willingdon, became viceroy of India. Initially, for my father, a life of bears and broncos, then one of maharajas, elephants and tigers, times that no one will ever experience again.

On 6 May 1945, unknown to my father at the time, Monty had issued a directive stating 'Looting by individuals is strictly forbidden. Whatever their rank those found contravening this order will be tried by court marshal'. My father's reputation as a serving member of the Houses of Parliament was paramount, and the fact that I had mentioned bringing back souvenirs from Germany placed him in great danger. Luckily, however, he received my letter unopened and returned from Berlin later that month with his souvenirs in a suitcase without being asked questions.

Letter 2

The Town Council
Windsor
Berks

July 1952

Dear Sirs

I am alarmed by the number of hooligans on the Windsor stretch of the River Thames.

I was rowing my single skuller, referred to by my school as a rigger, when two boys swam out towards me and wrapped their legs around my boat, trying to capsize it. Although they failed it was suggested that I write to you in order to lodge a formal complaint. Can you do something about this?

Yours faithfully

RR

Comment: I was unsure what a 'formal complaint' actually meant other than writing an angry letter. However it was presented it would, no doubt, have been thought frivolous by the council who, I was sure, did not like Etonians.

House Bumping four

Stroking the second Eton eight at Henley Royal Regatta

It was all part of a young man's learning curve. I recognised that I was spoilt and had led far too sheltered a life but hopefully, I was not being arrogant. Perhaps a better solution would have been to knock the two pirates off my boat with an oar, thus inviting them to take a sip themselves from Father Thames. But it was more likely that I would have taken the sip! The river had been an important part of my upbringing, and it was probably due to my love of sport that I had been granted a place in the school at all. Education had always come second and I continued to hate the discipline of school life.

My first school, in the nearby town of Dawlish, had been for girls, where I had been sent to accompany my elder sister. I was the only boy there but not being old enough to appreciate it, I began to hate the silly girls so much that I ran away and was driven home by the local butcher.

My second school had been evacuated to a nearby castle to avoid the bombs being dropped on London. The cook thought she could avoid all the constraints of rationing by feeding us on leeks, which, when their smell became overpowering, I felt so unwell that I walked back home to my mother, who, for some reason, did not send me back again.

My father, in desperation, then escorted me to a school run by a far stricter headmaster in the seaside town of Teignmouth. There happened to be an old fox's 'earth' in the garden; and while the gardener was on holiday, I managed to pinch his spade and with five other boys dig the 'earth' out as our secret lair. We had been experimenting by smoking different varieties of leaves inside it, when, one day while I was out foraging for them, it caved in and four of the boys were buried. Although they were all dug out alive, I was expelled and sent home immediately.

It was therefore not surprising that for my next school I would be banished to Berkshire. It had a lake in the grounds surrounded by bushes where some boys had discovered an old rusty scythe hooked over a laurel branch. They had no idea how to use it, so I took a swing myself and almost severed the leg off a boy standing too close behind me. The boy later became an important minister; but although we managed to staunch his blood, I made it no further than to the headmaster's study.

So finally my exasperated parents sent me to a crammer in Hampshire, where my nose would be kept to the grindstone, until I had passed my exams into Eton. But before long I fell in love with the headmaster's 16 year old daughter. Although she was spirited away to London as soon as we were found together, on completing my exams my father was summoned, who, in a towering rage, drove me back fast to Devon.

At Eton, my life changed again dramatically but not always for the best. Old traditions died hard at the school, and my indoctrination as a 'fag', or as a new boy looking after an old boy in the house 'library', soon came unstuck when

I failed to answer his cry of 'Boy'! The result was a flogging by the captain of fives, a game that encouraged players with strong wrists. It was not the only game with a difference at Eton because there was also the field game and the wall game, neither having much to do with my passion for water.

The smell of fresh varnish in an Eton Boathouse and the sight of hundreds of shiny brown needles, all built there by craftsmen, stacked high up on shelves, will never leave anyone who became a 'wet bob'. I tried out all of them during my time there, graduating quickly to a 'rigger', which I rowed through 'Locks' on summer days to drink a pint of shandy at Queen's Eyot, an island that had a bar serving drinks, hopefully not diluted with Thames water. But my best fun was rowing in the house bumping four. On the bows I had attached a black and white swordfish with a moustache, representing our house master and our house colours, which terrorised the opposition. Finally, before leaving, I was invited to stroke the Eton second eight at the Henley Royal Regatta.

Letter 3

Major General Reginald Hobbs
Royal Military Academy Sandhurst
Camberley

June 1954

Dear General Hobbs

During my time at Sandhurst I have been trying my hand at most things including a fuels and explosive course, which I joined because I felt it would be an important addition to my military training. But I have now been taken off it. It was perhaps unfortunate that when I lit a bunsen burner in the lab, I had no idea that the asbestos surrounding it would explode if soaked, inadvertently, in TNT.

It was an accident and, although it broke a window, it was not a major catastrophe, so please may I now be reinstated on the course?

Yours sincerely

RR

Comment: Some officer cadets had previously placed notices on the road through Camberley, which was then a main route to the West Country, and diverted all the traffic through the Sandhurst grounds.

Testing stamina!

On parade (Author in the rear rank)

The finger had been pointed in my direction but on that occasion, although I was already regarded to be a loose cannon, I was innocent.

So, although in my letter to the Commandant I had thought of mentioning the idea of soaking cigarette papers in TNT and sending them to the enemy, luckily I had refrained from doing so.

After first driving to Sandhurst in an old 1934 two seater Wolseley Hornet, I had hidden it away in a Camberley garage as it greatly facilitated taking the girls out in London when I was not polishing my boots. But as it had no floorboards, all male passengers had to wear bicycle clips around their trouser legs while girls in skirts found the experience far more challenging. The Duke of Kent, who was a fellow cadet, also enjoyed the odd outing, but once, having invited him to join me in a car rally, he landed up pushing the Hornet for over a mile.

Sandhurst was an extraordinary-enough experience, meeting young men of my age from all over the world, many of whom were to return to command their national armies in due course or sometimes to run their countries. One of these was to become the King of Jordan. Years later, I was crossing from Le Havre to Southampton on a channel ferry when, over the Tannoy, I was instructed to report to a cabin on the upper deck. The king had noticed me on the boat and had invited me to tea with him.

While I was at Sandhurst one of my favourite extramural activities as they were called, was learning to fly a glider. Lasham Airfield was not far away and had a magnificent perimeter track. So when I became bored waiting for others to take their turn, I would set off in the Hornet to break the track record. Then, one afternoon, I lost two wheels, landing upside down in a hay stack. 'Bloody fool' swore my flying instructor.

For most officer cadets memories of Sandhurst were about being drilled to exhaustion on the square by a regimental sergeant major. 'Now work like black.., oriental gentlemen' yelled RSM Jackie Lord on a day to remember. He was still there five years later marching straight towards me with his pace stick, when I returned, to everyone's surprise, as an instructor. I flew to get my hat from my car in order to return his salute and to hide my hair as he hammered down his mirror like boots beside me. 'Good morning Captain' he said, and when I asked him how he remembered me, he simply replied, 'Long hair, sir.'

RSM Lord had been captured by the Germans at Arnhem, subsequently keeping up prisoners' morale in his POW camp by parading them with wooden rifles. Such men, I soon discovered, were the salt of the earth.

Letter 4

The War Graves Commission
Maidenhead, Berks

December 1955

Dear Sirs

Last month, after I had first joined my regiment on an exercise at the Hohne training area in North Germany, I was given the day off. Before returning to Detmold, however, I visited the Belsen concentration camp with two other officers.

We were particularly shocked by the mass graves but were surprised that the buildings had been destroyed. Then on walking into the pine trees, we came across a pile of the inmate's boots. Should they not be put on display somewhere?

Yours faithfully

RR

Comment: Belsen was not an extermination camp, but more than 50,000 wretched victims had died there through disease and malnutrition.

On exercise at Hohne   Irma Grese

Among them had been the young Jewish poet Anne Frank, the German girl snatched from the Holland. The British liberators found unburied corpses everywhere. But the camp workers from nearby Bergen denied all knowledge of its conditions and of its sadistic German guards. Two off these - Josef Kramer (The Beast of Belsen), who was the camp commandant, and Irma Grese (The beautiful beast), who carried a whip and ran the women's quarters - had both been at Auschwitz. They were later hanged for their appalling war crimes. However the War Graves Commission did not deal with such atrocities. Belsen had put the shivers down our spines for we had just experienced such extremes of cold weather in Northern Germany that the thought of fighting for your life in such a dreadful place, particularly during the winter, was for us unimaginable. When I joined my regiment at Hohne I will never forget the first freezing night I spent with my troop of tanks nearby on Luneburg Heath. Indeed it was hard to conjure up the image of Monty taking the German surrender there in May 1945, bathed in sunshine, only ten years previously. That occasion, watched by my father, is included in one of my letters much later in the book.

I had looked everywhere for a decent spot to park my troop of four tanks for the night but could find none. As far as the eye could see there was black mud covered with snow, with ice-covered pools everywhere. But worse were the trees, still recovering from heavy shelling during the war. They jutted up from the mud, through torn-off branches, like rotten teeth, and completed a horrifying scene of total devastation.

Jumping off my tank to find one of those trees during the night had been sheer lunacy. I had removed my thick tank gloves and then failed to put them on again before reaching up to the 20-pounder gun in order to hoist myself back up into the turret across the armoured plating. As I did so, my feet slipped on the front glacis plate, designed to deflect enemy shells; and I suddenly found myself suspended by one hand, now frozen solid to the gun barrel. I seemed to hang there for hours and then, as the cold crept into my body and my cries of help began to fade, unheeded by my three tank crew fast asleep behind the turret on the still warm engine deck, at last I saw the guard I had appointed, approaching the same tree. 'Stop' I croaked. 'Come quickly and pee over my frozen hand right here.'

He did; and for a long week, as we played soldiers with tanks that often failed to start in the subzero temperatures, I had to endure leading my troop through the mud and ice wearing a stinking heavy tank suit. Although nothing could equal the horrors of seeing that Nazi concentration camp with its fringe of dark pine trees outlined against a cruel sky, I will also not forget the wrath of my squadron leader. 'You bloody fool' he said.

Letter 5

Forstmeister Keimer
Bad Lippespringe
Germany

March 1956

Dear Forstmeister

I have to report that I was the officer in charge when one of our Centurion tanks caught fire on the edge of your forest during tank driving instruction Fortunately, due to the extreme winter weather conditions, it caused little more damage than destroying a few of your pine trees. Do you require compensation?

Our many apologies.

Yours sincerely

RR 2 Lt

Comment: Forstmeister Keimer had been one of Hitler's top foresters during WWII and had been awarded the Iron Cross. Indeed, I remember a room in his lodge being adorned with swastikas. He frowned on the British officer class and obviously thought that our tank driver training at Sennelager was a joke.

My tank driving course   Wild boar

He was also upset that we had not done considerably more damage; for the compensation paid to German farmers and foresters at that time was substantial when caused by British military vehicles.

The only reason for writing was that I had been ordered to do so by my irate commanding officer; indeed, the following winter, when Keimer, surprisingly, asked our colonel to send two officers to accompany him in the forests of the Teutoburger Wald wild boar shooting. I was one of those detailed.

Soon after returning from Hohne, the adjutant had summoned me to his office at our barracks in Detmold and asked me to run the tank driving instruction on the nearby Sennelager training area, where German Tiger tanks had limbered up during the war. There was still a hard frost and when trooper Brown, one of our regimental team of instructors, drove me up a steep hillside to show me the extent of the training area, I was unaware that I was about to undergo their young officers initiation test. But no one had ever taken a 50-tonne tank over a 20-metre long jump when the ground was so hard. So when Brown tried desperately to find a gear as the tank flew through the air, a fan blade flew off as we hit the ground with a crunch and punctured the fuel tanks. The Centurion immediately burst into flames and as we jumped for our lives while it careered off into the valley below, we could only watch as it crashed into the forest, burning fiercely. 'You have just written off £100,000 of Her Majesty's property,' scowled the colonel. 'How do you expect to pay for it?'

The forest, where the tank had expired covered over a thousand square kilometres, and it teemed with wild boar. I was therefore surprised when Forstmeister Keimer instructed us not to shoot the first tusker to break cover. Climbing up onto a high seat hidden in the snow-laden trees I at once took a bead though the sights of my army .303 rifle on a huge black boar as he charged towards me followed by some baying dachshunds. But I did not pull the trigger. 'If you shoot the first pig to break cover' Keimer had explained, they all scatter and are impossible to find again.' The pigs had not scattered; and after becoming a reluctant snowman, I descended my ladder to find out what was going on.

'You bloody fool' swore Keimer. 'You should have shot him for he was the only pig in there!' I was not invited back again.

Letter
6

Managing Director
Underwater products
Norfolk

June 1957

Dear Sir

I write only because I have had a near disaster while swimming with one of your aqualungs. Diving off Majorca with a friend who has written books about the sport of underwater spear fishing, my reserve valve became jammed at 120 feet. Had it not been for my friend releasing it, I would never have made it back to the surface.

The valve, as you well know, is situated at the top end of the air cylinder behind one's head. It is always awkward to manipulate, particularly if the valve is stiff. Is there any way you could re-design the valve before someone dies?

Yours faithfully

RR

Comment: The ancient sport of fishing with a spear benefited greatly from the advent of the aqualung developed by Jacques Cousteau just before the end of WWII. Indeed one of the first experimental models had been destroyed in 1944 by a shell during an assault by British troops on a beach in the South of France.

Our host and mentor

Armed with sea lances

My parents had built a holiday house looking over the water near Formentor in Majorca during the late 1930s and after the war were fortunate that a Yugoslavian ship owner had asked them if he could share the house with them, which was becoming too expensive to manage. He had competed for his country in the Olympics and was an expert scuba diver. Having arriving back on holiday there in May 1957 we did not have to wait long before a fast motor launch called *Taro*, equipped exclusively for spearfishing, dropped anchor beneath the house; and after a brief session in the villa's swimming pool, learning how to use compressed air equipment, early the following morning we were rowed out to *Taro by* a well known local smuggler to try it out. We lay for an hour on white towelled bunks, listening to the engines, before being squeezed into wetsuits and fitted with the re-charged aqualungs.

We noticed that we were not far from a high cliff and when our host explained how it shelved away steeply below, we realised that we were not just going for a trial run, but were off to find Davy Jones's locker. That first descent to 120 feet, carrying a sea lance rather than a spear gun, was, in hindsight, totally irresponsible. On reaching the rock-strewn bottom, I attempted to bag a large grouper; but when my lance became stuck in a crevice, I stupidly knocked my mask sideways while trying to retrieve it. Sea water was pouring in but as I struggled to replace the mask over my face, I exhausted my air supply. When I then discovered that the reserve valve would not turn on, I realised, trying not to panic, that I was about to die.

The Yugoslav wasn't watching, but my youngest brother Andrew managed to alert him. Thankfully, he swam back to free the valve giving me two more minutes of air, and pointed towards the surface. However, too hasty a swim from such a depth may give you the bends, or bubbles in the blood, which can be fatal; so I swam up slowly, only pausing to spear a moray eel, which I had spied hissing from a hole in the rock face with 20 feet still to go. But as I surfaced below the safety dinghy, now totally out of breath with the eel gnashing beneath my feet, I almost died for a second time. The untrained boatman had seen a patrol boat approaching and as we were fishing in a restricted area, he pushed my head underwater again and, despite my gesticulations, held it there. When the Yugoslav arrived to pull me out, they pumped my chest for an hour before I was pronounced to be still living.

Today, but not due to my letter, which could have seriously implicated the equipment manufacturers, diving gear has been so radically improved that scuba diving is controlled easily by pressing buttons.

Letter
7

Director Swiss Alpine Club
Postfach 2000. Bern
Switzerland

May 1962

Dear Director,

I recently completed the Haute Route from Verbier to Zermatt with a party of friends and was shocked to find the state of your mountain huts was so deplorable. While skiing over the pristine slopes of the alps our party were so inflicted by the bites from bed bugs that we were lucky, when trying to scratch them, not to fall into a crevasse.

I am currently writing the account about our ordeal for a magazine and would like your assurances that your mountain huts will be properly fumigated in future and cleaned to a more acceptable standard.

Your sincerely

RR

Comment: Today the Swiss Alpine Club advertises their huts - which are often built on steep mountainsides many miles from civilisation, only attainable on skis, or on foot in summer, as - 'providing basic, comfortable accommodation, where guests may enjoy an unforgettable mountain experience directly in contact with nature'.

Haute Route   Mountain Hut

Back in 1962, the huts could also have been described as 'basic' and that was totally understandable. But the 'unforgettable experience' would have been better described as 'directly in conflict with nature'.

The Haute Route, which crosses 50 miles of the roof of the world, normally starts at Chamonix but as we were foolishly setting out when it was not yet spring, and we had been told that it was the earliest in the year that the High Route had ever been attempted, we decided to miss out the first leg and set out from Verbier instead. In those days there was no lift up to the Cabin Mont Fort, which was the first mountain hut in which to spend the night, except to climb there on 'skins', or seal skins tied to the bottom of the skis, which, with their fur pointing backwards, provided sufficient grip on the snow to ski steeply upwards.

Our first night was an experience in itself for it was possible to see down over a thousand feet through the bottom of the loo. We were carrying all our rations with us in heavy knapsacks; but before we set out that first morning, we were, at least, given a crust of black bread and a mug of even blacker coffee. Then, of course, there were those bedbugs to attend to, for which we had no other answer than the now banned DDT powder, which we had been advised to take with us.

Some eight Frenchmen were also sleeping in the hut; and encouraged by our favourable weather report, they had the temerity to leave before us. We were rounding a bluff of rock when our guide, Rudi, who was finding it easier to follow in the tracks of the French who had kindly punched though the last heavy snowfall of winter, shouted 'Stop!' Slowly but surely, the mountain ahead of us was breaking away at the top; and we witnessed a mighty avalanche bouncing down over the crags with increasing velocity until it hit the glacier, now glinting in the sunlight far below, with a deafening roar.

'The French!' a friend shouted; and as we recovered from the shockwave of the avalanche, which had almost knocked some of us sideways, we could see that half of their party had been buried.

We threw our skis off and rushed forward to save those we could with our bare hands as Rudi dug frantically with his shovel. 'Quick, over here' he shouted at me 'this one is injured but still alive. Climb up to that window in the mountain, where they are building a hydro-electric tunnel, and you should be able to find a field telephone. Then call Hermann Geiger fast!' We waited for the sound of an aero engine but when at last the most famous mountain pilot in the world landed his Pilatus Porter ski plane deftly on the snow below us, the Frenchman had died.

Our six day ordeal was only just beginning. Between snow storms the sun became so hot that choosing the right protective gear became almost impossible. Then grabbing too hastily in my rucksack for a tube of factor 50 suncream, I covered my face in toothpaste! The result was so painful that I all I wanted to do was dive headfirst into the snow if there had been any, but we were climbing over bare rock and ice swept by such a cruel wind that there was no soft snow in sight.

Later, as we continued to follow the tracks of our guide, the cloud came down and completely enveloped us. 'Stop' shouted Rudi, who we could no longer see in the whiteout 'we have gone wrong. Below us is a very nasty drop.' Rather than investigate, and before any of us had attempted to creep any further forward, Rudi skied carefully back and told us to help him dig a deep snow hole for us to wait in until he could locate the route to the last of our mountain huts. It was an hour before he returned and when he did just as the cloud lifted and the blazing sun returned, we found ourselves teetering on the edge of a 3,000 foot abyss.

Finally, having somehow avoided the last crevasses, snow blindness prevented us from telling one girl friend waiting in Zermatt from another.

The Secretary, The Alpine Club
Charlotte Road, London.

May 1962

Dear Sir

I have just returned from climbing the Matterhorn. My Zermatt guide, Ricky Andermatten, with whom I have climbed and skied for many years, was determined that I should try to achieve the record time for an Englishman to reach the summit.

When we set out from the Hornli Hut in darkness, the only other climber, a Scotsman wearing a kilt, was asleep snoring. But after a strenuous climb, when we reached the top we found him already there, together with his guide waiting for us. Would he qualify for the record?

Yours sincerely

RR

Comment: I had bust a gut trying to achieve the record, whatever it was; and nothing was more aggravating than finding that hairy fellow waiting for us at the top!

The Matterhorn 14,692ft

But I still do not know what the record time is for an Englishman to reach the summit, although today's climbers bolstered by performance enhancers and better equipment, would make my attempt look pathetic.

Apart from Mount Everest, the Matterhorn is regarded as the most iconic mountain in the world. It is also considered to be one of the most dangerous. By 1980, 18 years after I had climbed the peak. it was calculated that over 500 people had perished on the mountain. Today, with so many attempting the climb the Matterhorn, that number of fatalities must have increased alarmingly. It is no wonder, therefore, that trying to break any record is frowned upon by the authorities.

Because the mountain originally instilled so much fear, it was one of the last peaks in the Alps to be conquered. That was finally achieved by a party led by the British mountaineer Edward Whymper in 1865, but it ended in tragedy when four of his companions fell thousands of feet to their deaths when descending near the summit. If the rope had not broken, Whymper, with two other climbers, would have died with them.

There are four sides to the Matterhorn which gives the impression of rising almost vertically above impressive glaciers with each side facing a point of the compass. These are intersected by four ridges, which have all since been climbed many times. Whymper chose the now popular Hornli ridge up which with my guide Ricky, I had climbed the mountain.

The Matterhorn is not as steep as it looks until you near the top when there is a frightening traverse across the apex of the North Face before reaching the summit at over 14,000 feet. But crossing that traverse, where it is better not to look down, is now made safer with fixed ropes.

Before tackling the Matterhorn it is normal for guides to take their clients to a lower peak from which, after sharing a bar of chocolate, they may be lowered over a precipice to test their courage. Too many guides have lost their lives due to their clients panicking. The mountain is particularly dangerous due to its isolation and therefore its tendency to experience rapid changes in the weather. Also, it is prone, like many others, to terrifying rock falls when the sun rises and its frozen surface starts heating up. For that reason climbers normally set out a long time before dawn hoping to return before the ice begins to melt. If the Hornli ridge is being attempted that means, as I had discovered, setting out the evening before and struggling up a very steep incline to the Hornli hut, which is perched on a precipice high above Zermatt, and then attempting to sleep on a straw filled pallias until woken by the guide - or, in my case, by that hairy kilted Scotsman.

Letter
9

Major-General George Gordon-Lennox
Commandant, Royal Military Academy Sandhurst
Camberley, Surrey

October 1962

Dear General

I am writing to explain my part in exercise 'Beau Geste'.

Before we left for Libya I invited my cadets to buy as many packets of cigarettes as possible. On arrival in Tripoli, we used them to hire a sufficient number of camels to mount every officer cadet and their kit under my command. We thus captured the objective a day early.

It may have been, as you say, 'gung ho,' but I can assure you that Cadet's Cavalry have not only learned all about surprise, but also how to use their initiative in any theatre of war, including the desert.

Yours sincerely

RR Captain.

Comment: Half of the eight hundred officer cadets at Sandhurst were to take part in operation 'Beau Geste' one of the military exercises arranged every year to test their fighting skills. 'Serve to Lead' was the Sandhurst motto, with its influence spreading throughout the world.

'Beau Geste' orders group   "Interested in hiring my camels?"

Officers in the British Army are subject to an annual report written by the senior officer commanding at the time. so I was concerned that the general who was a guardsman, better known as a 'beetle crusher' by the British cavalry, would frown on my attempt to take the objective by such foul means and would write me off as an eccentric young officer not fit to command anybody. There was no way back, so I devoted the remainder of my three years instructing at Sandhurst mostly to sport, while avoiding most field work, including too many exercises, or wearing military uniform more than absolutely necessary. Afterwards I was forced to when I went on an army flying course at Middle Wallop in Hampshire.

Sandhurst, surprisingly, suited my lifestyle extremely well; and the cadets who passed out despite my unconventional methods of instruction now remember me more as an officer who was seldom there. Being a cavalry officer, I was soon running every equine event on offer including the Sandhurst drag hunt, the saddle club, and the Sandhurst polo team. Life became even better when I was invited to take over the Sandhurst ski team. Then there was also sailing and paragliding. On one occasion, while being watched by some gaping cadets, I was descending by parachute directly onto my chasing black Labrador, when one of them tackled her in the nick of time. Infuriatingly, it led to me cancelling some London engagements while visiting him in hospital. I did, however, give him full marks on his confidential report for bravery.

My favourite subject was teaching military history, and the importance of reading letters written by such great leaders as Napoleon and Wellington. But only too often my cadets, one of whom Quaboos bin Said al Said, was later to become the Sultan of Oman, tended to nod off.

Perhaps I was taking advantage of the Queen's shilling, but as there were no wars to be fought at he time I felt, like many of my contemporaries, that the only way to be a successful soldier during peacetime was to lead from the front with compassion and common sense, to be competitive both in everyday life and in sport, and try one's hand at any worthwhile opportunity that presented itself. It was much the same spirit that I hoped to imbue in all those I was responsible for during my three years serving again at Camberley. Being the youngest of all the Sandhurst instructors at the time, many of the cadets, who were not far behind me in years, became friends for life, some even thanking me for what I had taught them when I was fortunate enough to catch up with them later. 'How did I manage to teach you anything?' I would ask them 'when I was so seldom on parade.' In fact most officers at Sandhurst were so determined to become generals, that whenever I wanted to escape they were only too eager to teach cadets in my place.

Letter 10

Chief of Staff Military Aviation
Ministry of Defence
Via Venti Settembre, Rome

September 1963

Dear Sir

You were contacted by our mutual friend Sheila about the aircraft I crashed with my brother north of the mountains near Albenga.

This is to thank you and the Italian Airforce for retrieving our crashed Auster, for repairing it superbly while most of your countrymen were on holiday, and for then delivering it to the airfield at Albenga.

We would now like to write up the story in your top aviation magazine. Please will you kindly tell me whom to contact?

Yours sincerely

RR

Comment: With my brother Nicholas, who was also an army pilot, we had decided that driving home to Devon from Middle Wallop took a tedious amount of time, particularly in summer, and was an unnecessary bore.

Refuelling   Buzzing Monte Carlo

So we drove to the nearby Thruxton civilian airfield and bought ourselves an ancient Auster aeroplane for £700, deciding that her proving flight would be to Rome.

We almost made it but off the coast of the Italian Riviera, we flew into a violent electrical storm and crashed into a field. Our army leave was expiring fast and if it had not been for the Italian Air Force, there would have been plenty of flack to deal with on our return. Sheila, the girlfriend we had flown to see in Porto Ercole, had told the Chief of Staff that we were reporters from England's *Flight Magazine*. We were therefore unlikely to get a reply, for having called on the Italian Air Force to repair our machine rather than a civilian outfit, the Italian general had probably broken every rule in the book.

The idea of flying such an antique aircraft to Rome, which had been built barely 30 to 40 years after that flown by Louis Bleriot across the English Channel, was crazy, but although the aircraft had no electrics, therefore no lights, radio or navigational aids and only a few crude instruments, we almost made it.

The flight had begun badly, for on looking for our newly acquired Auster in a hangar at Thruxton aerodrome, it had vanished. 'Just trying it out before your great expedition' joked the mechanic, who had been flying it somewhere up in the clouds without a pilot's license. He had already found that the pitot head, measuring the air speed, had a birds nest in it!

We had planned to cross over the channel the long way via the Isle of Wight. But we had flown in the wrong direction around the circuit of a small airfield there and had met another aircraft coming in the opposite direction.

The air had turned blue and we had been told to get the hell out of it almost before we had managed to refuel. It was then by dead reckoning across the channel to Le Mans, where we spent our first uncomfortable night on the concrete floor of an old Nissen hut built on the edge of the airfield. The next morning, closely following the roads to Clermont-Ferrand, we picked up more fuel before flying down the magnificent Rhone Valley and crossing the toe of the Alps to land, as it became dark, at Cannes Aero-Club d'Antibes.

We had not noticed that every other flying machine on the field was protected from the scorching August sun by a canopy and because all the pumps were closed, we had failed to fill up, which can be a fatal mistake, causing petrol fumes to expand and strain the seams of an aircraft's fuel tank. Our final mistake was to spend a foolish stop-over enjoying ourselves in Cannes before returning to the tiny airport.

We had tried to hitchhike into the town, but that does not work if you are just a couple of tramps.

So by then totally exhausted, we decided to sleep on the beach on a pile of umbrellas, only to be arrested by two Gendarmes the next morning. 'Non' said one of them; but before he was able to continue, we had thrown ourselves into the sea. Fortunately they found a more interesting couple farther along the beach; so in the end, they gave up. 'Sacre bleu,' they must have said.

I have always been lucky; but it was uncanny that on wading ashore we saw a rich banking friend of our parents jogging towards us.

'Boys' he exclaimed 'what the hell are you doing here in all that wet flying gear?' And when we explained our mission, which he did not understand, he invited us up to have breakfast at his penthouse suite in the Majestic Hotel. We soon discovered that he had a 'gin palace' tied up in the harbour in which we then sailed for St Tropez. There we spied a trawler full of girls from the Folies Bergere getting brown all over; but sadly, on returning by taxi to look for them, we drew a blank.

When we took off once more, although a week had gone by, we could not resist flying low past Monte Carlo harbour before heading east again.

A close shave!

The problem was that wind and weather were only forecast in French territorial waters at the time; and as we flew along the coast we hit such a violent electrical storm that it blocked our way, right from the foaming sea to a altitude higher than our little aircraft could achieve. So the only option left was to bank steeply away from the black wall of water and fly inland or farther out to sea. But as we banked the fuel tank, which was mounted in front of the instrument panel, suddenly burst along its seams sending petrol spewing over our legs. 'Unlatch the windows' I shouted at my brother, fearing we were about to catch fire, but a gust of wind then blew the partition out of the rear of the cabin into the fuselage, solidly jamming the flying controls.

Such moments are the stuff of nightmares, and as we fell into a frightening dive while my brother tried to free the controls, the engine stopped. High winged aircraft don't land in the sea; and the beaches of the Italian Riviera in high summer were still covered in umbrellas and shivering holiday makers. Worse still, behind line of the beach were higher mountains than we could easily glide over, stretching as far as the eye could see.

It was only by luck that in a fleeting moment we saw a tiny gap between two mountain tops through the driving rain, so we headed towards it and almost scraping our belly on the rocks, dropped like a stone into a field of hollyhocks, bending our propeller like a banana and ripping off the undercarriage. But for Sheila our dead aircraft would still be lying there.

Letter 11

Brigadier S. Meath
The Army Flying School
Middle Wallop

November 1963

Dear Brigadier

Before I started my flying course I asked you to release me for three weeks during January in order to continue captaining the Army Team on the Cresta Run in St Moritz if my flying was up to scratch. But, although first agreed, you have now refused to do so.

Although I had an earlier reprimand from you, I have since had an entirely clean sheet on my helicopter course. I must, therefore, ask your permission to write to an officer of more senior rank?

Yours sincerely

RR

Comment: Having received no reply, I wrote accordingly to a general I knew, who just happened to be second in command of the British Army. The letter came winging back covered in red ink where I had made spelling and punctuation mistakes; but the general, who later became the principal of London University, and was a Cresta enthusiast, said in his covering letter that although it was unusual for such a junior officer to write to one so senior in such terms, permission was granted.

The army flying school at Middle Wallop was renowned as being one of the top flyng schools in the world. Students were first trained to fly fixed-wing Chipmunks in all weathers; and if they qualified, they would then graduate from piston engine to gas-turbine-powered helicopters. The school was run by a mix of army and RAF personnel, Eddie my instructor being a former RAF aerobatic ace with a splendid beard. 'Take her up to 3,000ft' he had demanded on my first day flying solo 'then I want to see you recover from a spin.' It was a frightening command after less than ten hours of instruction, and I must have blanched visibly.

On our final day of the fixed-wing course I decided with Garry, an officer in the Irish Guards, that for our last hurrah we would switch to our own radio frequency and then fly west down Southampton Water. All was well until Garry saw a liner approaching. 'Hello Red Leader!' he yelled over the radio, 'Bandits 200!' Without a second thought, we both peeled off and dived steeply towards her masts.

The fully aerobatic Chipmunk

My hell to fly Hiller

You 'bloody idiots' Eddie spat through his beard, jumping onto the wing of my Chipmunk after we landed 'All my efforts have been in vain. Both of you have been low flying and you are to report to the CFI (chief flying instructor) immediately.'

The CFI was a RAF wing commander with a whacko moustache; and as he thumped his desk, I could see that he was in a towering rage. He hated me already for parking our scruffy Auster in one of his hangars and he spoke briefly and to the point. We had been spotted by the keeper of the Needles Lighthouse diving between the masts of the liner *United States of America*. We had, therefore, disobeyed every rule in the book. Unless we had something to say, we would be returned to our units forthwith. 'Sir' I said 'two days ago, I saw Alpha Romeo executing a loop over Basingstoke, also against rules. Looking the Chipmunk up in the log I found that you were flying it. 'Case dismissed' he growled.

The Chipmunk was a fully aerobatic but stable aircraft but the chopper which followed was a nightmare. The Hiller had been chosen for its instability. Moving one control meant adjusting four others. If you raised the lever with your left hand to apply pitch for takeoff, you then had to twist the grip on it to increase power while with your right hand move the stick forward, thus gaining speed and tilting the rotor to obtain lift, while operating the foot pedals to prevent yaw. It was tricky, but not as frightening as the Hiller's lack of power, which I soon discovered when aiming it at the trunks of trees to gain sufficient lift to get out of forest clearings. Helicopter controls are now far better integrated.

Letter 12

Captain Nick Ganter, Station Commander
Royal Naval Air Station Yeovilton
Ilchester, Somerset

October 1964

Dear Captain Ganter

I must apologise. Probably against regulations I had flown over to Yeovilton from Middle Wallop in my latest type of military helicopter yesterday with the intention of giving Mark my opposite number on the Cresta Run, a ride in it.

As a fair exchange he had taking me for a flight in your 'Captain's Barge', when I, stupidly, pulled the wrong lever.

Unknown to him your staff had fitted me with a pressure suit and believing I was 'aircrew', not a chopper pilot, had not put me through the normal cockpit drills. Thank you for such a stimulating flight!

RR

Comment: Ruddy Pongo the station commander must have thought, 'How can he pull a lever, so clearly painted in black and yellow stripes?'

The *Captain's Barge* was a Hawker Hunter training aircraft in which the pilot and his pupil sit side by side. Painted dark blue with naval insignia, it was the commander of the naval air station's pride and joy. Surprisingly, it was the same aircraft that later crashed at the 2015 Shoreham Air Show killing seven people on a nearby road but not the pilot. Although the Hunter was by then in its sunset years, it had been well maintained and was in excellent condition. It was therefore concluded that the pilot had foolishly looped the aircraft from a dangerously low altitude.

The helicopter I had since graduated to at Middle Wallop was an Alouette III straight from the Aerospatiale factory in France. I was proud of it, and it played an important role for me later in the Alps and then on my sales trip around the world. It had a gas turbine engine and a wrap around envelope affording good cockpit visibility, but after my mistake, my friend was no longer keen to fly with me! At first, however, we were unable even to find it, hidden away by the Navy between two hangars.

Mark was at that time captain of the Royal Navy team on the Cresta Run and I was captain of the British Army team, so we had plenty in common, particularly when it came to bravado.

The Captain's Barge

My Alouette helicopter at Yeovileton.

Like most of us he was always partial to the odd flirtation, this time, once we were airborne, with his female controllers on the ground. 'Hello, this is Mark in Hunter Victor Lima flying at Mach point eight directly over Bristol. How was that dinner last night?'

Mark had told me to prepare for some violent manoeuvres culminating with a Derry Turn, but had failed to ask me first if I was comfortable. I had already tried hard to get his attention as my bone dome was touching the canopy and I needed to adjust my seat. So I pointed at the black and yellow lever and thought he had agreed with a nod; but afterwards, he said he had nodded sideways. I pulled the lever and there was a terrifying bang. Being ejected at that speed may end you up with a broken back or far worse; but somehow I was still there, like a white ghost, not strapped in. I had pulled the crash-release lever, which had caused my stressed harness to slap against the side of the cockpit. It could not be refastened.

Looking across at Mark I could see a glint in his eye; as now totally loose in the Martin Baker ejector seat, I was no more secure than a pea in a drum. We had fought like demons on the Cresta Run and now pushing the stick forwards, while telling me to hold on, as I groped for everything I could find not painted black and yellow, he announced 'We will first have a go at the sound barrier!' As we turned steeply out of the dive that followed, I cursed that I had been given no cockpit instruction by the naval ground crew as I watched my knuckles turn white with fright.

'We are now descending to 10,000 feet from where I am going to execute an engine off carrier landing' came Mark's calm voice through the intercom. 'Hold on tight' as if I had not been doing so already!

Shutting off the power Mark then directed the jet vertically downwards at the grey scar of runway far below, and, as the tarmac jumped into our faces, he flared out, landing perfectly.

I had once been detailed by my commanding officer at a regimental ball to dance with our colonel in chief the Queen Mother. We had been talking about our mutual love of horses and why I had joined the cavalry when the army no longer depended on them. She had been well briefed, for her second question was. 'I have been told that you enjoy flying and riding the Cresta Run. What is it that you young men get from speed?'

Ma'am I replied hesitatingly, as I struggled to compare the sensation with any of her own experiences. 'To me speed means acceleration, but to you it more likely means exhilaration' I was being pathetic 'that wonderful feeling you get when you stand high up on a moor in your beloved Scotland with the wind blowing through your hair.'

Letter

13

Andrea Badrutt
Palace Hotel, St Moritz

February 1965

Dear Andrea

This is to thank you for allowing us to use your ballroom in order to celebrate my brother winning the Fairchild McCarthy handicap race on the Cresta Run.

Surprisingly when we returned to our table from dancing it was occupied by the Shah of Persia and his entourage. When my girlfriend tried to retrieve her handbag, two security men jumped up from either side of him with guns in their pockets. We, therefore, had to ask a waiter to fetch her bag for her.

Who comes first at the Palace?

Yours ever

R

Comment: The family Badrutt had been esteemed hoteliers in St Moritz ever since the mid-1880s when Johannes Badrutt had first recognised the town's considerable potential as a holiday destination.

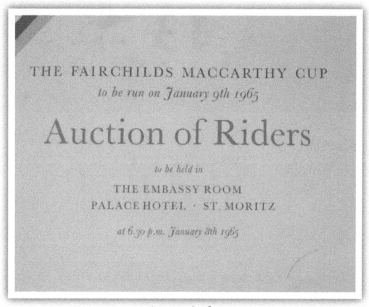

THE FAIRCHILDS MACCARTHY CUP
to be run on January 9th 1965

Auction of Riders

to be held in

THE EMBASSY ROOM
PALACE HOTEL · ST. MORITZ

at 6.30 p.m. January 8th 1965

Auction leaflet

Nicholas winning

In September1884 it happened that four Englishmen were about to leave the Kulm, the first hotel he had established there, when he stopped them with a wager.

If they came back during the winter not only would they find the weather warm and agreeable, but he would also pay for their whole stay. On the other hand should they find the weather disagreeable and they wished to return home, he would pay their travelling expenses. It was a win-win situation for both parties; and when the four Englishmen returned with their families and friends they stayed until the spring spending a fortune at the bar. The hotelier's shrewd move, became even more so when the Englishmen became bored and built themselves a town toboggan run. Before long the toboggan run had reached the tiny village of Cresta, later being extended to almost a mile long while dropping over 500 feet to the village of Celerina. At the same time by building icy walls down it's length, toboggan speeds were increased to nearly 80 miles per hour, while today newer and faster toboggans and skin suits have added to that figure. Badrutt through his generosity, had established the Alps as a place not only to spend the winter but also to enjoy skiing plus the other sports that were developing in the mountains, including the Cresta Run.

The Palace Hotel, commissioned by Johnnes Badrutt's son Caspar, opened its doors in 1897 and was immediately filled by many of the world's rich and famous, just as it is today. But when I first stayed there with my two brothers in 1960, we hardly had a bean between us. It was fortunate that Andrea Badrutt recognised the merit of giving young Cresta riders a special deal; and banished to the attic with the hotel maids, the times we spent staying at the Palace remain unforgettable.

During February 1965 an auction of Cresta riders had been held there the night before the popular Fairchild McCarthy Cup, with many of the hotel's super rich joining in the bidding, encouraged by the presence of Stavros Niarchos. Unknown to them my brother Nicholas, who had won the race previously and also the course record, had been given too generous a handicap so the three brothers bought him for just a few francs. It thus raised suspicion that we had been sticking our spikes in the ice previously, particularly when narrowly in the lead, I gave my faster toboggan to Nicholas and he won. We believed we had made a fortune but such thoughts were to be short lived. For while skiing down the mountains afterwards, on hearing loudspeakers blaring out, we knew that we had been rumbled. 'Tonight' some wag was announcing 'the three brothers are holding a party in the Palace Hotel and everyones welcome.' So 'Off to the Palace' did not mean going to see the Queen, but, instead, enjoying the hospitality of the three brothers in the most expensive hotel in Europe! Thus the St Mortitz Tobogganing Club and the Palace Hotel both made a fortune while the three brothers ended up with a deficit!

Letter 14

Chief of Police, Kanton Polizei
Via Greval, St Moritz, Switzerland

February 1965

Sir

Two mornings ago I visited your police station and reported that we had lost one of the friends staying in our chalet, when he failed to join us after riding down from the Chantarella Hotel at midnight on a wooden luge. But your police were unable to help me.

We continued to search for him both in the ravine beside the piste and throughout the town until this evening, when some of my friends called in at your police station and found that you had, indeed, arrested him.

Why was I not informed that he was locked in your cells all the time?

Sincerely

RR

Comment: All three of us brothers were having the time of our lives in the Alps that year and were up for anything. So one night, after our friend had vanished, we decided to ride down the notorious St Moritz Bob Run.

Workmen clearing
the bob run of icicles

Nash and Dixon winning the Olympics

It was the combination of luging down from the Chantarella and riding once previously on the bob that triggered one of our wildest escapades of all. Our friend, we discovered, was in prison for breaking off the aerial of a taxi as he tried to slow down that night before hitting the road through St Moritz. No one was prepared to pay a thousand francs to get him out so on our third visit, we took him a baguette with a nail file hidden in it and toasted both him and his guards with schnapps.

That evening there was a starry sky, so my brothers and I decided to go one better and take our three luges down the bob run. As far as we knew, it had never been attempted before and was not for the faint hearted. But that did not seem to matter when primed with schnapps. So we stepped onto the ice and set off into the dark one after the other.

The acceleration was frightening, even on wooden luges, but as we hit the first corner, half expecting to fly out over it, something slowed us down. The icy banks of the Cresta and also of the Bob are not created by magic but by a team of men, who, when temperatures drop sufficiently below freezing at night, spray the banks with water. So our headlong descent became an ordeal of wiping the spray from our eyes while trying steer the speeding luges in the right direction. Falling off as we somehow negotiated the high banks of blue ice, where a four man crew had died just a week earlier, was not an option.

The following morning, when the 'prisoner' suddenly turned up at our chalet, just as one of my brothers left for England, the magnitude of our folly became apparent. 'The police are now after you in a big way' he warned us. 'Thanks for writing that letter as they have let me off with a fine, but the bob run is now closed indefinitely while the police gather evidence and the workmen try to chop out the many thousands of icicles formed by all that water you threw up in gallons onto the banks. They know where to find you as you had, unfortunately, already given them our address, so I suggest you get the hell out of here fast!'

It was good advice and all seemed to be under control when just before we crossed the border into France our battered old Land Rover got a puncture. 'Look out, Police!' shouted my brother, but at that moment, stuck in the road, there was nothing much we could do about it. 'We noticed those two helmets in the back of your vehicle as you passed our check point' one of them said rather too directly 'and we know who you are for you must be returning home to England after riding the bobsleigh.' I shivered. 'But before we help you mend your puncture we must congratulate you, Mr Nash and Mr Dixon, for winning the Olympic gold medal at Innsbruck last year.'

Miss Henrietta Law
Flat 1, Mulberry Court
London

October 1966

My dear Henrietta

I am writing to say how sorry I am to have misled you about flying down to Devon in the aeroplane and to have given you such a scare in it.

I suppose we just got too late leaving and that dreadful rain storm just arrived from nowhere. Then, of course, my mother did not make things any easier!

I realise that you will not trust me about anything in future, or ever fly with me again, so all I can hope is that it is not all over between us.

Much Love

R

Comment: Girls are not always the best at being punctual but I admit that I had hoodwinked Henrietta by suggesting that she only brought a small suitcase as we were having a quiet weekend in the country.

Swinging the propeller to start the engine.

Crash landing

But as we had been late arriving at White Waltham aerodrome I had stupidly failed to look up the weather forecast or, for that matter, the times of daylight, as the nights were drawing in.

So as we flew west, and the sun started dropping below the horizon, I began to get worried. It was getting dark and through the windshield I could see that the sky was becoming increasingly obscured by a dense blanket of cloud

We were battling against a strong headwind; so on trying to land at Exeter, I found that the runway lights had already been switched off and the airport was closed. Even should I have been able to contact the control tower it was probably no longer occupied, and what was worse, I was neither trained or qualified to fly at night, and nor did I have enough fuel to turn back to London.

Fortunately, with my brothers, we had had cut the heather on part of the wartime landing ground situated on steep moorland not far from our house; but when heavy rain started driving in from the west, hitting a pin-point, which was impossible to see, and then stopping with no brakes as the strip fell increasingly away into a quarry, seemed impossible.

But my father, who had flown in the Royal Flying Corps during WWI, luckily twigged when we buzzed the family house making as much noise as possible. Grabbing a man, a fire extinguisher and our old battered Land Rover, he headed up to the moor and shone the truck's headlights correctly into wind from the higher eastern end of the landing strip.

During that summer, with my naval friend Mark, we had organised an inter-services flying circus there. Mark had encouraged some of his compatriots to bring the Fairy Swordfish from Yeovilton while my army friends arrived with a Miles Magister and a Tiger Moth. Crazily we then flew around the hill in each other's aeroplanes including the Auster. Somehow we all survived and, more importantly, I managed to find out more about our airstrip, where we had once watched the Blackburn Skuas crash land, than I would have done otherwise.

All would have been well if my mother had not tried to help. She had arrived in her own car, which could barely make it across the moor; then, determined to shed more light onto the strip, she had driven to the far end of it. I had done a couple of circuits, greatly relieved by my father's knowledge of flying, and was making my final approach when I became totally blinded by her headlights. But she would not budge despite the low passes I took over her car. Perhaps my father had not seen the lights, but as the Auster had no wipers, the windshield, lit up by bright raindrops, had become impossible to see through. So I took our lives in my hands and throttled back, hoping to hit the strip just where it started. I failed and after bouncing high into the air, the Auster skidded sideways into some gorse bushes, shearing off a wheel as my passenger fell out of her door head first, swearing 'You bloody fool' as she did so. She then took the first train back to London and I never saw her again.

Letter 16

Secretary of State to the War Office
LONDON W1.

December 1967

Sir

During July 1967 I moved with my squadron of the Royal Horse Guards to Cyprus. On 25 November when the Turks invaded and due to our Brigade Commander being re-located to the Army HQ at Paphos, I took over command of all British forces within the Eastern Sovereign Base, including half of Sandhurst then present on an exercise.

Apart from sending troops to help evacuate British citizens from Nicosia and Northern Cyprus, I also set up road blocks with my armoured cars, ordering my men to disarm all Turks and Greeks entering the Sovereign Base area. So I was amazed when told by the War Office to give all the large pile of weapons we had collected back. Why?

Yours sincerely

RR

Comment: Cyprus has always been dogged by an inflammable mix of Greeks and Turks. In November 1967, the Turkish leader Rauf Denktas, in order to take control of the island, carried out the first of two invasions from the Turkish mainland.

Road block

Natanis in Kyrenia harbour

But landing by rubber dinghy from a submarine in advance of his ships, he unfortunately chose the wrong beach and was arrested by the game keeper of the island's only nature reserve.

Taken to confront Archbishop Makarios, both Denktas and his troops were sent packing but not before the War Office had caused me considerable embarrassment!

Subsequently, in 1974, a Greek military junta carried out a coup d'etat in Nicosia, deposing Archbishop Makarios. But by attempting to unite the whole island, including the Turkish population in the north, under the Greek flag, they once again woke up the Ottoman Ogre, who then invaded northern Cyprus for a second time, bombing Kyrenia and dropping paratroops over the area. Later the Turks declaring much of the land, including mine, as The Turkish Republic of Northern Cyprus.

Restoring my men's morale after we had been ordered by the War Office to give the Turks and Greeks back their arms was difficult. As it happened, I had previously purchased an impressive plot of land to the east of Kyrenia and so, against all the rules, I arranged for groups of twelve of my men, to tidy up the ground, in turn, and plant it with fruit trees. At the time I had also discovered a fifteen ton yacht *The Natanis*, which, although owned by the army yacht club, had sadly been left drying out above the high water mark on the hard in Dhekalia harbour. Her planks had shrunk so badly in the sun that I detailed two more parties to hose her down, make her ship shape and then launch her in the briny. Taking on ten of the best of my men, plus my then girlfriend Annette and a ship's rat, we then sailed her round the panhandle to a berth in the magnificent crescent of Kyrenia harbour, narrowly avoiding a waterspout on the way.

Buying agricultural land in Cyprus is not to be recommended as Lawrence Durrell had once stated. First you negotiate for the soil, then for the olive trees, then for the olives and finally for the right to harvest them. I had left the hard bargaining to a Greek woman, who - once a road, a water main and a telephone line had crossed it - told me that she had found a buyer prepared to pay twenty times the price I had bought my nine donums of land for. I stupidly refused and therefore, because of her involvement, later lost it, probably for good, to the Turkish invaders.

The yacht was a great morale booster for I had obtained a dozen aqualungs through the Nuffield Foundation and we set up a diving school in Kyrenia for the whole squadron. One day while diving off the north coast, we were beckoned by a sponge fisherman who had just discovered the oldest wreck in history, now installed in Kyrenia Castle.

Letter
17

Count Frederic Chandon de Briailles
Moet & Chandon
Epernay, France

August 1968

Dear Fred

The flight back to England in the Moet et Chandon jet was spectacular, particularly when a bottle of Dom Perignon was uncorked. What a surprise it was when you called in your golden aeroplane to fly over the 'Madre Perle' off Bastia in order to give me a lift home. The cruise was delightful but the grounding quite an experience.

One day, if I get married in London, will you come and kiss the bride?

All best wishes

R

Comment: I would have been lucky to get a reply from such a busy Frenchman. I had met Fred in a Porto Cervo nightclub when I was only too pleased to shed one of the two girls I had with me.

The Madre Perle

Moet & Chandon Jet at Bastia

Peter the Black

The Aga Khan

He asked us to join him on his yacht the following morning, which was the largest in the harbour.

We then sailed from Sardinia to a bay in southern Corsica where we, unfortunately hit a rock and became jammed on it with our rudders. The British skipper had been covered by a jet of black hydraulic oil from the wheel mechanism and was in a poor mood; so when I found that his French crew had never used diving gear before and offered to help, he waved me aside. However, I soon managed to get the distraught man, who said he had never seen the bottom, to relent and, donning an aqualung, I then managed to shackle two weighty anchor chains through eyes at the back of the yacht's rudders. The crew then rowed out the anchors to drop them at ninety degrees to the boat.

When she swung in the evening breeze, the anchors pulled the rudders off the rocks for us.

Fred had been delighted by the unusual rescue of his yacht, although she had first sailed on to Bastia in embarrassing circles. Lending me his jet was unbelievable and two years later when Annette and I were married, he sent us enough Moet & Chandon champagne to fill a cellar.

Porto Cervo was the brainchild of the Aga Khan, which he started developing in the 1950s with other investors on the Costa Smeralda in Sardinia and It remains one of the most expensive resorts in the world.

I had arrived there with my brother Nicholas, hoping to buy some cheap land which was for sale not far to the west of the town. At first It looked like a good deal. However it was soon apparent that Peter the Black, the bandit trying to sell the land to us, was not to be trusted. We therefore set off to Olbia to search the registry and found to our horror that there was an arsenal hidden underground and that anyone who lit a cigarette there was in danger of being blown sky high. We had told the bandit that we would return that afternoon as the land had a white beach and azure blue water. But when we arrived the Aga Khan was there standing beside his helicopter. Maybe he bought the land; we hoped not.

Fred later invited me to his chateau at Epernay in order to see the Moet & Chandon cellars. 'You may know that many of the great captains of history have visited us, like Wellington before Waterloo. What is remarkable is that all of them were born in vintage years. Then, one day, the Russian premier Khrushchev turned up and was crestfallen when he found that in the year of his birth the vineyard had the worst drought on record, and the champagne was like vinegar and undrinkable. However, before leaving, he was assured that the year of his conception was the best year that Moet & Chandon had ever had.' Vive la France!

Letter
18

Mr Mark Grimes
CEO Lenkz Bank
London

October 1968

Dear Mr Grimes

I wish to draw your attention to a missing employee from your bank. A year ago I
was contacted by an American employee of yours called Rick Hanthorn who was
looking for a traditional sailing yacht. I told him that my family owned an eight
metre built in 1928, but that after a disastrous shipwreck we were looking for a
sailing partner prepared to pay for repairing her. This he agreed to do.

The work was carried out under Hanthorn at a Brixham shipyard but one night
six days ago she vanished. Can you help?

Yours sincerely

RR

Comment: We never discovered what happened either to *Moonshine* or to the wretched Hanthorn; and his bank was, obviously, not wishing to be involved in any of it.

Disaster!

We can only believe that one night, against our agreement, he sailed *Moonshine* out into the channel where the boat fell apart and went down without a trace in the Portland whirlpools.

Before the age of glass fibre, when boats were built of well-seasoned hardwood, it was possible to judge a boat's health as she got older from the fastenings, or copper rivets, which hold the planks together. When flaky rings start appearing around the fastenings, you know that the boat is in trouble; and *Moonshine* was beginning to get covered in them.

Hanthorn was fully aware of this, but we never had the opportunity of seeing her refit concluded; so it is possible that although he had seen to the storm damage being repaired, her planks had not been refastened.

On New Year's Eve 1968 we had sailed out from Torquay under a blue sky but in subzero temperatures to have *Moonshine's* engine repaired in a Teignmouth shipyard. There was a strong offshore breeze but no indication that it was blowing up to become a force nine gale and as we tacked four miles from the coast her forestay parted and the rig came crashing down, knocking my brother Nicholas overboard into the sea. When we pulled him out, he was crackling with ice. With no engine, no radio and no tools onboard, which I had taken off for the winter, we were suddenly in very serious trouble. It was impossible to keep the yacht heading into the rapidly rising sea owing to the rig lying against her side, which, normally, we would have been able to cut away with our tools.

Worse still, when we tried to light our flares we found that one by one each of them was damp and useless.

Moonshine in happier times

'The Major' is hero of rescue at sea off the South Devon coast.

Only wanting to be known as The Major, he has been the hero of a dramatic sea rescue off the South Devon coast involving two lifeboats and the crew of a gallant Brixham trawler.

Yesterday he rowed a tiny dinghy for almost three hours through heavy seas in sub zero temperatures to fetch help for his two brothers and two girls, all trapped aboard their 8-metre Bermudian sloop the *Moonshine*, which had been dismasted 4 miles off Berry Head in a force nine offshore gale. But when the major's mother was asked if she had been at all concerned by her sons being lost at sea, she replied 'No - my sons have been born and bred on the sea, but I am worried that they may have caught colds'.

Press report

Also with no engine, we were having to pump her out manually, and because she was shipping water faster than we could get rid of it, I knew she would soon be in danger of foundering. And I was responsible.

Having exhausted all but one option, I then decided that our only hope of survival was for me to jump into the dinghy we were towing and try to get help by some unlikely miracle. But it was only to find that its glass fibre bottom had been punctured by a cross-tree of the falling mast.

There was already no possibility of turning back, for the dinghy would have been smashed against the side of the yacht like an egg, so I just jammed my heel into the hole and started rowing, using all the skills I had once learned at Eton. The sky was was getting much darker; but after a time, when cresting a wave, I could tell from the loom of the Berry Head lighthouse that by taking an angle against the gale, now whipping the crests into streams of foaming white water, that I was inching towards the shore, still several miles away. It was only when, for an instant, I glimpsed the lights of a distant trawler it gave me hope that the fishing fleet were returning for shelter and we might yet be saved.

I thought about the pretty girl I had left onboard, who I hoped, one day, would become my wife. If it had not been for Annette's forethought we would not have survived, for shivering with cold, she had thrown the yellow jersey she was wearing into the dinghy - to wave as a flag.

It was about two hours later with the water beginning to lap at my knees, that I saw a second trawler returning to Brixham, mercifully heading my way. Although it was difficult to move, I somehow managed to wave the jersey. Then suddenly the trawler was alongside with arms being stretched out to pull me, like a dying fish, out of the sinking dinghy and onto their deck. They immediately called the coastguard who dispatched two lifeboats, but all was not yet over.

The hunt for *Moonshine* was not made any easier by the loss of her mast and her disappearing freeboard as she continued to fill with water almost to the brim of her cockpit. But the gallant crew of the trawler *Scaldis,* managed to spot her in the towering waves, and going about with a heavy catch on board, risked their own lives by taking her in tow.

The following morning the newspapers were full of it. When our mother was asked if she had been worried by her three sons being lost at sea, she retorted 'No, my sons have been brought up on the sea, but I am a little worried that they may have caught colds'. Some reporters quite wrongly called me a hero, for I had to save myself first, but Annette's uncle, who was a blustery old admiral, called me a 'Danger to the sea'.

Mr Christopher Hasson
General Manager. Dart Valley Steam Railway
Buckfastleigh, Devon.

February 1969

Dear Mr Hasson

We would like to borrow back my father's Dennis fire engine, which he kindly lent to the Dart Valley Railway two years ago.

Could you very kindly have it ready for us to collect at 1200 on Monday next week as we wish to use it for my brother's wedding?

Many thanks

RR

Comment: Sometimes when a letter is not answered you hope that it has been received and acted upon. But In this case, because I had not checked that my request had been heeded, our plan to borrow back the fire engine, although at first seeming to be a good one, turned out to be a catastrophe.

My father had bought the Dennis fire engine, armed with possibly the longest extension ladder in service at that time, not only as a long-term investment, but also because he was hooked on it. He liked it so much that he had built a large tin shed for it at home beyond the garages, which also served as a general workshop and the ideal place for its on-going maintenance. But as he was also a fan of steam engines and chairman of the Dart Valley Steam Railway, he misguidedly lent his treasured fire engine to the company for two years on condition that they looked after it, which they did not. Having driven it, carefully, back home for the wedding of my brother Nicholas to 'the girl from Rome', who with my future wife, had also narrowly escaped a watery death on the *Moonshine*, I had been amazed by the large number of people I had seen turning their heads as we drove past them on the road, for they don't usually gawp at anything other than at a decent car crash.

It made a sensational platform not only for the bride and bridegroom but also for the bridesmaids who waved their bouquets and blew their trumpets all the way back from our little Norman church in the valley.

Wedding

Going away!   Brotherly love!

Once the couple had changed, after the wedding feast, for their honeymoon, came the great moment of their departure.

I had parked the fire engine directly in front of the house so that my youngest brother Andrew could extend the ladder easily, which he did to a third-floor window. But when the bridegroom stepped out onto the top rung, carrying his suitcase, my brother extended it vertically to its maximum height, where it suddenly jammed. Those watching gasped; the bridegroom shouted down 'For God's sake do something!' and the bride broke into floods of tears.

The incident should have warned me for what was to come. For the fire engine had, obviously, not been topped up with oil or maintained at all, and although the ladder was freed and my brother rescued, when a party arrived from the Dart Valley Railway to take it back for a final month on display, I should have warned them not to drive it too fast. They did and sent the pistons flying up through the cylinder block.

The Dart Valley Railway never repaired our magnificent fire engine and left it to rust away to nothing. But they won a few points back when my sister had a party beside the Dart for a granddaughter's wedding. The young went skinny dipping in the river afterwards and the driver of the steam train on the opposite bank went toot - toot — toot with his whistle!

Letter 20

Harry Saltzman
Eon Film Productions
Audley Square, London

April 1969

Dear Mr Saltzman

Since you took me on over two years ago to recruit the skiers and plan the best skiing locations for OHMSS, I have diligently found the skiing doubles, including those to play James Bond and Stavros Blofeld, built a bob run for you and arranged the location of all the skiing scenes.

Your assistant, Jenny, has pointed out that army personnel may only be paid for work that is strictly detailed by them. The military did not know of my participation but I am surprised that Eon Studios are not prepared to reward me other than just with a ticket to the premier. Is that correct?

Yours sincerely

RR

Comment: Aware that other feature films were about to be shot in the Alps I had urged Harry Saltzman to get a toe in the door with OHMSS. Thus a year later I found myself showing him around St Moritz as the best possible location. A year passed before the film was shot in Murren instead, where poor weather conditions annoyed both Saltzman and his partner Cubby Broccoli by taking far longer to complete the film than expected.

A year earlier, while racing in the army downhill at St Moritz, I suffered such a serious skiing accident that I have never recovered since. I was heading down the mountain at nearly 70 miles per hour when a man walked across the racecourse. I tried to avoid him but collided with him so hard that my left leg was torn clean out of its socket leaving me with my skis pointing in opposite directions. There was no helicopter available; and as it was impossible to strap me to a blood waggon, I was manhandled down the mountain by friends and then taken to a St Moritz clinic to be told that, as my condition was too serious for them to deal with, I must be driven by ambulance to the main hospital in Chur. But as they had no driver or nurse available, one of my brothers had to take the wheel while, as I lay uncomfortably in the ambulance strapped to the roof like Humpty Dumpty, the other brother pumped me full of morphine.

'You have been very lucky' stated the famous Swiss surgeon Dr Algover, when he came to see me two days later. 'It is normal for the artery to be ruptured due to your type of injury. The victim will then die quickly from loss of blood'.

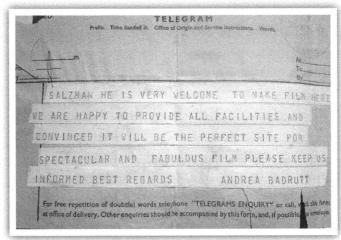

Telegram from Andrea Badrutt at the Palace Hotel St Moritz

Film clapper board   Choosing the skiing locations

Recognising his face from the cover of Life magazine I believed him. 'But since I came round does the fact that I have survived both that and you wrenching my leg around 180 degrees qualify me for being given bed baths every hour or so?' I asked him. 'Of course it does' he replied. 'As the hospital was full we had to find a room for you in the women's ward and the girls, who you will have discovered only speak Romansh, may never have seen a man before.'

When I returned to England, it took me a long time to recover; and because I had been reading about the exploits of 007 in OHMSS and was bored, I picked up the telephone and rang Harry Saltzman one of the two producers of the James Bond films. 'Who am I talking to? What der yer want?' he growled. I told him that I was an army Captain, injured in a skiing accident, and would like to talk about shooting OHMSS in St Moritz. 'Then come and see me Captain' he, replied. But when I staggered into his office on crutches he was so busy talking to other people, that I took the train home without saying a word to him.

It was a year later, while staying with my brother Nicholas in Italy, when his phone started ringing. 'This is Harry. Is that you Captain?' he drawled 'Hire a plane in Zurich and fly with me to St Moritz tomorrow morning.' So I immediately rang up Andrea Badrutt, owner and manager of the Palace Hotel in St Moritz, who was so thrilled, that on the following day, when we flew into Samedan aerodrome, not far below the town, the Palace limo was already waiting for us on the runway.

Willy Bogner filming the bob

Bogner with Cubby Broccoli

Jeremy skiing as Blofeld

At the time I was on the committee of the Cresta Run and my principal reason for contacting EON films had been to make the St Moritz Tobogganing Club some money for Fleming had mentioned the Cresta in his book. For the burghers of St Moritz it was a dream of riches about to come true. The lunch Andrea had laid on was sumptuous, and those invited to meet Saltzman included Gianni Agnelli and Stavros Niarchos.

We were just about to sit down when Saltzman pushing the vase directly in front of him down the table shouted at the waiter, 'Take them flowers away. I don't like flowers!' Although it grabbed everyones instant attention, his presence was to be short lived. Before my guest had finished, the second course of wild American turkey stuffed with Normandy truffles, he jumped up, thanked our host and asked me to take him, without further delay, to see all the locations I was so enthusiastic about. 'I want you to arrange the skiers and the ski scenes'.

I believed that the new cable lift rising to the Piz Corvatsch at nearly 10,000 feet, would make a stunning Piz Gloria. But after we reached the top station and climbed onto the metal platform to admire its long views stretching beyond the Matterhorn to Mont Blanc, a lift operator stuck his head out of a window and warned me that the weather was closing in and unless we left for Samedan immediately, Saltzman would be trapped in the Alps for at least two more days. Therefore we piled back into the cable car and then into the Palace limo before speeding down to the airfield to find it already closed. So he gave the pilot a fist full of dollars and told him to take off. We did, but unable to see the mountains rising 4,000 feet above us the young pilot fainted from Hypoxia and sheer terror. I fitted on his oxygen mask and, just as terrified, took over.

After a year waiting for further news I was dismayed when the location was changed from St Moritz to Murren due, they said, to the crowds. So instead I was flown out to Zurich early every Saturday morning and then picked up by chopper to fly to Murren for an early briefing. Choosing the skiing doubles, and locations, was simple but when I was asked to build the bob run life became more difficult. Having mapped it out, I then hired experts from St Moritz to build it and Willy Bogner, the former world ski champion, to film it. But the producers were not happy with the 'rushes' complaining that the run looked too tame. I had also hired the British ski ace, Jeremy Palmer Tomkinson, to take the part of Blofeld. Driving in his Porsche along a mountain road one day, we almost hit a horse drawn timber waggon. 'Bitte hilt mir' I asked the lumberjack 'I need a hundred of those trees, complete with branches, delivered to me tomorrow.' Planted at a forty five degree angle to the bob run, it worked.

Minister of State
Department of Trade and Industry
Victoria Street, London

January 1969

Dear Sir

I recently left Her Majesty's forces and have decided to travel around the world. But I do not wish to go empty handed.

Please would you very kindly suggest a suitable British export, or exports, particularly in the agricultural or aviation field, that I could promote during my years journey?

Yours sincerely

RR

Comment: The year 1969 was to be a record for British exports, totalling £7billion, an increase of 12 per cent over the previous year.

75000 MILES AROUND THE WORLD 1969

A world air ticket in one direction only cost £700. I crossed the equator many times.

With a burgeoning balance of payments surplus, the government was feeling so comfortable that the minister, if he ever received my letter, would have been complacent enough while sitting in his deep armchair, not to have given a monkeys about my pathetic attempt as an ex-soldier to further the situation. But as he had failed miserably to help me promote the two subjects I knew most about, farming and flying, and was not showing a spark of enthusiasm, I decided instead to try my luck in France.

The Alouette III, developed by Sud Aviation, was one of the most advanced helicopters at the time with the headquarters of Aerospatiale, the company who built it, in Paris. The marketing chief was charming, taking me that evening to enjoy the spicy atmosphere of the Crazy Horse Saloon. We met again in his office the following morning. 'We are putting a bundle together for you to include everything about the machine as you would find it difficult to pack our helicopter in your suitcase. We will pay you for you to carry out a world survey of helicopter operations and meanwhile offer you 3% commission on any you can manage to sell.' But as I still needed some ready cash for my journey, even if I drank only water and slept under the stars every night,

I rang up the editor of the Sunday Telegraph colour magazine, which no longer exists but in the late sixties often included world politics, asking him if he would be interested in a report on the emerging countries of the world. He said that they would and agreed to send me a reasonable amount for them.

Letter 22

The Governor General
Ali Qapu Palace
Isfahan, Persia

February 1969

Dear Governor General

I am writing to thank you for receiving me so generously in your splendid city of Isfahan. The Shah Abbas where I stayed must be the most beautiful hotel anywhere, and your streets, bordered by fine buildings and garlanded with flowers, make Isfahan a paradise I will never forget

I have been so impressed with the new way of life being created for your country.

You wanted the draft of my Sunday Telegraph article. If not to your palace, where shall I send it?

Yours sincerely

RR

Comment: Between 1963 and 1978 the Shah of Persia had been carrying out a wide range of reforms intended to turn Persia into a modern democracy.

Persepolis

The Blue Mosque, Isfahan

The Shah Abbas Hotel

Bringing home the caviar

His initiative was named the White Revolution as it was intended to be bloodless, whlle introducing a unique type of land reform to reduce the power of the middle classes.

But among many concerns, was the amount of money that the Shah and his Pahlavi family were siphoning off from Persia's new found oil wealth.

I had arrived right in the middle of his initiatives which were growing in unpopularity among the clerics, many rich landowners and others of the more fundamental section of the Persian community. I had flown initially to Shiraz, where, as I was writing for an English newspaper, I was immediately taken to meet the governor, a delightful man with a beard in his early fifties who immediately asked me about my first impressions. 'Having seen all the roses adorning every lamp post on the way in from the airport' I replied 'I now know why Persia is regarded in our country as the land of paradise.' He shook my hand as though I was already his friend and waving to an aid said that he was arranging for his personal driver to take me on a tour of the city and then to see the famous ruins of Persepolis 50 miles away. Persepolis, which had only been reclaimed from the sand dunes during the 1930s, less than 40 years before, had once been the richest city in the world. The sight of its tall columns and extraordinary freezes has never left me.

Moving on to Isfahan it had been recommended to me that I should stay in the Shah Abbas, supposedly the most beautiful hotel in the world where soon after my arrival the manager rang me. 'Major please do not hang your underclothes over your balcony. We have a perfectly good laundry.'

During the seventeenth century Isfahan had been one of the largest cities anywhere; but to me it seemed much smaller and a place full of mosques and minarets sitting peacefully, well to the south of Tehran, at the foot of the Zagros mountains. But what impressed me most was the governor's palace and the governor general himself. I had never seen a man wearing so much gold braid or such fine slippers. But I was no longer writing for the *Sunday Telegraph* it seemed, as he preferred to introduce me as The Major from the *Manchester Guardian*. Once again I was to be lent a state limousine with an English speaking driver, who, due to my interest in caviar, was told to drive me first 250 miles to an official residence in Tehran before taking me north through a steep sided gorge in the Elbutz mountains, to visit a caviar factory on the shores of the Caspian Sea. It was a privilege that few in the outside world had ever been allowed to experience. Run by Russians the 'factory' was only a small corrugated roofed shed to match the size of fishing boats themselves. Yet from it came some of the finest royal beluga caviar of all, the golden variety being kept only for the shah.

Today fishing for wild sturgeon in the Caspian has been banned forever; and the production of caviar is now limited to farming the fish, as practised on Exmoor in England and in many other parts of the world. Distressingly, I watched the magnificent fish being stripped of their eggs before being chopped into steaks. Today fish farms often manage to strip the sturgeon, once known to breed largely in the gin-clear mountain streams of Persia, without killing them. On leaving, when I was presented with a splendid can of their best blue-labelled caviar thanked the workers several times with 'Spa-see-ba' my only word of Russian.

Back in Tehran I had been impressed by many of the reforms the shah had instigated, particularly a type of conscription where the army was sent out to instruct in the remotest villages on medicine, agriculture and education. Also by a few of the benefits brought to the economy by the White Revolution. But the drive towards westernisation had not been popular and when, in 1979 the sickening shah fled to Egypt and the Ayatollah Khomeni returned from exile in Paris, he immediately started putting the clock back stating that the 'Western Plague should be eliminated.' As reported in the British press, the first to be shot were the governor general of Shiraz and the governor general of Isfahan.

His Highness the Tikka Sahib of Faridkot
Rajamal Palace, Faridkot
Punjab, India.

March 1969

Dear David

I would like to thank you for looking after me in Delhi and I hope that you have recovered from your mysterious illness and are now back at work looking after the new president.

Do you know yet when you will be coming to see us in England, where the weather is more important than politics?

Best wishes

R

Comment: The 'illness' David suffered from is better known as DT's, and I had not helped the situation. Soon after my visit I heard that he had sadly died.

Pastoral scene

Caught in the taxi's headlights

On my flight to New Delhi the American sitting next to me had ordered the air hostess to bring back my large tin of beluga from the fridge, which I was intending to give to David, and then shared it with me. I had mistakenly replaced it with a large bottle of Scotch

David Singh had studied politics with a friend of mine at Cambridge, who had assured me that he would be a perfect contact when I reached India. He was also certain that he would meet me at Delhi airport as his father, the Maharajah of Faridkot, owned, he said, 100 Rolls Royces. He was not at the airport; and I discovered, on later having dinner with him, that he had never ridden an elephant or seen a tiger.

So the following day I thumbed a taxi and asked the Sikh driver to find me one. He told me to get my toothbrush and then drove me south for many hours past fierce guards on the Rajasthan border to a tiger reserve called Seriska. We had arrived late, so the game warden was already out; but his wife told us where to look for him sitting high up on a tree platform in the forest with a young buffalo tethered underneath. It was a beautiful moonlit night and nothing stirred until we heard the shriek of peacocks echoing in the hills around us. 'Tiger' whispered the game warden 'Tiger.' But when we heard a twig break near the old Austin taxi, frightened that his only possession was about to be savaged, my driver jumped from the tree and ran towards it. 'Do not worry sahib' said the game warden 'we will take the taxi to look for him.' We did and found him, lit up by our headlights in a river wadi, and then he was gone.

Letter
24

The Minister. Department of Ecology
Bemina, Srinagar, Kashmir

March 1969

Dear Sir

While recently walking up a narrow valley in your Zabarwan mountains, I came across a man returning from the forest with two bear cubs tucked under his arms.

Surely it is an offence to steal such animals - right under the noses of your forest rangers?

Yours faithfully

RR

Comment: Before leaving New Delhi I had fortunately been invited to have dinner with the British high commissioner. 'Why not take the plane up to Kashmir' he said. 'I have a lovely friend there, who will look after you.'

Jammu and Kashmir, opened up to tourism again only recently after years of dangerous disputes between India and Pakistan, dating back to Partition in 1947, is one of the most beautiful countries on earth, but is still fraught with border problems.

Dhal lake

Old man with a hooker

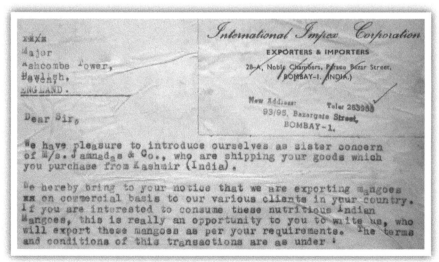

Letter from Bombay. The bed had cost, imported, just £70!

Bordering on the Western Himalayas, the Karakoram range is visible from many places with Nangar Parbat, at over 8,000 metres, standing amongst them as one of the highest mountains in the world.

Not far away is the North West Frontier, where my father had fought for the infamous Khyber Pass, likely to be the scene of conflict for ever.

My flight to this northernmost region of the subcontinent had been in a small aeroplane accompanied by an Indian prince and his wife, making it all the more fascinating when I spied her large ruby earrings and the sparkling diamond buttons on his smart jade-coloured tunic. I was soon to discover, however, that there were no such trimmings in Srinagar, the capital, which struck one as an ancient town of narrow streets with a jumble of wooden buildings lining either side; merchants, both very young and very old, selling carved and papier mache ornaments; or endless rows of finely stitched Kashmiri carpets.

As the streets faded into lush countryside I soon found the house with the pink veranda that I was looking for. Also the incumbent, a young Indian lady of great beauty. Then as she welcomed me into her house while clapping her hands to summon some boys to carry my cases, she sent others off to the market to collect some 'cheras'. 'What is cheras?' I enquired, having passed on the regards of the high commissioner. 'You are about to find out' she replied. I did.

First she had instructed me to roll some parings from what seemed to be a ball of putty in my cigarette. When that did not work, she then told me to breathe in the black smoke emitted from the nasty-looking ball, which she had held it in tongs over a blazing fire. But before discovering it was pure opium I had already lapsed into a deep slumber.

When I woke up three days later I felt amazingly happy. There was a cobra in the woodshed, which she told me to avoid; but apart from that, the rest was mine to enjoy. So we went fishing for trout in the clear mountain streams, and higher up went sledging at Gulmarg, where the snow had already fallen. Also there were more peaceful moments on a shikara gliding over the Dal Lake, and less peaceful moments when we went looking for bears in deep-wooded valleys in the foothills, where we saw the horrible fellow stealing their cubs.

While in Kashmir I was able to arrange for a young team of woodcarvers to make me a four poster bed from the root of a walnut tree. As I watched them fashion screws with penknives to join the sixteen deeply carved sections together, I should have told them to mark them, for when it arrived back in England, it took me over a week to put it together.

Letter 25

The British Ambassador
Kathmandu

April 1969

Dear Antony

You were kind to see me yesterday at such short notice and many thanks for passing me my envelope from England. But in particular for introducing me to Boris, his extraordinary Yak and Yeti bar and his Royal Hotel, where I am now staying.

Just one thing has been worrying me since, for I had wanted to see Edmund Hillary's ice axe, which, I am told, once hung on the wall of your office. What has happened to it?

Yours sincerely

RR

Comment: The First Secretary had rung me up in the Royal Hotel on the evening after my arrival to say 'The ambassador thanks you for your letter and has asked me to reply. He understands your concern about the Ice Axe but must remind you that Sir Edmund is not British.

Temple painting   Portrait of a Rana

His office is due to be redecorated soon, and once that is completed, he will re-consider placing the ice axe, which he previously discovered put away in the attic, back on the wall.'

Being only in Kathmandu for two days, I had given him little time to reply, but when his first secretary responded with such a lame excuse, I felt that I should get someone to call back later to see if the ice axe, had been hung, where it should have been, back on the wall of his office. Although Hillary came from New Zealand, it had been a British expedition that conquered Everest on 29 May 1953, led by John Hunt and announced at the time of the Queen's coronation two days later. It had made me feel prouder to be British than at any other occasion in my life. Surely the British ambassador felt similarly?

But, at least, I appreciated the ambassador's introduction to Boris, for he turned out to be one of the most remarkable characters I had ever met. Boris was a white Russian and a former Bolshoi ballet dancer, who it was said, had fled the Bolsheviks by crossing over the Himalayas during winter. It was a surprising feat but not as extraordinary as the situation he found on arriving in Nepal. Horrified by what he saw, he then walked on to India and, having made friends with the Maharajah of Cooch Behar, they approached the Indian government, who, as a result, set about re-instating the Nepalese monarchy, which had fallen, as it was due to do again later, on very bad times.

Boris had discovered that the King Mahendra of Nepal although parading through the streets of Kathmandu in a Rolls-Royce from time to time, was in fact only being used as a puppet by a family called Rana, and his feet were actually shackled to the floor of his car with chains.

Machapuchare. Otherwise known as The Fishtail Mountain

Beaver aircraft with *Machapuchare* behind

He also found that the Rana family, having locked up their king under guard for most of the time, had since 1846 been living the 'high life' in Nepal enjoying immense wealth and unlimited power, while building themselves astonishing palaces. So when the monarchy was duly reinstated and their period of tyranny and economic exploitation brought to an end, Boris was invited by the grateful king to choose a reward for himself. He naturally chose one of the Rana's royal palaces, which he then named the Royal Hotel, complete with the Yak and Yeti bar, which soon became famous amongst all Himalayan climbers. My two nights there, accompanied by an angry Himalayan bear living in the next door room, were remarkable. In my vast bathroom were taps of solid gold and everywhere there were paintings of the Rana family, all dressed in considerable finery. The Ranas had excluded all foreigners from their mountain kingdom for over a century; but King Mahendra now opened up the country and introduce a stimulating era of democracy, while building roads for the first time into India.

Eighteen years later, when I left the hotel and flew in an ancient Chinese biplane to the Himalayan town of Pokhara, Nepal had changed out of all recognition. While climbing up to the snow line to see Machapuchare, a towering white pyramid even more magnificent than the Matterhorn, I had met Colonel Jimmy Roberts, a retired Gurkha officer, returning from Annapurna. 'Christ

I'm thirsty' I had told him as he pointed down the mountain to a Buddist monk who was selling cans of ice cold Tiger beer.

Thoroughly refreshed, I had returned to the airfield to have a go at selling one of my high-altitude helicopters, when I spotted an army Beaver aircraft, that had since arrived, sitting beside the runway with its pilot asleep under a wing. I kicked him awake, thinking that I must know him, but I did not. 'Whoever you are,' he croaked 'I am bloody well dying of thirst. Just tell me how to find a drink?' So, when I asked him if he would like an ice-cold beer from a mountain stream, his tongue almost dropped out. 'But there is a catch' I continued. 'If I bring you a cold beer will you fly me around Mount Everest?' He had no alternative but to say yes, and for the next few days not only did we fly around Everest but much of Nepal as well; for he was delivering mail to the Gurkhas.

Unknown to me, however, while I was exploring the Himalayas, violent storms were gathering as Maoist terrorists plotted to overthrow the government. This was not helped when in 2001, many years later, Crown Prince Dipendra, walked into a Royal Palace and shot his father, King Birendra, his mother and seven other members of his family before shooting himself. The monarchy ended and the country quickly became Communist.

Letter 26

The Earl of Suffolk and Berkshire
The Royal Hotel
Kathmandu, Nepal

May 1969

Dear Micky

I hope you are now enjoying Nepal after meeting you so unexpectedly as the only other traveller among the ruins of Angkor Wat - but going around the world, thank heavens, in the opposite direction!

Just to say that I am sending you this letter quickly, before I leave Phnom Penh, because I am curious to know, should you meet our ambassador in Kathmandu, if he has yet hung up Hillary's ice axe?

Perhaps you could write to me at Government House in Perth. Meanwhile best wishes for the rest of your journey.

R

Comment: The ruins of Angkor Wat, covering over 400 acres, form the largest religious monument and one of the most striking in the world.

Angkor Wat - then overgrown with forest   Stone soldiers manning a bridge

Arriving in Cambodia in August 1969 I was not only confused by what was happening, but alarmed that a few bombs had just fallen on the perimeter of the airport and also on the outskirts of Phnom Penh itself.

There was a nasty situation developing, so considering it would be difficult to write about Cambodia as being an emerging nation, when the country was obviously going backwards faster than seemed possible, I decided, rather than talk helicopters, to take a small aircraft to Siem Reap, to the North West of the capital, and visit the ruins of Angkor Wat.

Built by a Khmer king during the early part of the twelfth century, they were, for a long time, to be the centre of grandeur of an empire stretching far across southern Asia. But in the fifteenth century the empire collapsed and Angkor Wat was abandoned to nature for over 400 years. It was not until 1860 that a French explorer, Henri Mouhot, re-discovered the ruins, saying they rivalled Soloman, although they remained hidden again from the outside world until the 1960s. I had been determined to see them, and they remain indelible in my memory as a vast area of closely built, sandstone temples, surrounded by lakes, with snaking forest tree roots trying to strangle them, while beautiful butterflies flew around them everywhere.

The situation in Cambodia was dire. Believing that the Viet Kong, who were infiltrating in large numbers over the borders from Viet Nam, were about to overrun the country, President Nixon, supported by the American Secretary of State, Henry Kissinger, had instructed the American airforce to carry out secret carpet bombing raids over the country, named 'Operation Menu,' in order to stop them.

Butterflies

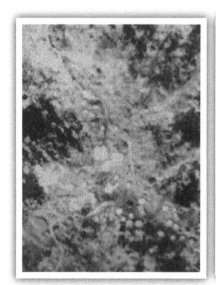

Ho Chi Minh Trail

Pol Pot

At that time ninety per cent of the peasants owned their own land, and by growing an abundance of rice, the country was still prospering.

However, on my arrival, I found that the Cambodian economy was already faltering after a growing number of communists under the banner of the 'Khmer Rouge', had started calling the landowning peasants 'parasites', made worse by 'Brother Number One', their ruthless leader Pol Pot, who, later in 1969, orchestrated the most horrific period in their history. Having ordered that the output of rice should be doubled, he drove all those living in Phnom Penh into the fields, where they either died of malnutrition, or, if found foraging, were executed.

But when I arrived, the most obvious enemies in Cambodia were the Americans due to their irresponsible bombing of an essentially neutral country, as I witnessed later when I flew over the Ho Chi Minh Trail, the Viet Kong supply route, targeted by the greatest concentration of bombs in history. I doubt that I would have gone to Ankor Wat if I had not been oblivious to the dangerous situation developing in Cambodia, but as the ruins were still largely unknown to tourism, the challenge was irresistible.

Micky told me much later 'You know already about the Killing Fields but what you don't know is on the day we left, because the Khmer Rouge thought the name Earl was American, both our guides were shot dead'.

Letter 27

General Richard Wolseley OBE
Chief of Staff. HQ Far East Land Forces
Tanglin Barracks. Singapore

May 1969

Dear General

I must apologise for turning up out of the blue at Flagstaff House without knowing who the incumbent was, and it was most kind of you to have me to stay the night. But I was sad not to see more of Singapore.

When you asked the driver of your staff car to take me to the airport the following morning, with the promise of a first class Cathay Pacific ticket to Hong Kong and a car to collect me at the airport, there was no ticket or anyone there to meet me! Perhaps you thought that before my arrival I knew who the nice lady was living at Flagstaff House?

With kind regards

RR

Comment: Although the general, better known to many as 'tricky Dicky', had once commanded a cavalry regiment; he was at heart a foot soldier and I was certain that he thoroughly disliked my cavalier initiatives.

Junks

Fish market

Castle Hill

He had also been suspicious of my motives because I had known his wife and her family when her father was the military attache in Paris.

So there was no one to meet me at Hong Kong airport as the general had promised, while having no alternative idea where to stay, I once again headed for a second Flagstaff House. The door was opened to my horror by a very different sort of general, a guards officer who I had got to know only too well before I left the army. Nor was he slow to remind me of the occasion when I had taken my squadron of armoured cars home to South Devon and had ordered my troop leaders to snatch the enemy's girlfriends and my men to lower the tents of B squadron; then camped in the grounds of a grand house, an hour away in North Devon, called Castle Hill.

Exercise Castle Hill had gone without a hitch but just as the girls were dismounting from the armoured cars my telephone rang. 'Is that you major?' the voice rasped 'this is the Commanding Officer London District. Am I correct in saying that some young officers under your command have just broken into Castle Hill?' I hesitated 'Well not exactly broken in sir' I replied. 'Oh yes you have' he retorted 'apparently one of your officers, known as fingers Steel, climbed through a skylight and abducted Lady Margaret's only daughter. She is **on fire!**'

Later at a pool he asked me 'So what did you do about it?' 'I detailed a dispatch rider to take her 100 red roses'. He stopped swimming 'Did that work?' 'No' I gasped, 'Lady Margaret never spoke to me again!'

Letter
28

Major General Sir Douglas Kendrew KCMG CB CBE DSO
Government House, Perth, Western Australia

June 1969

Dear Governor

I am writing from New Guinea sitting opposite to a man with a human bone through his nose.

Thank you for your great kindness in looking after me so well at Government House. Your lovely daughter Marcia was a star for introducing me to such a distinguished, yet down-to-earth, father.

It was such fun, surfing every morning with your ADC and then being asked by you to inspect your latest batch of debutants. 'You do the long white gloves' James said 'and I'll see that they are wearing knickers.'

Is life at Government House always like that?

Yours sincerely

RR

Comment: Douglas Kendrew the third British General I was to stay with over a period of a very few weeks, was the most outstanding of the lot.

Mining in Western Australia   Government House

He had played rugger for England, captaining the side during the year I was born. During WWII he had been awarded no less than four Distinguished Service Crosses for bravery, more than any soldier I had ever heard of.

Despite representing Her Majesty the Queen in his retirement, he had such a naughty sense of humour that the Australians loved him, and once, when mistaken for him while being driven in his Bentley to the beach and a crowd had shouted 'Good old Gov', I knew they meant it.

I am never likely to be much of a businessman, but the two weeks I spent in Western Australia were to make me feel like one for a while. For years, I had been dribbling some of my meagre army pay into a Swiss bank account, hoping to buy a chalet in the Alps one day. But the man I was sending it to, knowing that it was strictly against the rules, had told me annoyingly, just before I left England, that due to an error of judgement, which I found hard to believe, he had invested all my money in a dud Canadian mining company and had lost the lot. Now, like manna from heaven, when I arrived in Western Australia, it was mining that was nearly to claw it all back.

I had arrived right at the start of the famous mining boom, which was to make many men rich and was lucky that a friend, who had served in my regiment and afterwards in MI6, was not only living near Perth close to the action, but also knew a great deal about mining shares already.

The governor had very kindly invited Tony and his wife to have dinner one night, so on Tony telling me about Poseidon and some of the other exciting mining activities going on, I suggested, that as he was a trained spy, he should gather all the information he could and then pass it on to my brother-in-law a geologist living in England, who would evaluate the information and then, if satisfied, would notify the British stock market.

Stirred on by the fact that the Sunday Telegraph had sent a cheque to me me at Government House, only my second pre-arranged address, and not knowing if I would ever sell a helicopter, I therefore set about writing for them again. The governor had lent me his open Land Rover; so packing a suitcase I set out to find a friend from school who was farming somewhere north of Perth. But going 'somewhere' in Australia is like looking for a needle in a haystack, and it was a very long journey indeed. As I drove through the tinder dry countryside, I thought I would soon come across a kangaroo, but only when I drove down the track leading to my friends farm, did I first see one. Rather I heard one as a 'boomer', or male kangaroo, whistled over my Land Rover, just avoiding my head by a whisker. 'That was a close shave!' exclaimed my friend Tom, who appeared from nowhere 'Good ter see yer mate.'

'Have you heard about the nickel being found by Poseidon at Windarra?' Tom started off. 'Trading recently at less than a dollar, the value of Poseidon shares has risen twelve times in just a month so get in there quick mate. We call this the Mid West but north of here is Pilbara' Tom continued 'the scene of yet another success story. Lang Hancock was flying his Auster near there one day in the late 1950's when he was forced down by a storm and noticed that the earth was red with iron. Today he is a multi millionaire due to Japan's insatiable demand for the stuff. Then farther north is Kimberley where about a third of the world's diamonds are mined.' Afterwards I drove back, via a coastal lobster farm, to Perth in order to meet another tycoon, Alan Bond, who years previously, had left England with his parents, aged 12, to start life there by painting windows. He then began building houses on the steep land not considered suitable by other builders, and In 1983, after amassing squillions in property deals, he famously won the America's Cup.

When I returned to England, Poseidon shares had climbed to 300 times their initial value; but before those like myself with insider knowledge could celebrate, the nickel was found to be of such poor quality that instead I was cursed when shares in Poseidon dived together with my own through the floor!

Letter 29

Jack Amnier. General Manager
Lae Helicopters, Port Moresby
Papua New Guinea.

July 1969

Dear Jack

First I must thank you for flying me into such an extraordinary and remote corner of PNG, an experience I will never forget. I have provisionally arranged for an Alouette III to be delivered to you, in your company livery plus all the necessary spares, early in February 1970. Aerospatiale will contact you on confirmation.

I am now leaving for Fiji worried if you have received the approval yet from your parent company RTZ. I am expecting to find a letter waiting for me at the Tokatoka Hotel. Was approval granted?

Best wishes

RR

Comment: This was to be my only opportunity of selling a helicopter during my year-long travels; but until reached Rio de Janeiro during the following January, I had still received no letter or call from Jack and I was growing increasingly desperate to find out if the sale had gone through. Although I had tried telephoning him from several places, communications at the time were very difficult; and I was unable to get through. For his reason for buying my French helicopter was only due to my enthusiasm about its high-altitude performance, which I had particularly appreciated when flying an Alouette III during the filming of the movie OHMSS in the Alps.

The year 1969 was the year when copper mining and, to a lesser extent gold mining were first recognised as being of great importance to the future economy of Papua New Guinea. Ultimately, with the help of companies like Rio Tinto Zinc (RTZ), mining was to provide some 70 per cent of their export earnings and helicopters were needed to reach places which could not be accessed by the few roads built into the interior, which had remained largely unexplored until the 1930s.

New Guinea, unlike its southern neighbour Australia, is a largely wooded country complete with a spine of mountains rising to about 15,000 feet.

Within the forest are birds of paradise, some wild pig and many clearings carved out by a forgotten people obsessed by the cargo cult.

Headhunter

Shrunken head

During the war in the Pacific, when thousands of New Guineans, Australians and Japanese died, if an aircraft flew over the jungle, the natives, certain that it would be carrying some food, would cut down the trees for the aeroplane to land and kindly spew its contents for them out on the ground. Today they are useful as landing strips for mineral exploration and mining operations. I had discovered that Jack was operating an old Bell 47 helicopter from a tin shed on the edge of Port Moresby's Jackson airfield, which I was sure had been named after him. I had flown with him and two Australian patrol officers to just such a place cleared at the head of a distant tributary of the Sepik River, in the far north-west of the country. I knew that the area had a reputation for cannibalism but had no idea that the indigenous people we were to meet had never seen a white man. 'That's right, mate' stated one of the Australians 'and we have flown here to look for them'.

Our intention, surprisingly, was to get those we found to sign their cross on a piece of paper; for not only was Papua New Guinea about to become independent, but also its population needed to cast their vote for joining the United Nations. So we followed a track along a stream until it became lost in the scrub. The stream had then plunged through a series of caves, which at first being empty were then filled by savages in grass skirts with long spears. They were holding flaming bunches of grass with which they lit up our cavern like a scene from *King Soloman's Mines*. I wanted to run, but the Aussies stopped me and speaking in Pidgin, the only common language known to some in New Guinea, they tried to get through to them.

Have you come here for breakfast?

They totally failed, passed them some gifts of Western shirts, and before being eaten for breakfast, we all quickly withdrew back to the chopper.

New Guinea had the remarkable record of comprising over eight hundred individual tongues, not dialects, amounting to 10 per cent of all spoken languages in the world. Most of the population live in remote valleys, safeguarding their villagers from those around them by listening to their voices. Those they disliked would often have their heads chopped off and shrunk in the sun as trophies:

> The process of creating a shrunken head begins with removing the skull from the neck. Incisions are then made behind the ears and the flesh removed from the cranium. Red seeds are now placed beneath the nostrils, and cowrie shells inserted in the eye sockets. Then, before drying the head, the lips are sewn shut with palm pins.

Head hunting was more of an occupation, but the reasons for cannibalism were quite different. In 1961 Michael Rockefeller - son of Nelson Rockefeller, Vice President of the United States - went missing after his yacht had capsized off the south-west coast of Papua New Guinea. Although it was first believed he had been taken by one of the huge marine crocodiles living there, when people from the local Asmat tribe were interviewed, it was discovered that he had been cooked to a turn in a cannibal pot. However, when asked later if they had enjoyed eating the flesh of a white man, they said that a diet of witches and sorcerers was far better or one of those captured in revenge for crimes committed against them. Witches and sorcerers were rife at that time in New Guinea and the crime level there is still one of the highest in the world. Indeed in 1976, 10 years after I left PNG, a Sorcery Act was passed in their parliament threatening all witches and sorcerers with imprisonment.

On the day I flew out of New Guinea towards the Solomon Islands I was surprised to see the front page of the *New Guinea Post and Courier* almost covered by the grisly details of the murder of a white missionary by cannibals. He must have been nicely tender, I thought, although today the people are more inclined to enjoy pork, both from pigs speared in the forests and from those they reared, plus chicken, corned beef and dried fish. For vegetables they had plentiful supplies of sago from their plantations of sago trees, sweet potatoes, and cassava. So Cannibalism, still practised in New Ireland and a few of the Solomon Islands was a mystery, for the population of Papua New Guinea were never going to go hungry. But more extraordinary was a statement in small print at the bottom of the page: **Yesterday two men landed on the moon.**

Letter

30

Bernard Moitessier
Yacht Joshua
Papeete, Tahiti

July 1969

Dear Bernard

On flying into Papeete yesterday, and seeing you standing beside Joshua, I congratulate you on your feat of endurance.

I wanted to invite you to Le Meridien, where I am staying until tomorrow, but you head so many admirers that I was unable to get near you.

I am writing an article for the Sunday Telegraph, so I am leaving this note on Joshua. As a fellow sailor would it be possible to talk to you?

Sincerely

RR

Comment: Bernard Moitessier was no ordinary yachtsman for he had just sailed his yacht *Joshua* almost one and a half times around the world without stopping. It was remarkable that I had arrived in Papeete the morning after he had stepped ashore, gaunt and haggard with a shaggy beard, from completing one of the most extraordinary voyages in history.

The throngs of admirers around the yacht did not appear to include a single Englishman or, most likely, anyone who knew anything about yachting; and because he had been competing in the British Sunday Times Round the World Golden Globe Race, I was certain that Moitessier would contact me. Sadly, for a reason I was not to find out until I returned home to England, he had no intention of doing so.

My flight from Papua New Guinea had been similarly dramatic. The first two of the legs had been in an old Dakota, which had been converted into their idea of an Airbus. Both sides of the cabin had been cut away almost completely with lengths of Plexiglass stretching from stem to stern. Indeed the top and bottom of the aircraft only seemed to be held together by a few ribs and I felt that I was mad to be flying in it. What was worse, the passengers, many in bare feet, had probably never been in a plane before. They jumped up from the rock-hard wooden seats every time there was something interesting to see out of the windows.

Joshua

Bernard Moitessier

When one of the passengers shouted 'sharks', for instance, most of the passengers would run to one side of the Dakota causing it to bank alarmingly.

We were only flying at about 500 feet and having crossed over New Ireland we first landed at Guadalcanal, where there were still many relics of war in the Pacific. Indeed, while I was there, I discovered that, after the aqualung had been developed, divers had managed to salvage many of the valuable bronze propellers from the warships sunk in the Battle of the Coral Sea. Because they found only a few Japanese vessels, they were convinced that some Australian ships had been mistakenly sunk by the US Navy.

Ultimately when we arrived in Fiji, I was amazed to see a plaque above the door reading **Presented to Monty by Ike October 1945.** It was the very same Dakota that had been declared unserviceable when Monty had intended flying in it down to inspect us all in Devon.

After arriving in Tahiti I took a ferry to the nearby Island of Mo'orea, hoping that Moitessier would contact me there. It was a rude awakening! To say that the bare-bosomed Polynesian girls who served me lunch in a huge rondavel, were exuberant would be an understatement. Seeing me looking too British, when it came to the pudding course of jelly, pineapple and pomegranate ice cream, they tipped it over my head!

Tahiti nestles in the Society Islands in the central South Pacific and is renowned for its landscape of jagged peaks rising from lush valleys. Famous for its black pearls and the Mutiny on the Bounty when Captain Bligh and his loyal crew were cast adrift by Lieutenant Christian, who with his mutineers then settled in Tahiti, its people are described as being welcoming, innocent and carefree. I found out later that Moitessier was none of those things, describing the Sunday Times race as an 'insult to the sea'. He would, no doubt, have treated my article the same!

Letter
31

Brigadier General Augusto Pinochet
Chief of Staff 2nd army Division. Metropolitan Region.
Santiago, Chile

September 1969

Dear Brigadier Pinochet

I am writing to you only that I am currently staying in Santiago while travelling the world selling the latest French Alouette III helicopter.

Your name was given to me by a friend of yours, Felipe Neruda, who I met recently while I was staying in Tahiti. He thought the high altitude helicopter would be the ideal aircraft for the Chilean Andes.

Who do you suggest I contact?

Your sincerely

RR (Major, British Army. Retired).

Comment: Felipe had suggested that the Chilean Air Force could be interested in my high-altitude helicopters for operating in the Andes, that great spine of mountains I had seen when flying down half the length of South America, after I had spent a month writing about life in Mexico followed by a week in Jamaica. What I did not know was that only three years previously the Chilean Air Force had ordered thirty-three American Bell 205s, known as Hueys, which had not only earned a great reputation in Vietnam, but had also become the most successful helicopters in history. What I also did not know were the macabre intentions of some members of the Chilean government for putting their helicopters to good use subsequently.

Arriving in a country as switched on as Chile, I thought I needed a better introduction than Brigadier Pinochet to tell me about the place; but I knew no one. Luckily, however, I remembered a Chilean friend called Lesser from school; so I looked up his name in the Santiago telephone book. 'Yes', answered a pleasant voice, 'I happen to be Anthony's uncle.' He then asked me what sports I enjoyed and when I replied 'flying, polo and skiing' he said, 'then come and stay'. First he lent me his ponies at Santiago's San Cristobal Polo Club; and, then he took me to fly a glider over the flanks of Aconcagua, which at near 7,000 metres is the highest mountain in the Southern Hemisphere. The views from the glider were magnificent while below I saw the ski lift which was to carry me up that mighty mountain a few days later.

BBQ at the top of Portillo's one ski lift then   General Pinochet

Portillo is a ski resort two hours from Santiago, often used by ski racers to limber up before the snow starts falling in the Alps. It still has a large, yellow-painted hotel and a car park, as it did then; and I found that the single chair lift, since added to, was somewhat disappointing as it ascended just 1,000 feet. But I cheered up on reaching the top when I spied a lonely girl dressed in furs. Perhaps, since Tahiti, I had forgotten about being British, for I asked her to share a steak at my wooden table. 'Te gustaría cenar conmigo?' a voice suddenly asked from behind me. Looking round I saw a tall handsome guy of about my age inviting my gorgeous Venezuelan girl to have dinner with him. 'Shove off' I said 'she is already having dinner with me!' There followed such an argument that much to the delight of the girl, we decided to fight a duel. 'You choose the weapons' the Argentinian said, so I chose skis. 'The first man to reach the door of the hotel taketh all' I added; but when I arrived there first, the girl never showed up. So, instead, I sat down for dinner with my new friend, both agreeing that we would continue having a duel over a pretty girl once a year for the rest of our lives.

Soon after I left Chile, Pinochet, now a general, having oused Allende, was to become president of the junta. Later, it was alleged, that some of his government joined other South American politicians in a notorious operation named 'Vuelos de la Muerte.' Helicopters were used to throw left wing agitators, or their bodies, down into the sea, or onto remote mountainsides in the Andes. My Alouettes would have been used similarly.

Letter
32

Tony de Almeida
Banco Bradesco, Osasco
Sau Paulo, Brazil.

October 1969

Dear Tony

I am writing this from a hospital in Brazilia, having been evacuated from the Pantanal with dysentery, which has now been dealt with.

You were kind to have suggested I look up Richard, who, unfortunately, had already left Cuiaba when I arrived there. But I caught up with him later after a terrifying journey.

What an amazing fellow he is and it has occurred to me that you must have experienced similar hunting expeditions with him?

With best wishes

RR

Comment: After my newfound friend from Portillo, Baron Johnny Winterhalder, had flown me around his vast cattle ranches in a twin engined Piper Comanche, before returning me to Buenos Aires airport, I had taken a plane to Rio de Janeiro, the first port of call in which I had some decent contacts. Rio is a mix of very poor people living in the favelas, or slums, and super-rich people living in fabulous houses like the one I had been directed to, where jungle vines complete with parrots and brightly coloured butterflies fell behind them onto immaculately mown lawns complete with swimming pools. But by evening my host, who I had been given the introduction to, and his guests were so far gone on the 'ganga' that they made little sense, knowing, it seemed, more about Paris, than Brazil's fascinating interior. I was itching to write an article about the country but was getting nowhere, when a young fellow called Samo turned up, who seemed to know more about the country. Although Samo admitted that he knew little about the interior, he told me that he knew a man in Sau Paulo, who did. 'I will take you to meet him on my Harley Davidson tomorrow morning, but not before showing you a stone in the British graveyard here.' The stone, I discovered, commemorated a British explorer Dr Richard Mason, who in 1961, as widely reported, had been killed by Kreen-Akrore Indians, a fierce but unknown indigenous tribe, while looking for the Iriri River in Brazil, a elusive tributary of the Xingu, 'You see my point' he said 'if you venture into the interior you also may not come back alive.'

We arrived in Sau Paulo a day later, after one of the most hairy pillion rides on a deeply potholed road ever. Tony, who was working in a bank there, told me, after being introduced, 'Samo is correct I spend my all my holidays there.'

Richard Mason I presume

Tarantula   Setting out hunting for what?

'You have come to see me at a very good moment' he said 'for there is an Englishman recovering from malaria in a town called Cuiaba, who knows even more than I do'. 'What is his name?' I asked.

When Tony said 'His name is Richard Mason' I must have gasped visibly. So was Richard not dead after all? But buttoning my lip I asked him how I could find him. 'Just take tomorrow's mail plane out to Cuiaba' he replied.

The flight to Cuiaba, capital of the Mato Grosso was almost as far from Sau Paulo as it is to fly across the whole width of Australia; and it took all day. Below the countryside was almost obscured by smoke as the rainforest was burned to grow crops for a moment before soil erosion took over and wrecked the land forever. I had noticed several packages of what could only be 'white powder' stacked in a corner of the small Cessna. 'Do tell me what is in those packages?' I asked the pilot when, at last, we landed. 'You will soon find out' he replied. The scene that unfolded was straight out of the Wild West. Horses stood tied to hitching rails along a narrow street bordered by wooden-faced saloons, while amongst them stood one taller than the rest with a faded sign saying HOTEL, secured above a bullet-riddled door. But more surprising were elegant girls in long evening ball gowns, who seemed to be hanging around everywhere. 'What the hell is happening to me?' I asked the pilot. 'Those beautiful girls' he said 'are of half-Portuguese, half-Indian descent, and they are waiting to grab a rich prospector returning from the mines stuffed with gold nuggets. They are great seamstresses and I have brought them a load of Paris pattern books, thrown out by all the rich ladies in Rio.'

I asked as scruffy looking fellow behind the hotel desk for Richard but was totally shattered when he replied 'The guy left for the jungle two days ago'.

A tortoise for supper?

Or a slice of Anaconda?

It was lucky that the pilot had taken me to a sleazy bar that night and introduced me to a slim, olive-skinned beauty called Ana, who must have been Richard's girlfriend. 'Yes I can help you find him' she assured me in French. 'Tomorrow morning, pack some clothes, some drink and a sandwich, then take the bus from the stop just out of town and stay on it until there is a bend in the road. Jump off, and, I believe, that you will then find a track leading to a farmhouse where the farmer will lead you to Richard, who looks after his wild cattle.' The bus stop was a tin can tied to a tree and the bus was a huge open-backed lorry full of cackling women, obviously returning from the market with squawking chickens and squealing guinea pigs. And there was no turn in that endless dusty red switchback to somewhere for two long days! Ana, obviously had no real idea of Richard's whereabouts, for when at last a corner appeared, the track was nowhere to be seen. The truck was not returning for a month, and it was only, as fear crept into my bones under the scorching sun, that I recalled her words 'I believe'.

It took me an hour to find the tiny picada, or sheep trail, hidden amongst the thorn trees. But when I eventually reached the *fazenda*, a ramshackle Brazilian farmhouse, there were two gauchos sitting there on a plank, threatening me with six-shooters with no farmer in sight. Apparently, some Nazis had fled from Germany to the area after the war, and the farmhouse was so far-off the beaten track that I could easily have been shot as one of them. However, when the farmer, a wizened old man who had not shaved for years, turned up, saving me from summary execution, he took me in and offered me some life saving black bread and a mug of brackish water.

'Richard Mason?' I asked, and thankfully he must have understood that I was looking for him.

Jaguar pug mark

Richard with alligator behind

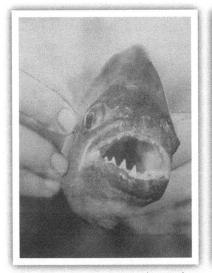

The water was teaming with piranhas

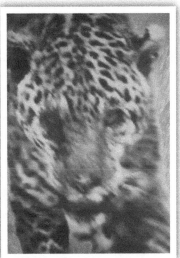

The Jaguar charged over the dogs

At dawn the following morning, he got out an emaciated pony and, mounting it, set off into the dry scrub as I followed behind on blistered feet, carrying my few belongings tied up within a towel to a stick.

We marched on until, on the second day, as the sun was setting, we reached an escarpment looking far down to the edge of the Pantanal, the largest swamp in the world, its green surface stretching as far as the eye could see. The old man then left me there, pointing to a track and his white cattle, which had once been imported through Manaus before going wild and spreading everywhere. So, as it got dark, I descended into the surrounding rain forest where, on seeing a glimmer of flame through the trees, I knew I had arrived.

'Richard Mason, I presume' I said thumping on the underside of one of three hammocks slung under a straw roof lashed between the trees. 'Who the bloody hell are you?' came back a gruff voice from under a blanket; and, turning over, he immediately went back to sleep. At four in the morning I was woken by loud barking from a pack of hounds; and all hell broke loose. 'I don't care who you are and how you found me here but make the bloody coffee.' 'How?' I asked him. 'Just pull up the canvas bucket, tip it into the can there and place it over the fire.' I did, but the bucket was alive with squirming black creatures and when I tipped it out, it was full of hand-size tarantulas.

Before I could think straight, while deciding not to find out his real name until later, we were off hunting lead by the pack of twelve hounds and an Indian tracker with a machete while I followed behind holding a Remington 700 rifle.

Richard, if that was his name, then formed the rearguard brandishing two Smith and Wesson .44 Magnums, with our Brazilian cook, armed with a sharp knife and a machete, in the rear.

My only shirt!   A sad sight

Family group

Taking turns we hacked our way through the clinging vines while the hounds fanned out ahead. 'What the hell are we hunting?' I asked Richard. 'Jaguar' he growled.

We soon found a large pug-mark in the soft earth and with the hounds fanning out ahead we hacked our way through thorn bushes, which tore my only shirt to pieces. That was fine until we swam across our first river. Holding our weapons above our heads we managed to avoid the alligators but, because of my scratches, it was the piraña fish that terrified me most. After three weeks of misery the hounds finally bayed up a jaguar, which, on charging towards me, Richard shot over my head before I had time to raise my rifle. Meanwhile, plagued by stinging insects and living largely off a diet alligator tails, marsh deer and tortoise, while, leaving a 20ft anaconda to look after itself, I contracted dysentery and had to be carried back to the farm, then by pickup to Cuiaba, and finally on by plane to a hospital in their capital Brasilia.

So who was Richard and what was his excuse for shooting protected Jaguar, apparently in a game reserve. I checked him out on returning home and it all rang true. He had been at Stonyhurst, a British public school, and had stowed away on a ship with a Brazilian friend to work on a ranch in Argentina as confirmed by the Vestey family. So there had been two Richard Masons amongst only five Englishmen living in the rain forests of the Amazon during 1961! One of them was looking for a river and the other hunting Jaguar to stop them killing a farmer's cattle, or so he said. I wondered, when Tony de Almeida later wrote a book about hunting jaguar, what his excuse would be!

Letter 33

To: Officer Commanding Police
Vigilance House, Nairobi. Kenya

November 1969

Statement

A police officer will deliver this to you about my hired car which disappeared from the car park of the New Stanley Hotel, where I have been staying for two nights.

I arrived at Nairobi airport on a flight from Cape Town arriving at 1825 on 24 October and immediately hired the VW drop-head Beetle. Yesterday morning, when I went to look for it in the car park I found the car missing with a few of my items still in it, which I reported to Herz at 1000.

I am leaving a suitcase at the hotel to collect before flying on to Cairo. Would you kindly leave a note there to say if you have found the car?

RR

Reporting for the Sunday Telegraph colour magazine 26 10 1969.

Comment: I had spied Tony, who I had met the year before in England, as he was coming out from attending a game conference in my hotel the night after my arrival. He was a 'white hunter' who ran safaris; and when I told him about my missing hired car and that I wanted to see Kenya, he offered to fly me up to Nanyuki in his new Cessna 172 the following day as he was due to meet a party of Americans there. However I was concerned when I discovered that he had only passed his pilot's licence the morning before. Even more so when I found out that there were three other white hunters waiting to board his four-seater aeroplane. But somehow we all squeezed in and Tony managed to lift off into a fast-blackening sky. As we hit the storm, the Kenyan countryside was momentarily blotted out. But after a short flight, as we began to lose altitude through the driving rain, I could see a small airstrip ahead where we landed with a splash, but, luckily, without further incident. It was only when we tried to take off again that Tony realised there was a problem.

Two of the white hunters had disembarked to meet their clients; but because the grass strip had become waterlogged and the three of us remaining were too heavy for the Cessna to 'unstick', I knew that a decision had to be made, which was unlikely to be in my favour. 'I am sorry' said Tony 'but we all have clients waiting for us at Nanyuki and so, I'm afraid, you who will have to get out.' So I asked Tony how the hell to get there on my feet. 'You follow that track,' he explained, 'which after 25 miles crosses the Nairobi to Nanyuki road, where I am sure you will be able to thumb a lift.' I gulped 'But what about lions?' I asked. 'Well there are a few trees to climb on the way' he reassured me 'but you will be unlucky to meet one at this time of day.' The sun was creating mirages, hoping that all the lions would stay very fast asleep, I started walking.

I had not gone far when much to my relief I saw a plume of dust coming fast towards me from the direction in which I was walking. 'Hullo Hullo!' said a voice I remembered from my army days in Germany 'What the bloody hell are you doing out here all on your own - feeding the lions?' I was choking in the dust thrown up by his Toyota Land Cruiser, but managed to rasp 'I was just thrown out of an aeroplane, Hilary.' Hilary Hook, who was collecting the strip's windsock, since leaving the army, had become a respected white hunter, concentrating on photographic safaris in the region of Mount Kenya. But, he told me, that like most of those in his profession, he had access to all the game parks in the land. 'Why not come and stay with my wife Jane and myself, you could be very useful.'

They lived in a delightful wooden colonial-style lodge sitting snugly on a wide shelf of land carved into the flanks of Mount Kenya. Because it was directly after the storm we had flown through but before the beginning of the 'small rains', the crystal-clear air provided view stretching on forever.

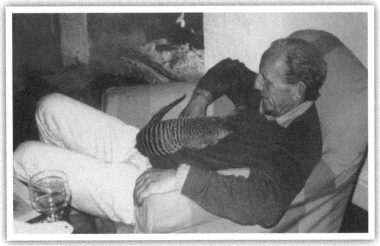

Hilary with Balu, his banded (bandit) mongoose - to be handled with care!

On Safari with the girls and a Somali guard

'We have two girls coming to stay' Hilary's wife, Jane, told me, once I had settled in, 'but Hilary has told me that you have first kindly agreed to lay out an airstrip for me and then teach me to fly my new Piper Cub.'

The airstrip was simple. I collected some rocks, painted them white, positioned them in the right places and hoisted the windsock. But the flying was more difficult as there were often strong winds on the mountain and Jane wanted to go solo before I had hardly got to know her properly. Then Hilary announced, 'Those girls are now arriving from England this afternoon. I'm busy for several days so I'm lending you my Toyota and I want you to show them some of the game parks. Are you on?'

The game parks were, but it turned out that the girls were not. Each clung to the other like two clams in deep water throughout my safari. Particularly when we had a tall Somali, armed with a rifle, standing on the back of the Toyota to guard us from some fierce Samburu warriors, he had told us about. I had to pay him most of the cash in my pocket, but the landscape - full of giraffe, zebra and elephant, with crocodile in the rivers, lion stalking wildebeest and leopard after impala, was stunning, as it was brimming with game.

We had been invited to the opening night of The Ark, a Treetops-style game-viewing lodge set facing a large waterhole deep in the Aberdare mountains. All was well until a rare, beautifully marked antelope called a bongo appeared; and an over-enthusiastic white hunter, donning an American lady's leopard skin coat, dived into the waterhole, scattering not only some dangerous buffalo, but also the bongo, perhaps forever.

Leopard with a kill   Jomo Kenyatta

It was yet another insight into Kenya rounded off when we were then invited to spend a few days down by the sea at Lamu, where Arab dhows sailed past us along the coast while we speared fish and spotted many varieties of birds, like paradise fly catchers, we had never seen before.

It was all very different from what was happening in Kenyan politics at the time. Most of those I know who served in the British Army against the Mau Mau in Kenya, some in the Kings African Rifles and others in regiments such as the Rifle Brigade are still proud of it. The Mau Mau rebellion had started in 1952 when the Kikuyu, Kamba and Maasai people plus other smaller tribes rose up against British colonial rule. There followed a period when the British Army tried their best to crush the Mau Mau. Although they may have killed many of them, they found their guerrilla tactics hard to beat and decided that by pitting one tribe against another it was a better way to reach a conclusion. The fighting was finally brought to an end in 1956, when one of the leading generals of the Mau Mau was mortally wounded by a patrol of the Rifle Brigade, and another later surrendered. But not before nearly 11,000 of their people had died, most of them while fighting against themselves.

One other Mau Mau chief, Jomo Kenyatta, was accused of plotting the rebellion in the first place. Although imprisoned by the British from 1952 until 1959, he was, however, not to be silenced. So In 1963 he became prime minister of Kenya and a year later their president, a post he held until 1978 when he died aged 80.

Under Jomo Kenyatta, it was said that the Mau Mau rebellion finally succeeded. Soon afterwards in 1964, Kenya ceased being a British colony and was renamed the Independent Republic of Kenya, with Jomo Kenyatta leading a one-party government manned by KANU the Kenyan, African, National Union.

When I arrived in Nairobi, Kenya was in its sixth year of independence. With its first general election due to be held in December, it was going through a period of considerable unrest. While I was enjoying myself going on safari and writing about the country, it was surprising that I was totally unaware of this. For me Kenya was an emerging African nation with vast resources and a growing economy based on tourism, agriculture, and later the large quantities of flowers being flown to Europe daily.

However, a feud was developing between Jomo Kenyatta and his long time partner Jeramogi Oginga Odinga in rebuilding Kenya, ending on 25th October with the 'Kisumu Massacre' in Kenya's Nyanza province, when twelve people were killed. The first I knew about it was when Hilary told me that an open VW had been found with two stiffs in it. I was lucky not to be delayed by the police at Nairobi's international airport.

Before leaving Nairobi, in thanking Hilary and Jane, I wrote a poem.

Balu the bandit mongoose

I have a pink nose
not to sneeze with
or find flees with as any mongoose does,
but to tease with and when its twitching'
to poke legs with, smash eggs with
and terrorise the kitchen.
So I'm called a bandit
not to steal with
or even deal with
but as I understand it to make 'em squeal with
and when the'm squealin'
to just close with -
my nose with -
the'm appealin' to the ceilin'.

Balu smashing eggs

Letter 34

El Ingles, Frank Evans
Salford, Lancashire

September 1970

Dear Frank

We met at a Tienta near Ronda, you will remember, when Annette and I were on our honeymoon in Spain. I will not forget you sending me into that small bullring erected on your friend's farm where I was encouraged to cape a young bull to test its bravery. I was the one who was not brave, although, only last year, I was almost as terrified by a wild cow I was asked to lasso on a ranch in the Andes watched by some cheering gauchos. But this time it was worse, being watched by those who understood the 'sport' of bullfighting, which I have never enjoyed myself.

El Cordobez with his Beatle haircut, who we met at Ronda afterwards, told us that you had already given up fighting bulls. Why?

Yours ever

RR

Comment: By 1970 El Cordobez, with his unorthodox method of fighting, often with his back turned to the bull, had won more money than any other matador in history, said to top $80 million.

My wife Annette at last.

El Cordobez. Met on honeymoon

So, just as El Ingles had done, he had decided to retire for ever. However, In 1979 both he and El Ingles, one of only three British matadors, returned to the bullring as they were unable to stay away.

After nine months on the loose I was amazed to find Annette, who had saved my life by throwing her yellow jersey to me when we were shipwrecked off the South Devon coast, waiting to welcome me home at Heathrow airport. And once again, she saved me very soon afterwards by agreeing to marry me. So, having sworn that I would become more responsible, we were hitched at the Guards Chapel in London.

Our honeymoon started off by being a disaster. I had booked a room in a smart hotel in Barcelona for our first night. However not only was my new wife disappointed by being flown only to Spain, but during our first night we were kept awake all night by the constant din of jack hammers. They seemed to chatter away in every place we then visited, where planning regulations had been consigned to the bin and buildings were being thrown up like concrete confetti. As we drove south down the coast, at one town, where we stopped for a couple of days, we found the swimming pool full of workmen still wearing their boots; and the sea beyond, so grey with cement dust that we could not swim in it. Occasionally, glimpses of the true-blue Mediterranean beckoned. Then, as the towering hotels diminished, our confidence began to grow as we neared our destination near Marbella.

A friend had invited us to stay in a new villa she and her husband had built on the Sotogrande, south of the town. Only his wife was there to greet us; and being a follower of everything Spanish - from the influence of Moorish African art from nearby North Africa, to be seen in towns such as Cordoba and Grenada, to every tradition of the Andalusian community around us - she gave us one of the most interesting times possible. Also she knew the Domecq family, famous for the production of sherry. We went to visit them in Jerez where we met Alvaro Domecq, who, in 1935, the year of my birth, while running the family business, had made his debut in the bullring by becoming a rejoneador, or a horseman carrying a lance called a *rejon* rather than the curved sword of a matador. Alvaro also had a passion not only for breeding beautiful horses but also Veragua bulls. But his life had changed considerably after becoming a respected member of the Spanish Parliament.

Our friend knew all about Veragua bulls, otherwise known as Domecq bulls, plus many of the young matadors, giving us an insight into of every aspect of bullfighting including most of its formalities. But there was one rule she did not know about - what happens on an afternoon when there is no matador left to fight the bull, for I was one of the few people to have ever experienced it. Years before I had been taken to a fiesta in Majorca when the first matador to enter the bull ring was a *novillero* (novice). The Miura bull confronting him was a breed from Seville, renowned for their intelligence, and it killed him. So when the second of three matadors booked that day was also badly gored by the bull, the third matador refused to enter the ring. It is Spanish law that three bulls should be killed, so he was marched off into custody. 'So what happens now' I asked our expert. 'By Spanish law' he replied 'if there is no matador left to fight the bull, it is the responsibility of the president of the bullring'. In this case the president was a priest, who by saying that his religion forbade him to commit suicide, got away with it.

Killing bulls in the bullring is fast losing its appeal in Majorca, as in Spain, with only a reducing number of afficionados still supporting it. But there is no reason why bullfighting should be stopped where the bulls are not killed, their horns having been tipped with leather. But it was going too far when inflatable bulls were marched through the bull fighting town of Inca, just as I had gone too far by asking El Ingles why he was giving up as a matador. For he had no more intention of doing so than I had of fighting another bull while I was on our honeymoon!

Letter 35

Richard Mason
Hotel Perola, Cuiaba
Mato Grosso, Brazil

January 1972

Dear Richard

Over two years have passed since I met you under that straw roof in the rain forests. Since then I hope you and your two men have survived your increasingly dangerous way of living. I also hope this finds you.

On returning home I got married and I am now trying to set up a sporting agency - so I thought we might co-operate. Before I left, you told me that you were building a lodge, then offering hunting and fishing safaris to Americans. I always wanted to catch your Dorado and Pintado.

Has your lodge been built yet?

Best wishes.

R

Comment: My journey around the world had taken me over 75,000 miles, or three times the length of its circumference, on a 'one direction only' air ticket costing me just £700. The helicopter sale plus my report, together with my articles for the *Sunday Telegraph* colour magazine, had more than paid for my year away, but now I needed to start earning a living with few ideas on how to achieve it. A friend of mine in Devon had a rich contact in Hereford who was a keen a game shot and suggested that, because of my contacts, particularly in South America and Africa, we should all club together and start an agency to promote hunting, fishing and shooting. We called it, rather grandly, Sporting Services International.

While in Brazil, I had discovered that Richard Mason was already compiling a list of prospective American clients. But when he told me that he was planning to run safaris in the Pantanal, I had not realised that he was talking again about hunting Jaguar. That worried me because, if Mason was no longer shooting the animals just to protect the farmer's wild cattle, and was going to organise hunting Jaguar commercially in a protected area, he would be in big trouble. I also found that he was already selling Jaguar skins in America. So, when he did not answer my letter, I thought that he could easily be in prison.

All would have gone well with the idea if the company had been introduced more gradually through our existing contacts. But our partner from Hereford disagreed as he was in far too much of a hurry.

Was John Wayne to be our best and last client!

We opened a smart-looking office in London's Dover Street, with an experienced sportsman to run it; and then, after an expensive advertising campaign, all foreign ambassadors were invited to a party.

The winter passed by with an occasional shoot being booked; and when spring came some fishing was sold but none to international clients. Meanwhile, I had been hatching up some other business plans, which would not materialise until the following year. I had made friends with Prince Bernhard, the German-born consort of Queen Beatrix of the Netherlands, after meeting him, a keen skier, while riding in a cable car at St Anton in Austria. Some considered Prince Bernhard to have been a Nazi, who fraternised with the Germans during WWII, but that was nonsense. I found him a nice enough fellow, particularly, when he asked if I could arrange some challenging pheasant shooting for him in England together with a party of his friends. It resulted not only in him bringing a party of Dutch to shoot with us every winter in Devon, and a fascinating introduction to the World Wild Life Fund of which he was president.

In hindsight we were too early into the sporting market. Ultimately a Hereford accountant rang our friend up to say he was throwing his money away needlessly. So we were forced to sell SSI for one pound!

The Right Honourable Jeremy Thorpe MP
House of Commons
Westminster. London SW1

February 1973

Dear Jeremy,

You will remember visiting my impressive (your words) frozen food emporium in Exeter two months ago, just before Christmas.

You told me a joke about the family who tried to avoid the seven year tax rule by popping their father into their freezer. The Exeter City Council are no such joke, and after seven months, without warning, they have painted double lines around our car park, making trading impossible!

Please would you help us get the lines removed?

Yours sincerely

RR

Comment: I thought, for a moment, that my first failed business idea was going to lead to a better one, although throughout the remainder of my working life that seems, fortunately, to have happened. An army friend, who had once considered letting his shoot through SSI, suggested that I should abandon the sporting agency and join him as a shop keeper instead.

Raymond was then associated with one of the major frozen food distributors in Europe, so, before the advent of much larger fish in the pond, we decided to set up a retail empire selling freezers and frozen food throughout England. So we leased a large building in Exeter with a window fronting onto the street, extensive storage capacity and a large rear car park, suitable for both customers and delivery lorries. But Crystal Foods was never to expand beyond that first unit, when, out of the blue, the Exeter City Council, decided for reasons unknown, to close off our main and essential artery of a car park.

My father would have preferred his eldest son to have followed him into politics which I almost did by fighting for Jeremy Thorpe's seat in North Devon. But as politics had changed and everything you should not do as an MP is now monitored, I pulled the plug, knowing how quickly I would be found out.

It was lucky that I was not followed the day, I went to see my wife in hospital. She had just produced our first son and as It was outside visiting hours, I kept my white coat on and located Annette's room without being challenged. But hardly had I jumped into bed with her, when the door flew open and a nurse came in. At first I hid behind a newspaper, but when I dropped it 'Oh dear!' she shrieked 'are you the new young doctor we have all been waiting for?' I should have answered yes!

Although the shop had been a success and was making the odd bean, without the car park our aspirations were already going down the drain when a well known Exeter accountant walked in. 'I would like you to deliver the largest deep freeze you have' he said 'and then fill it up with the best food on offer.' But better still was the letter he sent thanking us, which we pinned up on our notice board. He returned to top up his freezer on the day we closed, and when I congratulated him on his letter, something not normally sent to ordinary shop keepers, he looked me in the eye, saying 'So what are you going to do next?'

Replying that I was off to agricultural college, it sparked off a far more exciting business. 'Then come and see me when you get back' he said.

Letter 37

The Managing Director
Head Office, Barclays Bank
Lombard Street, London

November 1978

Dear Sir

It is with regret that I am finishing working for Barclays Bank on such a bad note at the end of my short contract. When Barclays and ICL (BARIC) bought my company Agricultural Computing Limited. (ACL), we had many of the most important farms and estates in the country using our accountancy system, but although I have tried my best for you, none now remain.

Rather than say 'I told you so,' why you did not see that ACL was already a busted flush because of the plethora of small personal computers and bespoke farm software systems coming over the horizon?

Yours Sincerely

RR

Comment: I had not seen the revolution in smaller personal computers coming either, no more than I had seen the dangerous competition emerging in the world of frozen food. So when BARIC bought ACL, I had just been very lucky as now seemed to be happening frequently in my life.

Meanwhile, just before Crystal Foods had bitten the dust I had tried one other venture selling frozen Oysters, which I was helping to grow on the River Dart. They were beautifully packed, with the 'Oyster and the Carpenter' poem enclosed, but on receiving no re-orders from Harrods and Fortnum & Mason, my luck almost ran out. Before the time of bespoke distribution, it was impossible to get frozen food to its final destination unless you had your own transport. So accompanied by Annette I used to take the oysters by train to London with all the windows wide open. 'Shut em!' would be shouted at us by the other passengers, but explaining that we were transporting urgent medical supplies, for oysters are supposed to be an aphrodisiac, we somehow got away with it. Should they have thawed out on the train, or later in our taxi, I was concerned that if I poisoned half of London, I would soon end up in the cooler myself.

During April 1974, soon after my year away at agricultural college, Paul, keeping to his word, welcomed me into his office. 'I miss your frozen food' he started 'but I expect you learned all about new computer software systems at agricultural college, and about how to use them on farm. You know, as I have many agricultural clients I am thinking they would be better off financially if they were able to analyse the results of each of their enterprises more precisely every month. Will you help me achieve this?' So I asked him when we were going to start.

It was certainly an innovative idea, which no one else had yet thought of. So we approached ICL, International Computers Limited, who then leased us two machines, each larger than a country bus, while with my limited knowledge of their abilities, I specified the programmes and others wrote them. Then, accompanied by someone expert at farm accounting, I set about marketing ACL throughout the British Isles. One of the initial prospects we approached was Lord Rayleigh's Farms in Essex. They farmed some 25,000 acres and provided much of the milk for London, and were so taken by our computer system that we later installed and programmed their own number-crunching machine, which we acquired for them. Next was a 15,000 acre farm in Lincolnshire followed by a farm in Wales where they were milking over 10,000 cows a day, said to be the largest dairy farm of its kind anywhere. They also seemed to be thrilled, until it was discovered that their manager was siphoning off some of the profits and we were told that we were no longer needed. Next was a farm in Herefordshire run by Monsanto, an American company, milking over a thousand cows under one roof. Indeed with more farms and estates joining ACL every day, Paul, who had recently married rather well, became so happy with his life that he decided, aged only forty four, to emigrate as a tax exile to Malta.

Because I had not enough enough skill to continue running ACL on my tod, it was sold to BARIC on condition I stayed on for six months.

What I had learned during my four years promoting ACL was that the computer world is mighty fickle and fast moving. So there are rules to obey. Firstly watch the opposition like a hawk. Secondly get ready to abandon ship at an instance. Thirdly never know too much about the wretched machines, or pretend that you do.

It was during this time that Richard Mason turned up at our house in Devon saying that he had been in the jungle for so long that he was frightened to cross the road. He was, he said, on his way to Africa for a while before returning to Brazil to finally set up his lodge. After he had left us for Angola, his old nanny, the only other person in England he talked to, rang us. "Richard was turned down by Mad Mike Hoare the British mercenary, he wished to join, and was starting a safari business there. But while he was looking for clients in Lisbon, he learned that Zambian terrorists had set fire to his three Land Rovers and killed all his men. So I told him to get back there and deal with them. He did and Richard has just sent me an envelope containing the head terrorist's ear.'

Derek Kimber. Managing Director
Neale Fruit Growers Ltd.
Sissinghurst, Kent

September 1980

Dear Mr Kimber

You will remember me calling in two years ago when attempting to get you interested
in our ACL computer system. I have now sold the company and returned to Devon
to set up my proposed fruit farm.

You promised to look me up and give me some expert advice. I have now planted
the first fruit trees and am about to plough up some virgin land to plant over 15
acres of fruit.

Any chance now of your professional help?

Yours sincerely

RR

Comment: I had never contemplated farming any land myself and, without help, immediately made a mess of it by planting too many cherry trees.

Dashcombe Balloon   Strawberries as large as plums

Then, without being given the professional advice I was looking for, I discovered only too quickly that without netting the trees, my cherries became a feast for every bird in Devon.

Matters were to get worse when I bought an extraordinary 'push me pull you' type of agricultural machine that could operate between the rows of strawberries. Not only did the machine fail to bank them up correctly, but also it gave me an excruciating backache. Perhaps I was not cut out to be a manual labourer. Then, in late May, on the day we opened our self-pick fruit farm, just as my wife arrived to receive our first customers, it started snowing and soon the whole strawberry crop was covered with a white blanket. Most of our prospective pickers managed to turn back before entering the steep road leading up to the farm, but those that failed became stuck for hours, causing mayhem.

The fruit farm business had started so disastrously that my brother Nicholas, who was then living in Italy, suddenly arrived to help me with a hot air balloon. One day, when we were flying over Exeter inviting people down in the street below to come a pick our strawberries, the pilot said suddenly 'You have control.' The wind was from the north west and he warned me that if we passed to the left of a tall chimney, we would be swept out to sea. We did. Balloons make up their own minds, and as we flew down the river Exe, heading for France, the bearded pilot intervened. 'Try spilling air' he shouted. 'Our only hope is to descend and find a different wind direction.' We found one but it blew us almost sideways towards a fringe of trees where having desperately re-lit the burner in order to lift over them, the pilot shouted again 'Quick - pull the plonker!' I hesitated for an instant, but there were cliffs not far beyond. Only when we hit the ground did I notice the fruit pickers scattering in all directions. We had landed slap in the middle of our opposition's strawberry farm. Next day the local rags were full of it. 'The major finding out how to grow strawberries' was one of the headlines.

The second year strawberries, due to the virgin soil they had been planted in, were as large as plums. But there was another problem. Although the till was churning over nicely there would have been considerably more cash if not for so many children stuffing strawberries into their tummies and, although we began weighing them in and out of the farm shop, they cleverly filled their pockets with stones first. So I stocked a barn with farm animals believing that we could occupy them by showing where milk comes from and the difference between a sheep and a goat. Then one day an irate woman appeared, holding a miserable child by the hand. 'Are you the owner here?' she demanded.

'I am madam' I replied. 'Well you should be ashamed of yourself.' Then, dragging along her weeping daughter, she beckoned me to the barn. The first stall had a South Devon cow looking over the door. 'Just read that' she ordered. Pinned on the door was a notice. 'The South Devon cow is the largest domestic cow it the world, noted for its easy carving.'

As most children were still more interested in plundering my strawberries I quickly abandoned my educational idea in favour of a 'Tarzan Trail' built to include tree platforms and ropes so that children could swing through the woods. Charging each of child a pound, it was so successful that when things soon started going from bad to worse, It solved everything.

But my fruit-growing efforts did not fail due to children, weather, Spanish imports or the British public's diminishing desire to go fruit picking. It was purely due to vandalism. The new manager, who I had taken on to organise the fruit growing, had invited his sister-in-law to help. Then, just a day later, when she returned from spraying some fruit trees I had suggested, he accused me of poisoning her with the spray, summoned an ambulance and notified the press. When I sacked him, as the girl was completely unharmed, he destroyed all my crops one night with weed killer.

Letter
39

Ted Turner. CNN
Atlanta, Georgia, USA

September 1983.

Dear Ted

Meeting you during Cowes Week was so special, not only for myself but also for my artist friend, Tim Thompson.

Tim will now concentrate on the two paintings you have commissioned, which, when completed, we will send to your office at CNN.

Both of us thank you for your interest and ask if you would also like Tim to paint Courageous, your winning America's Cup yacht in 1977.

Yours ever

R

Comment: Why would I expect a reply, I then thought, from someone who at that time was fast becoming one of the richest men in the world. For Cable News Network, founded in 1980 by Ted Turner, an American media promoter, was the only broadcasting station then providing Americans with news coverage for 24 hours per day, now available everywhere.

I had met Ted at an exhibition I had lain on for Tim in the Cowes Week race office, which every competing sailor had to pass through. Tim's work was selling like hotcakes, and when the loud American asked me to sell him the one in the window and then another on the wall to be told that they were both sold, he said 'By the time I come back from Beken the photographers I want to see your prices doubled. Your paintings are just too darned cheap!' So when he returned, encouraged by his remarks, business had been so brisk that there was not a painting left.

It had all started three years earlier when we moved into the family house to find that all the paintings had either been given away to siblings or sold. We were feeling pretty miserable looking at the bare walls when we were told about a similar looking painting to the eightieth-century oil which had been in the dining room, on sale in Plymouth. I took my wife to have a look at it only to find that it had already been sold, not from a gallery but from a junk shop. 'Who was it by?' Annette asked the owner. 'By a man called Thompson, but that's all I know' he replied.

Ted Turner outside a pub next to our painting exhibition at Cowes

So that winter, determined to find the artist, we rang up every Thompson in the Plymouth telephone book until at last, on reaching the initial *T*, the right man answered. 'Yes I do paint' he said 'but currently I am working as a gardener in the Plymouth Parks department.'

Tim had invited us to meet him at his cottage on Dartmoor where he explained that he had studied an eighteenth-century Dutch artist called Van de Velde while feeling bored when living in the Channel Islands. We asked to see one of his paintings, but he only had one photograph to show us. Having studied art at school, I could see immediately that his work was astonishingly good, so we commissioned him to paint us two seascapes for just a few pounds. They were so good that I asked Tim if he would like to be promoted, not on a commission basis, but in exchange for paintings for our house. 'Then let's think about an exhibition.' Thus started one of the most exhilarating art businesses imaginable, although, sadly, it was to have an unhappy ending.

I was sorry that Ted did not jump at us painting *Courageous*. There is a plaque on the pavement outside the New York Yacht Club, which celebrates his win stating 'This is where Ted Turner fell in 1977'. He was a great sailor, also winning the notorious Fastnet Race two years later. But his pride and joy were the Atlanta Braves baseball team plus the vast herd of bison he kept in Montana on just a small part of his million acre landholding in the USA. Also a philanthropist, Turner was famous for donating a billion dollars towards the United Nations Foundation, and, as a ladies' man, for marrying Jane Fonda. But for us The Mouth from the South as he was known, was to become a hero for other reasons.

Letter 40

Mlle Mariella de Spirlet
Neuilly-sur-Seine
Paris, France

February 1985

My dear Mariella

Congratulate you on getting engaged. Extraordinary enough I met Starling again at your party, who has now decided to go into business selling mega yachts. He wants me to join him, but, although he has experience in the big boat world, I have none.

As you know, I also have a passion for sailing, so my part in the new business would be to sell the marine paintings I have recently been dealing in. Because you are the only person I know who may understand Starling, what do you think?

Fondest love

R

Comment: I had met Starling during 1967 while serving in the army in Cyprus. Mariella was the daughter of the Belgian ambassador to the Lebanon and, as Beirut was so close, I used to fly over to see her at weekends. Then, one Saturday, she told me she was meeting a friend at the airport. It was Starling, who had just flown in piloting his own twin-engined aircraft. From where we were standing high up on a hill, she then pointed out his impressive-looking schooner lying just offshore below us. I had been totally outgunned and that was the last time I was to see her.

Subsequently, Starling, who was the son of a Chicago banking family, lived with my former girlfriend in London for a few years before discarding her while continuing to sail the world in his yacht having fun. I was therefore surprised when he told me his business ideas, knowing that he had never thought about earning a living! However, when I saw the plans for the shop - with its walnut panelling, dark-blue carpets and large window facing from London's Mayfair Hotel on to Berkeley Street, I agreed to join him, although I could hardly afford to, as it was the ideal location for selling Tim Thompson's paintings. Later those who passed by the window always stopped, riveted by a portrait of a yacht costing millions of pounds with a tiny note saying **The yacht is thrown in for free.**

Mayfair Marine was never going to be the success that Starling dreamt of because we needed other offices in Monte Carlo and Fort Lauderdale in the United States, which even he could not afford.

Mayfair Marine.

Before long it was also obvious that I could no longer afford continuing as his partner. Although I was beginning to sell more paintings than he sold yachts, I realised that, unless there was a miracle, I would have to fold. 'There could be salvation for you on the horizon,' Starling announced one morning, 'I have a Swiss banking friend coming to see us next week who has a great idea for an investment up his sleeve.'

If you let him have that money you received from the sale of your cattle recently, he says that he will be able to double it within three months.' Perhaps foolishly I let the gnome have it, but although my shares had dropped after three months to just 2 percent of the purchase price, knowing that I had to leave Mayfair Marine fast, I failed to redeem them.

While commuting from Devon every week, yet trying to make a living elsewhere, I was becoming worried. Although I was never to become rich, my fortunes were soon to change dramatically, not due to any success at Mayfair Marine, which was then to become another company, but due to a profitable business born directly from it. It had all started when a pretty girl arrived in my office one day and said that she wanted to borrow the two paintings of the America's Cup I had hung on the walls of our reception area. Having explained that it was not possible I told her why I had first become involved in the Cup. 'I wrote to Ted Turner of CNN suggesting that Tim Thompson painted *Courageous*, his America's Cup winning yacht' I explained 'but when he did not reply I had an inspiration. I rang Thompson suggesting we painted the yacht in any case and with it every winning moment of every race since 1851, when the yacht *America* won.' She looked excited. 'Let me ring my boss' she said.

Letter 41

The Honourable Patrick Lindsay Esq
Fine Art Director, Christies
King Street, St James's, London
London

January 1986

Dear Patrick

Nicholas and myself are once more together in the Alps. He says that has just heard through the auctioneering network about your illness. We are both so concerned that you, of all people, should be struck down in this way and wish you a speedy recovery.

No one will forget how you charged the Sotheby's banner, flying from two strong posts planted in the ice at the finish of my brother's car rally from London to St Moritz last year. What a sportsman!

Is your Porsche, with the 'otheby's' logo on it, still in two halves?

R

Comment: Unfortunately Patrick was never able to read my letter. His wife Annabel, in thanking me for sending it, told us that he had very sadly died before it arrived.

Driving the Benz - parent of Mercedes   Three little girls from school

He was a keen sailor, the owner and pilot of a Spitfire and other veteran aircraft, and had competed successfully in countless classic car races. Not very long before he had obtained the record price for a painting at Christies. When he charged one of the two solid wooden posts holding up the Sotheby's banner, it had split his car right down the middle. It must have been his final fling. He had always been one of my heroes.

The centenary of the Cresta Run had been an unforgettable occasion by my brother holding a Sotheby's/Cresta car rally starting in London. Driving a 1934 Aston Martin, with exhaust pipes sticking out of the bonnet, he had told the eighty drivers taking part, that it was a rally and not a race. But when the drivers were later topped up with champagne, kindly provided by my friend Fred Chandon at Les Caves de Moet et Chandon in Epernay, most of them disobeyed and after the pit stop stamped on their accelerators. Thus the first man to arrive on the lake in St Moritz, a Swiss racing driver, had not only completed it in record time, but also won another record by driving his Porsche down the hairpin bends of the Julia Pass in a straight line, with it finishing up as a tin can. Unfortunately my brother was unable to join us at the finish, because his Aston had broken down somewhere in France. But having rung up the firm, a new distributor head had been fitted by a mechanic from nearby farm within two hours. So that evening he and his brothers celebrated by performing 'Three little girls from school' at a raucous Cresta dinner.

The rally had not been popular with the police for by then car racing on the lake was strictly forbidden because, they said, when the ice melted the exhaust fumes would still harm the fish! So one day the British sat down in the main street and blocked the traffic for several hours. When, later, a tall policeman asked us what else we had in mind, we passed him a 'dirty book' from a joke shop and when he opened it, the electric shock passing through his metal-studded boots felled him to the snow.

The centenary celebrations were sensational with air displays and parachutists, plenty of bagpipe music and finally the best firework display many of us had ever seen. Our mother had sworn that she would never travel out to Switzerland to see her miscreant sons again. 'But Mama' we had begged her 'this is a once in a lifetime experience and your three sons promise to behave.' I had picked my mother up at the railway station, but as I was late for a briefing, instead of driving around the town to her hotel, which was at the far end of the circuit, I drove her just twenty metres up the street the wrong way. Unfortunately the same tall policeman was standing by the door of the hotel. Thinking that my mother, sitting in the left hand seat, was driving, he pulled her out by the collar and arrested her within five minutes of her arrival!

Letter

42

Graham Walker Esq. Royal Thames Yacht Club
Knightsbridge, London

December 1986

Dear Graham

I am indebted to you for arranging that my whole collection of twenty six paintings
of the America's Cup should be exhibited at the Dorchester Hotel and then viewed
by Prince Charles and Lady Diana on the occasion of the America's Cup ball.

I am also grateful to you for asking British Airways to fly my wife and myself to
Western Australia in order to hang them on the panelled walls of your British club
in Fremantle. We wish you luck with White Crusader.

But should the whole collection be sold in your club, will you accept the commission
you are asking, only if you complete the sale personally?

Yours sincerely

RR

Comment: Graham Walker was a busy man involved in both the food industry and White Horse Scotch Whisky, thus adding White to the name Crusader.

White Crusader   Our paintings at the America's Cup ball

I had made it clear, that as I had lent Graham the collection, I was not giving away any commission lightly. Meanwhile, while I and my wife were hanging the paintings, we had met Graham's club manager who I agreed to send me an urgent telex if he saw anyone interested in them.

It now seemed to me that Mayfair Marine, which had first appeared to be a waste of my time and money, was rapidly proving to be one of the best investments I had ever made. Firstly due to meeting Graham Walker, then surprisingly, as described later, due to Starling's introduction to his gnome friend from Switzerland.

I had started working on the Americas Cup in the magnificent library of the New York Yacht Club and then in that of the Royal Yacht Squadron in Cowes, eventually taking three years to research and to finally complete with Tim, twenty six accurate paintings. When that girl had rung Graham Walker to tell him about them he had responded immediately. He said 'I understand from Sophie that these paintings are are so remarkable that I would first like to show them off at our fund raising ball in the Dorchester and then have them flown out to Australia to hang in my White Crusader Club, headquarters of the British challenge.'

Somehow a photographer had concealed himself behind the ballroom curtains, and although using royalty to promote anything commercial is forbidden, the photographs of Prince Charles and Princess Diana viewing the paintings with the artist were seen everywhere, particularly in America.

Letter 43

Sandro Petinelli
Via Luigi Tosti, Rome, Italy

May 1987

Dear Mr Petinelli

We met last month at Sotheby's sale of the Duchess of Windsor's jewels, where you said you were hoping to buy a piece of British history. You will recall that we had been discussing the Duke of Windsor meeting with Hitler. I then told you about my father being presented by the Russians with Hitler's hot line red telephone in the Fuhrerbunker.

When I asked you if, as a dealer, you would be interested in buying this important piece of history as no British auction house would touch it, you said that you would send me eighty thousand pounds sterling - unseen.

Why has the money never arrived?

Yours sincerely

RR

Comment: As I had not sold the America's Cup collection yet and my adventures in Mayfair Marine had left me seriously out of pocket, I had been tempted to sell the red telephone, which friends had said would only bring me bad luck, having offered it first to the Imperial War Museum.

Although the dealer obviously had no intention of paying me for the telephone, at least I was now aware of its potential value, which encouraged me to investigate it further. So I approached a friend I had met on the Cresta Run named Peter von Siemens, who was to become president of Siemens, the German company that had manufactured Hitler's 'instrument of death'. Apart from it being a standard army telephone he was unable to help, but it was to trigger another drama.

'This is going to be the most exciting jewellery sale ever.' announced my brother Nicholas, by then heading Sotheby's office in Geneva. Now solely responsible for the acquisition and sale of the Duchess of Windsor's jewels after a tip off by The Hon Angus Ogilvy, Princess Alexandra's husband and a director of Sotheby's. The two-day auction was to be held in a vast marquee erected overlooking Lake Geneva in the grounds of the Beau-Rivage Hotel, where the Duke and Duchess had stayed in 1939 prior to meeting Hitler.

Nicholas at work

Jewels

My brother realised that the Duchess's unique jewellery collection was of such excellent workmanship and intimacy, with words, such as 'We are ours now' from the Duke inscribed on them, that it was going to be worth far more than the jewels themselves. So the sale was advertised widely.

On Friday 3 April 1987 my brother's efforts were to be rewarded when no less than 1,500 bidders, including many of the richest people and most famous jewellery dealers in the world, crammed into the lavish marquee, accompanied by 250 members of the world's press and countless TV crews. Eagerly awaiting my brother to stand up on the podium were also many celebrities such as Shirley Bassey and Elton John while over 300 telephone lines were opened to outside bidders such as Elizabeth Taylor, who, apparently, was waiting to put in a bid while sitting by her swimming pool in Los Angeles.

Nicholas, then appeared accompanied by beautiful models, destined to wear the jewels as they were auctioned, also being shown on large screens erected both inside the and outside the marquee for the crowds thronging the hotel lawns. There was a roar as lot 1 was announced and then a louder one when it sold at eight times its estimated value as printed in the Sotheby's catalogue. We realised immediately, just as my brother had said, that we were about to experience one of the greatest jewellery auctions of all time, ultimately to raise over £30 million for the Pasteur Institute in Paris. When I returned home I found that Sandro's cheque had not arrived, which I was to be very grateful for later.

Letter 44

Dennis Conner. San Diego Yacht Club
USA Dock, Fremantle, Australia

December 1986

Dear Dennis

We met at the Crusader Club in Fremantle yesterday, when you refused to back down from your accusations about Michael Fay and his America's Cup yachts the 'Plastic Fantastics'.

Michael Fay has invited me to fly to New Zealand to reassure the Royal New Zealand Yacht Squadron that, as a member of Lloyds Register was present throughout the build, his yachts were within the rules.

Because your allegations are therefore directed at our British Lloyds Register, I have been instructed to ask you to kindly retract them?

Sincerely

RR

Comment: Dennis Conner, who at that time was acknowledged to be the top America's Cup helmsman in the world, was just making things difficult for the New Zealanders. But he was wrong about Fay's Plastic Fantastics. 'Those boats' he told me 'sail straight and level like friggin' darts. You know why, sir? Because they have been built light at both ends.' What Conner meant was that the GRP had been laid down thicker at the centre of the yachts rather than at bow and stern. In order to prove his point, he had then asked for holes to be drilled through their hulls, which Fay, needless to say, had angrily rejected.

Michael Fay had approached me earlier in the Crusader Club, where, accompanied by my wife, I was hanging the last of the paintings of the America's Cup. 'As you have studied the Cup's history as much as anyone' he said 'would you agree to fly to Auckland to see the Royal New Zealand Yacht Squadron on my behalf, who have put their name behind my challenge, and explain that Conner is spouting a load of hot air? They have nothing to fear as you, as an Englishman, can vouch for the validity of my yachts certification by Lloyds Register of London.'

Two days later, while Annette took an aeroplane to Sydney in order to enjoy riding horses on a friend's sheep station, I flew to Auckland to be met by a man from Michael's merchant bank, Fay Richwhite, and then driven by him to spend the night at a hotel.

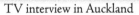
TV interview in Auckland   No better than a bunch of bloody pirates

The following morning I was picked up and taken to meet the somewhat austere looking gentlemen waiting for me at the Royal New Zealand Yacht Squadron.

Then, having then been introduced by the commodore, I gave the easiest rebuttal of one man's complaints than I have ever given. That was fine but not so good when I was afterwards besieged by the press asking me to give the same reassurances many times over. But at least I was able to spend two more days on North Island, managing to visit the Hauraki Gulf, where, during the millennium, I was able to write about New Zealand winning the America's Cup for the first time.

We had flown back by San Diego, expecting to find the book which I had just written about the Cup, with a foreword by Ted Turner, on the shelves of every bookstore, but had failed to do so. So the friend we were staying with telephoned the American co-publishers in New York saying 'If the major's book is not on sale here by the morning, I'll come and break yer legs'. Later I had the honour of being invited by the commodore of the New York Yacht Club to give their after-dinner speech. In talking about my ancestors, who, under the guise of being French Huguenot shipping merchants had prevented with their cutlasses the sport of yachting from developing for over 50 years, I told them that by hanging onto the Cup for 132 years they, themselves, were no better than a bunch of bloody pirates. I was lucky to return home!

Letter 45

Starling Hemmel Esq
10 Cadogan Square, London

January 1987

Dear Starling

It was a pity that I joined you in the first place for I never really had the money to invest in the company. The overheads have been killing us.

Thank goodness that my paintings have sold so well and helped shore up the lack of yacht sales, but now that I am leaving Mayfair Marine with the potential of selling the 120ft Motor Yacht Walanka I need your reassurance that I am to be paid my half share of the commission. Also, after three years creating and promoting the America's Cup collection of paintings, that if sold, I split the proceeds between the artist and myself.

Do you agree?

Yours ever

R

Comment: 'Never go into business with friends', they say. I had written the letter the day after our Telex machine had started chattering about the American determined to buy the collection.

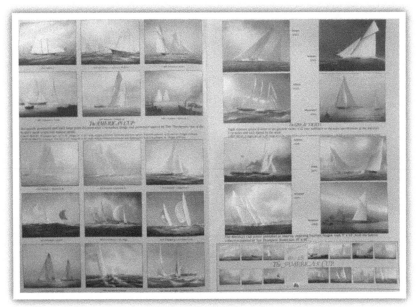

America's Cup prints

MY Walanka

A girl had entered the shop that morning and asked me if she could purchase the whole set of fifteen America's Cup prints I had just produced. She wanted them for her fiancé.

I had selected the best plates from the two books about yachting and yacht racing I had completed by then. A friend, who worked in the Tate Gallery, then asked me to send the transparencies to their exclusive printers, who finished them beautifully with a thin coat of varnish. I was soon selling them in batches of up to a hundred at a time.

When she told me that her fiancé was an 'America's Cup buff' I asked her, 'So is he out in Fremantle watching the racing?' Amazingly she answered yes. 'In that case I am buying you a return air ticket to Perth later today, so that you can deliver them yourself'. She looked totally mystified. 'You can't be serious?' she said. I was serious for not only was Rosie, aged 32, extremely good looking, but she also had her own PR agency. 'Just help me when you arrive there by finding the American interested in buying the originals, take him back to the White Crusader club, where all the paintings are hung, then, if you manage to sell them for the price Jack, who runs the office there tells you, ask him to telex me here immediately.' 'I will' she said. 'Yipee!'

I waited for ages with bated breath for the telex to arrive as the hours ticked by. Then it happened. 'The eagle has landed' is all it had said.

Getting myself out of the partnership had been difficult and resulted in an extraordinary manoeuvre. We had understood that the most esteemed yacht brokers of them all, Camper and Nicholson, were on the market. So we bought them. Of course I was unable to pay my half of the deal, so I sold my worthless shares in the new business to a Greek.

I would have danced with joy if Starling had agreed to my terms but he did not, getting back to me not until eight days later after I had left the company. 'Dear friend' he said over the telephone 'there is no way I can agree to the terms you have put on paper. Those two America's Cup paintings hung on the wall when that girl came in, were the only reason that we, as a company, were able to sell the collection and that was achieved by you using the office telex machine. Thompson will take half and we will share the balance. Regarding the sale of *Walanka*, she was only referred to, not because you were an individual, but because you were a partner in the company. So again the profit will be shared between us. In total the amount you receive should just about cover what you owe us from the last six months trading.

'Damn you' I swore under my breath. Another business down the drain.

David Rosow. Stratton Mountain ski resort
Vermont. USA

March 1988

Dear David

I was delighted when you acquired our paintings of the America's Cup and it should become an important collection in the USA.

While staying with you I apologise for skiing over the speed limit and being escorted to the compound. Although Tim Thompson tried his hardest, I just had to leave him for a burn up. I also apologise for complaining about the drains when I arrived. You correctly told me it was a skunk!

Having met Dennis Conner again, I was dismayed to hear of his plans, for defeating Michael Fay's megayacht later this year. Can you not stop him building what is so obviously going to be catamaran?

Yours sincerely

RR

Comment: David Rosow, a former naval officer, had made a pocket full of dollars out of establishing tennis and other sports facilities throughout the United States.

David Rosow with an America's Cup painting behind at Stratton Mountain

Dennis Conner in London signing my America's Cup limited edition prints

I had been invited by David to hang the first of his America's Cup pictures at Stratton Mountain after they had been imported into the USA. But before I set out I was prevailed on by Thompson, to buy him an air ticket as well, for he said that after all the time we had spent together since I first discovered him as a gardener living on Dartmoor, I had never taken him to meet any of our clients. It was a major mistake.

On returning to Devon I was due to meet Tim in Plymouth to discuss a new commission, but he did not turn up, later telling me that, as I no longer was involved with Mayfair Marine, he had become wedded to another gallery. Then thanking me for all my introductions in the States, he announced that I was no longer his agent. After everything I had done for the man, and all the money I had made him, I could not believe what I was hearing.

Suddenly all had fallen apart, just as was happening on my fruit farm and in San Diego. Michael Fay, incensed by the behaviour of Dennis Conner the previous year in Fremantle, had decided to ask Bruce Farr to build him a leviathan of a yacht to be sailed by no less than thirty-two sailors. That was a mistake; for in 1988, it was unlikely that the American courts would support such a controversial move against the American skipper. Conner had told me at Stratton Mountain that he had a secret weapon to defeat the leviathan which he was not going to copy, as it was up to the defender to decide on the specifications for the next America's Cup yachts. Fay was not the defender and Dennis would blow him out of the water with a yacht carrying a quarter of his crew. The race that followed was no match at all. A catamaran had never been entered for the America's Cup previously, and Conner beat the New Zealander's yacht over two courses by a considerable distance.

My involvement in the Cup paintings was becoming a sad story, only relieved by the fact that I still owned the copyright to the Thompson prints, which I had not only specified but also created with compositions in my own watercolours first. So I have continued to sell them through distributors that I have since often visited in countries with an interest in yachting throughout the world.

Later in 1987, when Dennis Conner had announced he was passing through London, he agreed to sign my special-edition prints of his American yacht *Stars & Stripes* defeating the Australian yacht *Kookaburra III* in the finals of the America's Cup held previously in Fremantle. After his defeat by Alan Bond with *Australia II* at Newport in 1983, Conner had shown obsessive grit and determination as a skipper rather than as a billionaire to win the Cup back four years later. By recruiting Merrill Lynch and Ford to put up the cash and NASA to provide figures from the most powerful computers known to man, he had been able to design four gunsmoke-blue yachts to compete against one another in order to choose the best boat to fight for the Cup in Australia. Dennis, who had started life with a draper's shop in San Diego, and was by now the first skipper to train a crew, known as 'my guys', for 365 days of the year without a lunch break, had been named as America's greatest sailor, winning the Cup four times.

On meeting Dennis at Heathrow Airport, where we were soon surrounded by a noisy crowd, he immediately asked me, 'Where's the rester ....' However, neither hearing or fully understanding his broad southern drawl, I must have told him at least twice, 'Don't worry Dennis. I have booked lunch at a restaurant overlooking the Thames' knowing that he could only eat when looking over water. It was only after I had twigged that the poor fellow was begging for the restroom, did we avoid an embarrassing shipwreck! When later I took the prints in my small dory to be signed also by the defeated skipper on the Isle of Wight, I almost lost the lot when swamped by a passing oil tanker.

Planning Officer
South Western Gas Supplies
Broad Street, Bath, Somerset

February 1990

Dear Sir

I understand that a new gas main is to be installed in the ground running between Exeter and Plymouth close to our village.

Please would you kindly send me a map of its precise direction as soon as its known?

Yours faithfully

RR Chairman Dashcombe Parish Council.

Comment: I may not have received a reply either because it was discreet information, or they feared that objections would be raised. Or, perhaps, that local businesses and residents would plan to tap into it.

That, although not possible, would have caused mayhem. But on hearing nothing from the planning officer, I, one day, tackled a man doing a survey on a nearby estate who told me everything.

The gas pipe was going to be approximately 5 feet in diameter and would be dug to a depth approaching 20 feet in most places, he told me and he was only too happy to peg out the route of the proposed pipeline on the ground. I was correct, it was going to pass through Dashcombe. Each section of the pipe would be joined by welders, who would finally inspect it by riding through the pipe on trolleys. Finally he told me that the land above the pipe would be restored to its previous state; and if there were any problems they paid excellent compensation.

I had pricked up my ears on hearing that, for after my fruit farm had been trashed by the person I had trusted to run it; I was already planning the next step, which I knew was far beyond my resources. They included a possible nine-hole golf course as we were intending to run the farm for corporate team building and entertainment. So I learned how to build golf greens and then completed all nine of them myself with the farm JCB, costing me peanuts.

Dashcombe quad bike

It was unfortunate for British Gas, therefore, that when their huge diggers arrived plus lorries stacked with gas pipes, they found that they had to pass through no less than four of my golf greens!

They called up their chief inspector immediately, who being under duress, asked me to meet him on site as soon as possible.

The crashed aeroplane   Paintball notice

'Well' he said 'as we are now running short of time we have no other alternative than to pay you twenty five thousand pounds for each green. 'Would you be happy with that?'

Some fifty quad bikes were then purchased plus a number of automatic clay pigeon traps, while anything to do with golf was abandoned immediately. Meanwhile I drove up to Gatwick airport with a low loader and purchased a crashed aeroplane. This we painted with Columbian markings; and having carried it into the nearby woodlands, we bolted the wings back on and secured it up in a tree to look as though it had just crashed through the branches. We then cordoned off the area as a paintball site crisscrossed by wooden bridges over a deep ravine and added an assault course built by the Royal Marines, and a zip wire, which, at that time, was the longest in the country. But the bob run was best, sporting bobs on wheels, which negotiated a half mile banked up track snaking down the steep hillside behind the farm

The next job was to adapt the farm buildings. First the hayloft where a bull had once fallen through onto a cow below, became a club room with antlers mounted on the walls and a 'Stagger Inn' bar. Then we created an office and a kitchen, while outside the barn we built the first amphitheatre since the Romans, wired up for giving lectures. Also twelve twin en-suite bedrooms and a lecture room. All we needed then was to build a helipad for the air ambulance to take the injured away.

Letter

48

The Chief Executive
David & Charles publishers
Newton Abbot, South Devon

January 1989

Dear Sir

I have just heard the unwelcome news that David & Charles have been sold to Readers Digest, who, I understand, will no longer be interested in continuing to publish my 'Story of' books.

Please will you kindly suggest another publisher. But more importantly, explain to me how you can feel justified, without any warning, to sell my latest book 'The Story of Skiing' in its entirety to Canada?

Yours faithfully

RR

Comment: Perhaps foolishly, I had never employed an agent over my first five years of writing books. David & Charles had blatantly started selling their stock to the highest bidders without any regard to authors such as myself in order to bolster their accounts when flogging their publishing business to *Readers Digest*. My *Story of Skiing* had only just been published, when, after travelling most of the ski resorts in Europe and then to two in the USA, I was informed by letter that they had sold my book with all its rights to a publishing company in Canada.

When a book is distributed in a foreign land the author will only benefit from reduced royalties, but should a book be sold to a foreign publisher, unless authors have a watertight contract, then they are lucky to benefit from much of a return at all. Therefore, as David & Charles had already ceased to exist, I had little chance of claiming anything back although the book had cost me a fortune in expenses. The first book I had written *The Story of Yachting* had been subsequently translated into two other languages. It was a good start, for shortly after it was published, while visiting the London Boat Show, I was presented with The Nautical Book of the Year award by the First Sea Lord. For a moment, I thought that I was becoming a reasonable writer but I quickly realised that the award was just as much due to the paintings. My second book *The Story of the Sporting Gun*, which I had again been encouraged to write by David & Charles, was more difficult, for I needed a new artist to illustrate it.

Story of Yachting: Reliance 1903 had the largest sail area ever.

Story of the Sporting Gun: Ptarmigan in Scotland in winter.

So stirred on by the success with my yachting artist, I arranged to visit the Exeter University Arts Department and find someone suitable.

It was a good move, for one young wildlife artist stood out so clearly among the rest of the students that I had no need to create a short list. His name was Andrew Ellis, later to become one of the most celebrated bird artists, particularly of raptors, in Europe. But at first, he needed some practical experience.

I had taken Tim out sailing initially, so I soon introduced Andrew to a shooting party in Scotland where I had a friend who owned a grouse moor. He watched an October shoot taking place and then met the game keepers. He was soon being told about black game, capercaillie and ptarmigan while finally being taken to see them all in their particular habitats. These were in the heather, deep in the pine forests or high up on the snow-sprinkled peaks, where the ptarmigan were already changing into their white winter plumage. Andrew was captivated and It also became a new and enthralling chapter in my life. I learned not only about the development of guns and gunpowder from their inception but also about the sport of shooting as it spread internationally to embrace every variety of bird shooting from sandgrouse in Africa to partridges in Spain, doves in South America, and quail in North America, all conducted in totally different ways.

If you write about a subject that is often in the news but not always understood, then the book may be a winner. *The Story of the America's Cup* was just that and a natural progression from finding out the facts, often from original newspapers, studying every situation very carefully and then, in watercolour, composing the scene I wanted the artist to paint in oils. Wherever I had travelled during my three years of extensive research, I had written down all the facts and figures of every match since 1851 in considerable detail. Then, after I had taken all the paintings to be professionally photographed in London, David & Charles printed them to a format, which they assured me could only be achieved by them and no one else in the business.

The beauty of this, my third book, was that it was then to be republished after every America's Cup, held at three-to four-year intervals according to it being held north or south of the equator. Meanwhile it became fatter with every commentary, painting, line drawing and sometimes a portrait of the winning skipper by my wife, every time it is printed. I have therefore updated the book ten times, with it also being translated into French and Italian. But when David & Charles ceased trading, my book was sold to a publisher in New Zealand who now pays me a pittance!

Letter
49

The Director Autoritat Portuaria De Balears
Moli Interior, Elvissa, Spain

August 1989

Dear Sir

I have recently returned from sailing around the Balearic Islands with my wife, our two young sons and one of their friends.

Knowing that most of your harbours are at least one thousand years old, there is still no excuse for the filthy state of the one we sailed into on the east coast of Ibiza. We left there immediately in case the children might catch an unpleasant disease.

Please will you revise your sewage systems before too many other sailors suffer the same fate and re-assure me, before my next visit, that suitable steps have been taken to clean your harbours up?

Yours faithfully

RR

Comment: We had sailed the 50 foot yacht *Narooma* out into the azure blue mediterranean looking for the small island of Ibiza about six hours away.

Narooma

Giles at the helm

As our bad memories of arriving there linger on, we have no wish to return, although, the harbours may now be immaculate. But our memories of sailing past Cape Salinas, the southernmost tip of Majorca, will never be forgotten as they would have terrified the toughest sailor.

I had come across the splendid-looking ketch one day in Torquay harbour. The owner had taken me out for a sail; and, because he was too busy producing fibre optics, we had agreed to share her for six months of the year. Since I had then encouraged him to sail her down to the Mediterranean, we enjoyed her for six years while teaching our children to sail. Ulysses is said to have met the Sirens in the seas off Ibiza, but the wind we met later off the south-eastern coast of Majorca resembled a hurricane. The Garbi is a wind revved up by thermal depressions in North Africa; and although summer squalls are rare on the Island, this one came gusting in from the Sahara like a born killer. I had seen it coming and rushed forward to reduce the canvas as were flying a genoa jib, a full mainsail and a mizzen. Our two boys were already struggling on the jib halyard; but before I could join them, their young friend, who we had left at the wheel shouted 'I can't hold her!' as the yacht veered suddenly at 90 degrees to port, directly towards the cliffs only a hundred yards away. As she heeled over alarmingly, it was difficult to crawl astern again but far more frightening to find that George, the auto pilot, had not only gone crazy, but now refused to be switched off. It was impossible to override the steering system; and only at the last minute, as the wind howled in from astern and we were nearly on the rocks did I remember the circuit breakers under the companionway.

AN EXPLANATION!

Half way through my book I believe it necessary to answer three questions the reader may have been wanting to ask from the outset.

Why did you keep so many of your letters?
Apart from photographs and cuttings, they were the only dated record of my parents lives and we just followed their splendid example.

Why are only the unanswered ones printed?
It was not possible to include all my many letters. Those not answered better illustrate the ups and downs of life.

Why did you treat life as such an adventure?
Life must always be an adventure. John Masefield says it all for us:

> The power of man is as his hopes
> in darkest hour the cocks are crowing.
> With the sea roaring and the wind blowing;
> Adventure. Man the ropes.

Miss Tracy Edwards. Yacht Maiden
Royal Southampton Yacht Club.

September 1989

Dear Tracy,

We cannot thank you enough for bringing your team of twelve girls to train at Dashcombe before what must be the first ever encounter by a ladies crew with the world's fiercest oceans.

Perhaps we were a bit tough on you, but that is what you wanted. We must apologise, however, for having to send two of your team to hospital by air ambulance, although one of them returned immediately.

As you were the first ladies team to come to our Adventure Centre, before you set sail would you kindly agree to writing an enthusiastic testimonial for us to use for advertising purposes?

Yours ever

R

Comment: I had employed a retired army colonel to run our team-building courses at was now my new training centre, formerly my pick-your-own fruit farm.

Explorer praises new valley centre

Dashcombe Valley's new training and business centre could pioneer similar projects throughout the country.

That was the hope expressed by Devon explorer Sir Ranulph Fiennes when he officially opened the centre after flying in by helicopter last Friday.

Sir Ranulph spoke, at the opening ceremony, of the 'enormous shortage' of similar establishments throughout the country.

He said the centre's business function was to provide the training which led to successful trade, and attacked the lack of training Britain's managers received compared with their counterparts in countries such as Japan and Germany.

'Forty per cent of UK managers have no training. This is pitiful, and I hope it will be put right through places such as Dashcombe Valley.'

had realised the importance of training during his four years as a Junior Employment Minister.

He also believed the centre would show businessmen the importance of teamwork, adding that he hoped Dashcombe Valley would be 'a great success.'

Indoor facilities available include a barn-style conference or dining room for up to 60 delegates; two spacious lecture rooms for up to 30 people; a 4,000 square feet training hall; and single and twin cabins all fitted with showers.

Around 2,500 acres of surrounding land include extensive woodlands with forest paths and bridges; steep hillsides, ravines, two lakes, a nature trail and orienteering course.

Dashcombe Valley also employs between 15 and 20 trained part-time instructors - the majority women - whose other jobs range from train drivers to secretaries and housewives.

Ranulph Fiennes opened the centre once it was fully established

The Dashcombe team

The colonel, who I believed to be the right man for the job, had once shouted at me so fiercely to quit and cross my stirrups in our regimental riding school that I have been in pain ever since. Nor did the girls learn to love him, as I thought they would, for one soon damaged her leg and broke a wrist when falling off a quad bike, and another had to leave the field when hit smack in the face by a paint ball. But they did learn about toughness, leadership and bravery resulting in *Maiden*, which features again in the book, completing her world circumnavigation with honours.

It had taken me almost two years since leaving Mayfair Marine to create the Adventure Centre as a new, and profitable enterprise, helped greatly by the money from British Gas. wishing to start on the right foot I invited Sir Ranulph Fiennes to open it. Ran was the son of my father's greatest friend of the same name, who in 1944 had been killed in Italy at the battle of Monte Cassino. Ran's greatest exploit, in my mind, was climbing the notorious North Face of the Eiger, in the Alps, with four fingers missing from his left hand. So when I invited him to become a director of my Adventure Centre he must have thought it remarkably tame.

His supposition was wrong. Anywhere less tame would have been hard to find. When parties first arrived, they were told about a siren. Should it go off during the night they had to be out of their huts within seconds. It did, always at two o clock on their first morning. 'There is an emergency!' an instructor would shout. 'An aeroplane has crashed in the woods somewhere, shot down yesterday evening by the clay shooters due to it's Columbian markings. Your task, in teams of three, is to look for the plane, the parachute and then the pilot plus the canister of white powder he was carrying. The first team to report back here with it will be given a full English breakfast. The rest of you will receive nothing.'

Often it would take them more than an hour to find the aeroplane hidden high up in the trees, then another hour to find the distant parachute and one more the dead pilot, who was concealed in the deep, thorny, undergrowth. But the canister of white powder was more difficult as the pilot had buried it. It was only the start of their mission for on returning they would be tackled by drug dealers and warned by notices saying 'minefield'. The only safe route was to cross over a deep ravine on a bridge also primed with explosives. A team had safely crossed it once when the instructor following them was blown clean over the side!

Letter 51

The Attorney. The America's Cup Organising Committee
San Diego Yacht Club. California. USA

January 1991

Sir

You have sent us a letter stating that the America's Cup Organising Committee are now holders of the state registered logo of the America's Cup and that we, a British company, are in contravention of the law because, without your permission, the words 'America's Cup' have been printed below the images on our fine art prints. You have also pointed out to me that a Japanese company has just paid the America's Cup Organising Committee 3,000 dollars to settle a similar breach of your law because they had been selling America's Cup T shirts. The America's Cup was named by the British after the yacht America won the race around the Isle of Wight in 1851. Do you honestly believe that rights to the name are now American property?

Yours faithfully

RR

Comment: My first reaction was that the Yanks were just trying it on. But I was wrong for the America's Cup Organising Committee ACOC were, in fact, broke having failed to appreciate the huge costs of running the event in San Diego. It was true that they were also suffering from a lack of challengers for 1992; but once again, as it happened all too frequently in America's Cup history, the law was partly to blame, not that their attorney would admit it. The raid by the New Zealand Leviathan against Conner's much smaller catamaran in 1988 had drained their coffers dry due to fighting the result in the court rooms,. For that reason, when a second letter arrived from the ACOC doubling the amount of money first demanded while insisting that we destroyed all our stock, I knew that they were being serious. Rather than answer the letter, I took immediate action by closing our bank account and moving the money elsewhere. So, fed up by being treated like criminals, when 3,000 dollars plus three times the costs were next demanded by ACOC, I flew with my wife to confront their wretched attorney in San Diego. We were staying with friends and when the fellow arrived in his new Porsche we discovered that he thought we were an international company operating from a skyscraper like Trump Tower. We gave him a scotch and he left, promising that the ACOC would willingly market our prints for us in 1992.

Letter 52

Maurizio Gucci. Yacht Creole
Astilleros de Mallorca, Palma, Majorca

May 1994

Dear Mr Gucci

You have stated that you would like to purchase the painting of your yacht Creole, by the marine artist Tim Thompson. Tim has been working with me since 1987. Apart from the America's Cup Collection in Connecticut, his work hangs in some of the finest houses in world including a royal palace belonging to the Sultan of Oman.

I understand you are on Creole at the yard in Majorca, just for a few days, supervising some of the work being carried out on her during her extensive refit. I shall be flying to Palma on the last day of the month and should you have left I will give the painting to your captain. Or will you still be on board?

Yours sincerely

RR

Comment: I had not met Maurizio Gucci before, but hoped I was about to do so, as the name of his company was famous throughout the world. He had passed by Mayfair Marine one day while I was on another mission.

Painting of *Creole* by Tim Thompson

Maurizio Gucci

But when I arrived in Palma with Annette, each holding one side of the large gilt framed painting above the roof of a taxi, we met his Italian captain but not, unfortunately, Maurizio who had already left for Milan.

The 200ft three masted *Creole* is considered the largest wooden sailing yacht in the world and is certainly one of the most famous. Currently owned by Allegra and Alessandra Gucci, the two daughters of the late Mauritzio and his wife, Patrizia, the black-hulled schooner is maintained in mint condition, to be seen sailing at some classic yacht regattas around the Mediterranean. But that hides the extraordinary story of her shadowy past involving jealousy, suicide, and murder.

She started life with a curse on her when, in 1927, the third magnum of champagne aimed at her bows on the slip at Camper & Nicholsons yard in Gosport, England, failed to shatter. First commissioned as *Vira* by a rich American carpet manufacturer, she passed through British ownership, renamed as *Creole*, to be commandeered during WWII, with her rig removed, as a mine hunter. When the war ended, like many other vessels, she was left in a sorry state until Stavros Niarchos, the Greek shipping magnate, took pity on her. However, while she was being restored at vast cost, and her cabins hung with priceless works of art, Niarchos fell in love with Eugenia Livanos, the beautiful daughter of another shipping millionaire whose bruised body was later found on *Creole* during May 1970. Some said it was as the result of an overdose.

With her death, Niarchos lost interest in *Creole*, and she then became a Danish training ship until 1982 when she was bought by the Italian Mauritzio Gucci. But by 1995, having moved the yacht to Majorca due to jealousy amongst his family over the success of the brand Gucci, it all went horribly wrong again. Accused by his wife of overspending on *Creole's* lavish restoration, then of courting a young girlfriend Paola Franchi, Maurizio was found shot dead in his Milan office, supposedly murdered by a hit man hired by his wife Patrizia, who was subsequently to spend sixteen years in jail.

After meeting *Creole's* captain, knowing nothing of this gathering storm, while being shown around her resplendent interior, being enhanced with carved ebony and marble floors, he rang Mauritzio in Milan to announce that the painting had arrived. 'Ancient or modern?' I clearly overheard his boss say. 'Modern' replied her captain, for the yacht was less than seventy years old. 'I do not want it then' Gucci concluded abruptly. So we had to smuggle the painting back to Exeter airport, where by my wife's slight of hand, we avoided the customs officer and the duty he would have charged us. We sold it the next day to Arthur Maiden an advertising tycoon and sponsor of the yacht *Maiden*, for the same price.

Letter 53

The Chief Constable. Devon & Cornwall Police
Middlemoor, Exeter, Devon

September 1994

Dear Chief Constable

Our problem with the 400 Travellers camped on our land is becoming far worse. Not only have we now lost at least 100 sheep to their dogs on the surrounding farms, but our home is increasingly becoming an island, cut off by those of them so high on magic mushrooms that they lie down on the road and swear at all who try to remove them. Although the law has to date prevented us from evicting them, we are now fearful that they intend to stay camped on Haldon Moor, just half a mile away, which they have now been occupying for over four months, permanently. Today we heard that one of them had murdered another with a shovel.

Please kindly let us know what action you are taking to remove them?

Yours sincerely

RR

Comment: The small patch of moorland near our house, on which we had carved out an airstrip, was a natural target for nomadic Travellers, often purporting themselves to be Romany Gypsies, but obviously not.

A police officer arrived in full rubber gear, but brought none for myself

They had arrived one night like a swarm of locusts, in the most shabby collection of vehicles we had ever seen. Although we always received warning through our local publican, who would also alert local farmers, on this occasion the large number of tractors and other farm machinery deployed in order to prevent their arrival were of no consequence.

On previous occasions, I had managed to avoid both the law and the police, who had their hands tied too securely behind their backs. British law stated that the police could only intervene either when criminal damage had been caused or if the the Travellers were proved to have used violence and obscene language.

So my answer had been to fasten an eviction notice to a fat fencing post driven into the ground in the centre of their encampment. Firewood was not easy to find on the moor; so before long I was usually able to take a photograph of them burning my precious fencing post, thus providing sufficient evidence of criminal damage to call the police. Going to the law was a non starter.

On this occasion there was plenty of evidence without such a ruse and perhaps spurred on by the murder perhaps, the deputy chief constable replied immediately. 'You will be relieved to hear that the police are taking all necessary action in this case.' That was all that I heard until I answered our door bell on the following morning. 'Who the hell are you?' I asked the terrifying looking figure who confronted me, for he was clad from head to foot in black rubber gear. 'I'm from Special Branch' he replied 'and I'm accompanied by a hundred men all dressed like myself in riot vans with orders to get rid of your gentlemen immediately, sir!'

'They are not gentlemen I can assure you, but why the hell are you all dressed in such ridiculous outfits?' I enquired. 'We are all dressed like this' he explained, 'because, sir, we believe they are armed with AIDS-infected hypodermic syringes and we need you, as the landowner, to come and tell 'em to get the hell out of here.' 'Thanks for your kind invitation' I said. 'Just give me a rubber suit and obeying the law, I will also then have to risk my neck confronting those four hundred bastards.' He looked confused. 'Sorry, sir, we have not brought one for yourself, sir.'

The women Travellers were even more frightening than the men; and as we approached their sprawling campsite, apart from the rancid odour that burned our nostrils, the cacophony of screams and curses that greeted our black phalanx of policemen must have been heard several miles away. 'You just stand out in front, sir, and we'll take care of you' their officer in charge tried to reassure me, but they nearly failed.

Waiting out of sight down the adjoining road was a convoy of tractors and diggers stretching for several hundred yards. When they advanced I instantly recognised our own yellow JCB leading the pack, driven by one of our gallant farmhands. But as soon as I started reading out the riot act to the hornet's nest of angry Travellers with a megaphone, telling them to get out fast in order to avoid the Black Death, I saw the poor man set upon and dragged out of his cab by the hair, while others slashed the digger's expensive tyres to ribbons. 'Let battle commence then!' I shouted down the megaphone. 'You had also better get your wheels back on those vehicles fast before they are towed out onto the road by our tractors, or watch them being trashed.' It worked, and as a trench was dug to stop them re-entering, I felt like rounding them up again to clear all the filthy refuse left on our beautiful moorland. For It was spiked with so many hypodermic needles that, although the litter was removed, the area has had to be avoided ever since.

Subsequently, I thanked the chief constable for his successful intervention; and we travelled together by train to London and then on to Westminster, where we met the secretary of state for the Home Office. Our intention was to stop such a large number of Travellers ever congregating again by limiting the number of vehicles in any one place to six only. But when the law was finally passed the Travellers congregated in other locations no differently. Instead they gathered in groups of six vehicles but placed a little farther apart from one another!

Letter 54

Mr Howard Green. Keepers Cottage
Ashcombe, Near Dawlish, Devon

January 1996

Dear Mr Green

Notice to leave my employment.

I have now sent you three warning letters about your behaviour as our game keeper but they seem to have been disregarded.

It has since been reported to me that you have made some derogatory comments about a party from Dorset who recently booked the last Saturday of our pheasant shooting season.

I therefore have no hesitation in dismissing you with a months notice. I also ask you to quit Keepers Cottage by the last day of February 1996. Meanwhile please continue feeding the birds, unless you do not wish to?

Yours sincerely

RR

Comment: Although I had dismissed the keeper by the book, I was surprised not to receive a reply from him when I discovered that the shooting party had never, ultimately, turned up. I also felt uneasy when, on further investigation, I could find no evidence that the shooting party had ever been booked, unless by the keeper himself. But that was also unlikely unless he was angling for me to sack him without sufficient reason in which case he could pursue me for compensation.

Perhaps it was no surprise when six months later, on the last day that any claim for unfair dismissal would be accepted by the courts, a nasty letter from Green's lawyer came winging through the post. Determined not to spend a fortune on defending myself against a man who was spending too many hours in the local boozer, I then started preparing my own defence, conscious of the fact that I had insufficient evidence about his final misdemeanour. Worse still I had also discovered that Green may have been consorting with the Travellers, who had blighted our lives for so long, when they all visited the local pub together. As a result I searched the hedgerows whenever I walked through the village, knowing that some years before, due to a family feud, one old dear had been hit over the head with a tractor engine starting handle.

As I lived on an agricultural estate in the tiny hamlet of Dashcombe, which I was to manage as a trustee but never to own, it was always a joy meeting our few villagers, like our 90 year old blacksmith who had once shod our children's ponies from soon after the war.

Press report

The Earl of Devon kindly brings us a pheasant

But now there was an enemy in our midst. Because Green had starred in a BBC documentary I had asked them to produce about our shoot, he was strutting around like a film star and convincing others of his innocence. So when it came to the court case I was not surprised, when I arrived with only our youngest son Giles, and found half the press in England gathered around the Exeter Courts of Justice, waiting for me.

The first day, the only one of my defence, seemed to go well except when the court clerk suggested I should use the fire escape to avoid the cameras. Instead, Giles, fetched his battered old car to collect me from the underground car park, where I was jumped on by the press anyway.

'Call the first witness for the prosecution' came the cry as I entered the courtroom on the second day of the proceedings; and when the first witness turned out to be a detective, my heart stopped beating. 'I understand stated Green's lawyer 'that you have enquired throughout Dorset about the shooting party, which was the cause of Mr Green's dismissal. Is it true that you found no such shooting party ever existed?'

'My Lord' I begged the judge 'this is such new, damning evidence that I am only able to defend myself if I may call the witness who reported Green.' But the judge explained that I had already had that opportunity.

My son had quickly telephoned my wife, and she luckily found the farm mechanic, who had spilt the beans on Green's behaviour, lying under a tractor. He had never been to court before and was scared stiff when the judge finally on seeing him arrive, relented and called him into the witness box. 'Then tell me precisely what happened that day Mr Gay?'

'Well it was like this milord' Gay managed to blurt out. 'Mr Green, who had asked me to repair his Land Rover for the umpteenth time, told me, that due to a shoot being booked on the last day of the season, when he had invited friends of his to shoot, he was going to give them a bloody awful day. So I rang Major, who said, "Write your statement down, sign it and bring it to me immediately" which is what I did, milord.' But the judge did not believe him. 'That is nonsense Mr Gay 'Well, milord, I must admit that as my writing is no good, I did ask the wife to write it down.'

I knew that my case was going disastrously wrong. More so when the judge still seemed to be unhappy while the press wrote away frantically. 'Mr Gay' he continued, 'if you do not tell me the truth and the whole truth you will be taken down to the cells for perjury.' 'Milord' after a long pause Gay stuttered 'Yes I was lying milord for she is not actually my wife.'

I soon realised that the judge had been cleverly proving to the court that Gay was a reliable witness, and because I had believed him when he came to see me before I sacked the keeper, it really did not matter if the shoot from Dorset existed or not. The court was therefore dismissed and I returned home relieved that it was all over. But I was wrong. *Who then*, I thought to myself, *had made that shoot booking and why?* Three weeks later I was to find out.

The door bell had rung and when I opened it I had found a nice enough looking young man in plus fours waiting to see me. 'Major' he stated 'I understand you are looking for a new keeper. Give me a year's trial and apart from rearing stock for other shoots, I will give you all your pheasants for next season just for the cost of the food bill.' He had taken me to the cleaners for when, already worried, I discovered that he was rearing many more pheasants than I had agreed to, my final jolt came when I went to see our promised poults released into the pens that June. There were none. He had sold the lot and vanished!

And so the Dashcombe shoot was left without any pheasants that winter, only saved by the Earl of Devon, who kindly brought me one in a basket.

The Chief Constable. Devon & Cornwall Police
Middlemoor. Exeter, Devon

November 1995

Dear Chief Constable

It is probably out of order to be writing to you so soon after your help in getting rid of our Travellers.

Alex, who runs our local Elizabethan Inn, and who has been our eyes and ears when warning us of approaching Travellers, has yesterday been threatened with immediate closure for not reporting a fire arms incident that took place in his pub's car park. Alex is a good man who runs a reputable business, well supported by our villagers.

Alex did not witness the event but while investigating it, may have been slow reporting it. Would you very kindly look into it further?

Yours sincerely

RR

'The Chief Constable thanks you for your letter and reassures you that, as this is a serious offence, the matter will be thoroughly investigated.'

The Dashcombe Skeet Shoot

The Stagger Inn Bar

Following the sacking of Green the gamekeeper, and despite the fact that we had been left without pheasants for the season by the man who had instigated it, I attempted to continue with a couple of days' shooting by appointing our tractor mechanic, the man who had reported Green, as our keeper. But, for a moment, it was to be a baptism of fire!

Our clay pigeon shoot at the Dashcombe Adventure Centre had been improved free of charge, surprisingly, by a man called Marker, who had kindly added a skeet range. Skeet shooting, unknown to many, is an Olympic competition where shooters move through seven stands set in a semicircle, and then from one in the centre, and aim at clays fired fast at a standard number of angles from two trap houses placed in precise locations.

I was only to discover why Marker had been so generous when he gave an attractive girl we employed a shotgun and invited her to shoot with him. Pheasants were thin on the ground, so Marker had booked the day from the new keeper at a considerable discount. The day had gone reasonably well without the girl shooting anyone, until they retired to the Stagger Inn bar at the adventure centre, where they drank themselves stupid before staggering out to the local pub for a very late bite of food. However what Marker had failed to realise was that Liz, the other girl in his life, who was the daughter of the owner of one of the top hotels in Torquay, and the person who, behind the scenes, had been financing the skeet range, was already waiting at the pub with bared teeth ready to bite him to the bone.

Hardly had Marker's shooting party flopped down to eat when Liz made her appearance and immediately slapped her disloyal boyfriend hard across the face. She would probably have left it like that; but, as described to me shortly afterwards, our girl from the centre somehow managed to lurch up from the table and strike her back. The cat fight that followed would have tested any pub owner's nerves to the limit; and fearing for his other regular customers, Alex had the two brawling women, followed by Marker, thrown out, bleeding, into the car park.

'Marker, you left the shoot without paying me' stated our new keeper, who happened to be waiting for him there. 'Nor will I, you bastard!' he replied. Whereupon our keeper punched him so hard on the nose that he ran, bleeding, to his new Mercedes, grabbed his shotgun, loaded it, and stuck it in the keeper's ribs. For Alex it was particularly unlucky. Unknown to any of us, our girl was already married to a man in the Special Branch, and when she got home, she had told him everything.

Andrew Gaunt Esq. The Gauntlet Syndicate
Lloyds of London, One Lime Street, London

September 1996

Dear Andrew

Following your letter about the insurance crisis at Lloyds, I fail to understand how
I and, presumably, all the other 'names' on your syndicate, were not informed about
the looming problems of Asbestosis.

It is obvious both to myself and to my many friends, who have been members of
Lloyds for many years, that we have been hoodwinked into believing that all was
well with our Lloyds insurance syndicates, including yours, and that we should
continue underwriting.

Why did you keep the problems so secret?

Yours sincerely

RR

Comment: The famous Lloyds of London *Lutine bell* had last been rung in the late seventies when a ship sank and Lloyds syndicates at the time had to honour the annual premiums by paying out on them. However when the Asbestosis problem became known, the losses, some going back as far as WWII, but most not disclosed until the late 1980s, would have meant tolling the *Lutine bell* continuously until it crashed to the ground.

 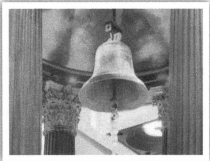

LLoyds building   Lutine Bell

The Asbestosis crises was not only to create mayhem at Lloyds, however, but to cause many individual underwriters, known as 'names', to fall to the ground with it, and, in the worst cases, to commit suicide.

I, like many others, did not have the resources to be a member of Lloyds in the first place, and as a 'burnt name', which we came to be called, my losses were unsustainable. At least Lloyds had subscribed to our children's education by then, but now it was payback time and I could see ourselves having to sell everything. How could Lloyds have continued recruiting new names, I thought, knowing that their house was about to fall down and many of their underwriters with it? Indeed the scourge of asbestosis had already become frighteningly visible to me while waiting to see my doctor on a bench in our local surgery. A man had lurched past looking very much on his last legs; and when I asked him what was wrong, he replied 'That bloody asbestos the Navy got me to install in their effing ships during the war is about to kill me.'

'Hold your nerve' my wife Annette had implored me when the demand from Lloyds arrived, 'let's think this through carefully and decide what we can flog first while we look for a better solution.' But I knew of none.

'Twelve years ago' I explained to a girl sitting in an office in London's Curzon Street 'I invested some money in a business named Amarindo. through my company Mayfair Marine. Although I immediately lost most of it, I was hoping to find them still here, but now, blast it, they have disappeared and have no doubt gone to the wall.' She looked at me smiling. 'No, not at all' she answered. 'You will find their new offices in Grosvenor Square next-door to the American embassy.' I must have run there faster than anywhere in my life and when I saw the impressive building and burst through its burnished doors, I could not believe my eyes. Sitting alone at a gilded desk in a vast atrium, with the name Amarindo embroidered on the carpet and all the way up the stairs, was a lovely girl with auburn hair. 'Can I help?' she asked. 'Yes' I replied, I have been away a long time, and, as I had asked you not to send me any correspondence, I was looking for Amarindo back in Curzon Street. But you have moved here!' She hesitated, then replied calmly. 'We have also been looking for you, for you have the privilege of being our very last private shareholder. Go upstairs and meet Garry one of our partners. He will be waiting for you.'

'Major' the Japanese-American, exclaimed, shooting out a hand. 'We have been looking for you everywhere. You see those few shares you still had with us have since been leveraged at six times their value and then compounded over all those years. You are now a very rich man!'

Letter 57

His Grace The Duke of Roxburghe
Floors Castle, Kelso
Northumberland

October 1996

Dear Duke

I have returned recently from fishing your Driburgh beat on the river Tweed.

It is a lovely stretch of water, but I hope you will not think me impertinent in telling you that one of your ghillies was being disloyal to you. I told him that I strongly objected to what he was saying.

Would you like me to give you his name?

Your sincerely

RR

Comment: My luck at Amarindo must made me far too cocky at the time, although, after paying off my huge losses at Lloyds, there was not too much left in the kitty. It had been an amazing investment for which, ultimately, I had to be grateful to my former partner in Mayfair Marine.

Fishing   Bertie our terrier, surveys the catch.

At first I had cursed his Swiss banking friend who had encouraged me to invest in the high tec company, which also had an office in Silicon Valley, USA. It had subsequently been so successful that Garry had donated £27 million of their profits towards a new business school at Cambridge University, while building up a stable of classic racehorses.

So happy with a few more bob in our pockets we started taking holidays. For years a great friend had been inviting us to stalk the stag and fish for salmon on his beautiful estate in Wester Ross on the north-west coast of Scotland, and we revelled in it. But I was a rotten fisherman and remembered the day that his uncle, who we had named Black Rod, had caught seven salmon within just an hour. When he put his rod down for a moment, I had crept over from my position on the river bank and having snipped off the fly he was using with my scissors, landed a fish immediately. They were great times as was stalking on the high peaks.

Fishing the Driburgh beat on the Tweed, owned jointly by the noble Dukes of Northumberland and Roxburghe, had been another experience. I had hooked the seat of my waders as my fly had been blown by the wind, and when I had to take them down in order to retrieve it, the ghilly, who I had just berated for bad mouthing the duke, had peered down over the river bank saying 'We have a perfectly good loo in the hut you know,' thinking I was about to have a crap!

Letter
58

Mr Edward Rice
Manager
Lloyds Bank
Exeter

January 1997

Dear Edward

We are finding life difficult. The weather this winter continues to be appalling! Now, because of the torrential rain, the road up to our building site has, in one place, been washed away.

As the lorries bringing the workmen their cement are now unable to reach them, the men are having to carry the sacks considerable distances in order to keep going.

Please will you consider extending our loan should we be unable to fulfil your requirement of finishing the barn conversions by Easter?

Your sincerely

RR

Comment: I was becoming frightened. The home farm was now starting to making some money and combined with the meagre profits from the Adventure Centre and the income from my fine art print business, I had felt that it was the right moment to take another step forward in ensuring the estate's future solvency. Meanwhile the dairy farm I had decided to convert into holiday cottages was too small to be profitable as a farm any longer, so, once the cows were gone, the builders had moved in.

But as it was all going wrong due to the weather I urgently needed confidence that the additional loan from the bank would still be secure if we did not open the new enterprise in time and thus fulfil the income projections I had promised the bank manager. It was only after many sleepless nights we at last heard that he agreed to giving us an extension.

Starting a holiday cottage business, as well as my other enterprises, was not what I really needed to do with my life. But the hamlet of Dashcombe nestled in one of the most attractive valleys in England, just four miles from the sea in one direction, and eight miles from the wilds of Dartmoor in the other, while blessed with a micro climate to die for, I was confident that it would be step in the right direction.

The problem was that I was converting seven farm buildings at once after the dairy farmer, like so many others in our valley, had retired, and it was not possible to build them in stages.

The first holiday cottage development

The indoor pool

Also, because one of the cow barns was going to be left unattractively empty, I had decided that we would need it for an indoor swimming pool. It was only by greatly increasing the workforce that we finished most of the development in time only to see our guests moving in through the front door as the workmen crept out of the back doors of each building.

The worst ordeal for both myself and Annette, had been shopping for fifty beds with the bedclothes to go with them plus buying the material for some sixty curtains and countless other furnishings. To do so I would arrive early with our horse trailer at a local emporium to be met by men with mill boards. 'Major' they would say 'what do you want to tackle first, lamps or lavatories?'

The swimming pool had also been a problem for it could only be completed in year two. As the farm stood on one of our steep Devon hillsides, it had to be made doubly secure by our men pouring tons of concrete before it could be signed off as safe and unlikely to cause a flood, by the district building inspector. But when it came to the following spring the building inspector had been sacked, taking his notes with him! So it cost us another fortune having to pour all the concrete again.

But my most anxious moment came later when we were converting a farmhouse with an adjoining barn into just one holiday cottage sleeping twenty eight people. The man supervising the work suddenly left us without warning just days before our first party was to arrive for the New Year. Worse still, in order to try and finish on time before he became fed up and threw in the towel, we discovered that not only had he been paying unprofessional, last minute, labour in cash without declaring tax, leaving us with a nasty problem for later, but the fire doors were not up to specification, the decorating was far from finished and many of the bedrooms had not yet had their doors fitted.

By then it was approaching Christmas with all the suppliers shutting shop and every man who could handle a screw driver, or even a paintbrush, going into hiding. So there was nothing for it but for the family to get stuck in ourselves.

All seemed to have gone well until the day after the party arrived. 'I would like to inform you' complained their leader, who we discovered ran a major travel business, 'that our holiday has been ruined as we have been unable to cook for twenty four hours.' 'Why I asked?' 'Because the range blew up in our faces' he spat out. 'So why you not use the gas cooker instead?' I replied. 'Because' he continued angrily, 'we found that it had never even been plumbed in!'

There was one other problem. It was no good having such a large holiday cottage without an equally large car park. So before we received any more flack it was imperative that we built one. That would have been easy if the only site possible had not been directly across the road running past the cottage and then over the river beside it. So we built a substantial bridge wide enough and solid enough to take all the plant machinery but not, unfortunately, high enough to take what happened next. Devon is always blessed by decent rainfall but not by the sort of storm that then blocked the bridge with so much foliage that the river flowed out over the road and ripped up over a hundred yards of tarmac.

'Major', said the man from Devon Highways, who appeared as if by magic, 'this is going to cost you a lot of money'. 'Because of an act of God?' I asked innocently. 'If you mean that God gave you permission to build the bridge, that's fine Major, but even he could not grant you the planning permission!' I groped for an answer. 'No' I retorted 'but that is where we now have to sort our sheep so I did not require planning permission.' He had me by the short hairs. 'So your sheep do not swim?' he asked. 'Of course they do' I replied 'but they also know how to poo in the water and that is not longer permitted by Health and Safety regulations.'

Letter 59

General Manager, Stardust Marine
2 Rue d'Athènes, Paris, France

April 1997

Dear Sir

I recently chartered a yacht from your company to sail from the Island of St Martin via Nevis to Antigua in the Caribbean.

On sailing from the Island of Nevis it had to be at night and strictly against your rules. For no one had mentioned the volcano lighting up the sky over Montserrat. When we calculated that beating against a twenty knot wind in a six foot sea, it would take us fourteen hours to complete the revised passage, and we needed daylight to spot the reefs approaching English Harbour, there was no alternative.

Why did you not inform us about the erupting volcano?

Yours faithfully

RR

Comment: Fishing holidays were never going to be straightforward, but neither were sailing holidays. Perhaps the French did not mind if the English were inconvenienced either by an erupting volcano or by a reef. Stardust, which later sponsored a French yacht for the America's Cup, seemed to be far more dependent on their fellow citizens or on French Canadians from Montreal, and they were probably very well insured!

At last, now we had a little money in our pockets, we had discovered that chartering a 50 foot yacht with three other couples was one of the best and most reasonably priced holidays you could take during the winter. Thus every March we continued to hire a bareboat from Stardust Marine, who would promote me as skipper from aspirant to enseigne to lieutenant to capitaine and, finally, to amiral, over the next few years, with an increasing amount of discount. I admired their marketing skills and the excellent condition of their yachts except on that voyage from Nevis when the cockpit echo sounder went berserk. I had hit my head photographing some green monkeys on the island, and descending to the chart table in a violent sea, while trying to guide the yacht through a narrow gap in the reefs, I became unusually seasick. 'Is this really your idea of a holiday?' Our friends all asked.

It was not the first time we had been in trouble in the Caribbean. One stormy night on a previous voyage when we had taken up a mooring off Port Elizabeth on the Island of Bequia, we had hardly retired to our bunks when there was a massive jolt; and I flew up on deck believing that another boat had hit us. I was wrong. Our rotten mooring rope had parted and we had cannoned, luckily sideways, into another yacht.

Yellow Parker provides us with a lobster

Swimming pig. Note the plimsole line!   A pirate looking not best pleased.

'Say, have you your insurance papers there? We will be reporting this. We have sure gotten some damage.' It was pitch dark and when dawn came, not far away on the rocks lay a yacht with a mighty great hole in it. 'See what we've done' said one of my friends but the yacht we had hit was still bobbing on her mooring with not a scratch on it.

For me everything in life was an adventure and there was always one to be had wherever we sailed. Among our happier moments was when a fellow called Yellow Parker, brought us some lobsters on board. 'You must have met my brother Brown Parker' he said 'for he saw you off from Union Island.' We were beginning to like the Caribs until putting into the port of Kingstown on the Island of Saint Vincent, two 'pirates' started climbing up one of our warps tied to the quay. We grabbed some oars; and, as I had once learned at Eton, shoved them off into the drink. It was not much different when we sailed into a horseshoe cove further up the coast. After tying the yacht's stern to a palm tree, we had waded ashore amongst some amazing swimming pigs in order to have a bite in a corrugated hut, pretending to be a restaurant. Under the corrugated we could see eyes looking at us: for drugs were being traded. Then a man rushed in. 'Have you seen my pistol?' he demanded.

Letter

60

Brigadier Templer, Bee Keeper
Woodbury, Near Exeter, Devon

May 1977

Dear Brigadier

You assured me, when I purchased your twenty-five bee hives, that your bees were the most docile of any that you have known, yet when I collected them, I learned otherwise.

I have now been able to collect the first twelve hives in my horse trailer, but before I return to pick up the rest of them I need your re-assurance that, as my protective equipment has not yet arrived, I will not get stung so badly the second time.

Would you be able to lend me something more secure?

Yours sincerely

R

Comment: I had soon realised that the brigadier was not prepared to accept any criticism from a mere major. Furthermore, as was pointed out by a bee inspector later, that his bees were no different from anyone else's bees; it was just that, like many others involved in beekeeping, he was often able to handle them without gloves and a veil except in unusual circumstances. Perhaps I was the 'unusual circumstances' for the moment I walked towards the hives they started making a 'beeline' for me. On that first occasion, the Brigadier had given me an old bowler hat to wear with a veil attached to its brim; but what he had failed to point out, was that, when I pulled the bowler down on my head, the top of the hat flew up like a letter box encouraging his bees to fly straight in!

I had arrived at six o clock in the morning with a dreadful hangover, but, having been stung through the top of the hat by several of his bees, my headache had vanished. Despite the therapy, however, I thought it would be better to get there earlier when the bees were deeper asleep. So on the following day I arrived, with a man to help me, at half past five in the morning before the cocks had started crowing. It was still very dark, but we congratulated ourselves on loading the twelve remaining hives into the horse trailer without a problem. The problem came later.

We must have run over some barbed wire on leaving the field where the hives had been placed. Climbing up the steep hill halfway back home, I sensed the trailer was falling to one side and becoming difficult to tow.

Living dangerously!

Back home

Leaping out of the Land Rover we discovered that our worst fears had been realised, for both left-hand tyres had deflated. Worse still the spare wheel had never been used and that was flat as well.

It was before the time of mobile telephones; so all we could do was wait to be rescued, knowing, as we had no top doors on the ancient trailer, that once it became light, the bees would wake up and start flying out. Luckily, however, it was not long before a police car drew up. 'Please help us.' I asked. 'We have a load of bees onboard and they will soon become dangerous. Would you kindly arrange for someone to pick up the outfits we have ordered from the bee shop in Exeter and give them to the AA, asking them to bring two new wheels for our trailer as fast as possible?' Knowing that the shop would not open until nine o'clock, all we could do then was to hunker down and wait for mayhem.

It came quicker than expected. The dozen hives of bees all seemed to wake up together; and as they swarmed out of the back of our horse trailer, the early morning traffic slowed almost to a standstill as they were confronted by the black cloud of stinging insects. They were all over our truck, so we never saw the AA arrive until we had both been stung on the face trying to slightly open the windows. 'The two wheels are OK now sir, just give me your address and then drive on slowly home.' We did and all the bees followed us to return to their individual hives later. Amazingly, it was the honey they then produced that lead me to yet another far more exciting enterprise.

Letter 61

Mrs F Simon. The Crystal Palace
Fairway Road,
Blackpool,
Lancashire

June 1998

Dear Dorothy

Than you again for your purchase of the 'Weeping Tree' at the Chelsea Flower Show.
We hope that it is now connected up in your amazing greenhouse successfully. Do
let us know what your husband Frank thinks of it?

Yours sincerely

RR

Comment: It may not sound plausible but yet again one business in my life had lead to another, and this time it was because I had started to be a beekeeper!

'I'll have that' said the lady in the purple trouser suit, who had pushed her way through the crowd on the second day of the Chelsea Flower Show. 'How much?' Setting a price had never occurred to me 'No more than a small family car' I answered. 'Well don't tell husband and bring it up to our place in Blackpool we've called the Crystal Palace right away.' Noting down her address I replied 'Crystal was the name of my very first company.' But she had already disappeared back into the crowd again.

The ten foot high copper 'Weeping Tree' was only the second water sculpture I had ever attempted to build. But, not being able to weld, my work had come under considerable criticism from our youngest son Giles. 'Too bad' I said 'I'm joining the branches and trunk together with a marine glue which is stronger than the copper itself. Then I'm attaching the leaves to it with rivets.' However when Annette and I took the sculpture up to Blackpool in our horse trailer, many of the copper leaves blew off. So I riveted on replacements, which I then painted with a chlorine mix to turn them to a matching verdigris before our arrival.

'Take it to greenhouse' Dorothy ordered Jack, one of her four gardeners waiting for us 'then put t'hose on it to see how it works.'

The leaves of the Weeping Tree moved as water flowed from the waving branches.

She had not only one greenhouse but three of them, much resembling smaller versions of those at Kew Gardens in London. It was only when her four men had planted our tree in a basin prepared for it within the first greenhouse, that I suddenly noticed their large collection of Macaws sitting high above us on golden painted perches. Then it all went horribly wrong. Jack had just turned on his hose in order to make the branches wave, when the parrots, each worth a small fortune, began wobbling on their perches alarmingly. 'Chlorine' shouted Jack. 'Tis gas ma'am!' But by then, clutching Dorothy's cheque, we were already halfway towards our Land Rover, which we turned on her best lawn before speeding through their electric gates, which Frank, unknowingly, opened for us.

The sculpture business had not been started intentionally but accidentally, just as my computer business had evolved due to the intervention of the Exeter City Council and as my Adventure Centre had been born solely due to some greedy children eating too many of my strawberries. This time it was solely because I had tripped over our honey extractor when mixing some cement. The year before, while I was getting wet in the driving rain and bemoaning the difficulties in finishing our holiday cottages, a shaft of sunlight had lit up a cattle feeder situated in the centre of the farmyard. The workmen, using it as a bin, were busy chucking the last of their cement sacks into it when it suddenly came to me that the sacks looked like flying fish. So I rang up Giles at Exeter University. 'I'm going to build a fountain' I told him. 'Please see if you can find me a book in your library about making moulds out of latex?' The design was of four concrete salmon leaping over a waterfall and when they emerged from their latex moulds, they shone astonishingly like marble due to all the honey I had then mixed into the cement.

The four salmon were mounted on granite over which flowed a waterfall

I was therefore not surprised when a keen fisherman who had arrived at Dashcombe for a day's shooting, was determined to buy it. 'No' I said 'Bugger off. I have no intention of also becoming a *fountaineer!*'

But the man, who was president of a city company, who I met again later on the Cresta Run, was not to be put off. I had already named him 'Sir Brian, Sir Brian as brave as a lion', when he told me that his company was sponsoring the second largest stand at the Chelsea Flower Show that spring, so I reluctantly, gave in. 'OK I said 'I will design two water sculptures for your stand, but I am not prepared to build them. You can then choose the one you prefer. Of course he wanted both.

Giles, who after gaining his degree in business economics had already left for London to learn how to become a tycoon, on hearing about Brian's commission, rang me up immediately. 'Dad' he started 'I am coming back home to help you. I am not a city boy and you are not a welder, so why don't I find out how to do just that. Instead of you joining them with glue, let's build the two water sculptures you have designed for Brian together?' Knowing how Giles would jump on me when he saw my earlier *Weeping Tree* I did not hesitate. 'What a fantastic idea' I said.

The father-and-son partnership, which has continued ever since, was to become one of the most exciting ventures in my life, albeit that I was soon to accept that Giles was far better equipped to run it. He then went on to spend three more years studying sculpture at the University of Kingston, featuring in the *Sunday Times* magazine as being the 'next big thing'. Helped by Brian's friend Charles Williams, owner of the Burncoose Nurseries in Cornwall, on whose winning stand at Chelsea we have continued exhibiting our water sculptures ever since, due to him we soon received a commission to build one for the Royal Parks at Windsor and shortly afterwards obtained our first order from America. Indeed, following that initial flower show, which was to become our sole means of advertising, our water sculpture business never looked back, with Giles now busy installing water sculptures all over the world.

But learning the unusual art of water sculpture does not happen over night. After finishing the salmon sculpture we never used concrete again, first learning about the habits of non-ferrous metals and then building in copper, bronze and stainless steel instead. What became clear was not only the need to become competent engineers, but also metallurgists and specialists in fluid dynamics plus knowing how to design permanent structures with few demands on maintenance. Only due to this growing depth of knowledge, Giles, years later, was able to design a forty foot high water sculpture for the Sultanate of Oman.

Letter 62

Miles Downside. Hester Insurance
25a Lombard Street, London

July 1999

Dear Miles

I cannot believe that you are now unable to find insurance for the Dashcombe Adventure Centre anywhere in the world!

Although I must admit that we have suffered several accidents over the years, I must point out that the half million pound claim by the man who said he had hit his head on the tree at the bottom of our 'Death Slide' was agreed by his doctor to be totally false.

Please will you continue to search for other possibilities. Meanwhile are you really serious that we will have to close the Centre down immediately?

Yours sincerely

RR

Comment: We had built a helipad at the adventure centre, before it was first opened and had found that any casualties could be airlifted to the hospital in Exeter within five minutes from takeoff.

Adventure Centre with
Sea Eagle sculpture.

The Dashcombe Bob

Death slide

Also we had trained several of our staff to cope with any medical eventualities. Finally we had invited the Royal Marines to investigate every physical activity we were asking our customers to attempt.

I therefore felt very angry. How could a London insurance agent, who knew little about the countryside or my business, behave like that? if we failed to close the Adventure Centre down, the man had warned, and we had another accident it was unlikely that we would be able to pay for it. So, still fuming, I took Annette for a holiday in the South of France.

Yes I had built a bob run down the steep hillside and a man had broken his leg on his very first descent. Then there was the time when a guy playing paintball against Hell's Belles, our ladies' team had nearly lost an eye when he was shot in the face by a tough-looking dame at point- blank range. On another occasion, an instructor had fallen over the side of one of our wooden bridges, as described earlier, built some fifty foot over a deep ravine. But he had survived.

We had also tried paragliding and mountain biking at Dashcombe, but the most popular activity was definitely quad biking with 'quad bike safaris' being advertised out on the main road. It was unfortunate that some of the riders would not obey instructions and by deviating from the track had sometimes got themselves into serious trouble. None more so than a man who lost control and hurtled into our ravine, hitting a tree on the way down. Only Hell's Belles were on duty that day, so when they discovered that he had injured his credentials, they set about trying to repair him as best they could with unusual gusto. Apparently he thanked them afterwards by asking each nice lady to share two balls of ice cream with him. But I was not surprised when he also put in an insurance claim, which declared that his subsequent loss of performance had been certified by his wife.

We had arrived on the sunny French Riviera without incident, but as we were having a drink overlooking Monte Carlo harbour, my new mobile telephone started ringing. 'I thought you would be pleased to know' said Miles 'that after considerably more research, we have managed to obtain your insurance, Major, and you may open your gates and get going again.' *Blast*, I thought while ordering the most expensive bottle of champagne in history, for we would now have to return to England before we had even had time to drink it, lat alone cool off with a Mediterranean swim. Then the telephone rang again. 'Major, there is one other thing I did not tell you. I'm afraid that it is you who they consider to be the problem at the Adventure Centre, and they will only renew your insurance as long as you have nothing more to do with it.'

Lieutenant Sean Galway. HMCC Vigilant
H M Customs & Excise, Crownhill Court, Plymouth

August 2000

Dear Lieutenant Galway

Thank you for showing me around your Customs Cutter yesterday. Your merry Irish crew impressed on me how determined they were to stop drug runners, smugglers and freebooters by every means possible, but I wondered what 'means' they were referring to? Your Customs Cutter's top speed is only twenty six knots, so she is not going to stop anyone, and as your RIB is only twenty two foot long, it is useless in heavy seas. But what alarmed me most was that there are only four Customs Cutters operating in the UK, with at least one them always out of service.

Are you and your gallant crew seriously expected to guard with them some eight thousand miles of the British coastline?

Yours sincerely

RR

Comment: Earlier in that Millennium year I had been appointed High Sheriff of Devon, meaning that as I was to be the Queen's representative in charge of supporting the county police for a year, I would have little time for anything else.

Hanging Baskets! The High Sheriff was once responsible for hangings.

I was, therefore, happy that my insurance agents had relieved me of my responsibilities at the adventure centre, which I had leased subsequently to a more safety conscious farming family from Cornwall.

High Sheriffs are luckily allowed to set their own agenda apart from helping to look after the Royal Family if they visit the county, and my aim had been twofold. To better the lives of the wretched children excluded from our schools and to highlight those importing drugs through our frighteningly porous coastline. But after my visit to inspect the Customs Cutters, when I found out later that HM Customs and Revenue had insufficient staff to monitor both of the boats arriving from Le Havre in France and from Roscoff in Spain, and had received no new recruit for a countless number of years, I wrote to Michael Howard, leader of the Conservative opposition in parliament, about it. Sadly my letter was never actioned and the problem has never been resolved.

My concern about the excluded children was equally important. It would also save public money by reducing the number of such children turning to crime. On my tour of duty it had been pointed out to me that as many as fifty children in Devon's towns and cities such as Torquay and Plymouth, were being thrown onto the scrap heap every year. Yet in America, I knew that the problem had been relieved by placing many of their miscreants on an addictive computer system, backed by the Mayor of New York, who had placed his own children on it. So I then decided to approach the manager of the McDonalds fast food restaurant in Torquay, and investigate their method of installing 'pop-up' burger bars.

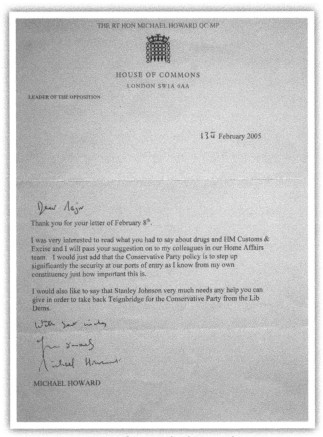

Letter from Michael Howard

We then earmarked a building for the first of the many proposed 'Achievement Centres' to be set up on McDonald lines, each equipped with from thirty to fifty sponsored computers as necessary, plus the brilliant American 'Pace' software system, which allowed children to learn at their own pace without teachers while conducting their own self-examinations.

Apart from meeting Princess Margaret for tea, when my wife and I were cheered by a large crowd for entering a public house in error, the year passed peacefully except when escorting my old friend from Sandhurst, the Duke of Kent.

Running short of time, as he had to go elsewhere, he had asked me to visit Great Torrington on his behalf, a North Devon town famous for the last stand of the Cavaliers, and with them King Charles I, before he was taken off to London by the Roundheads to have his head lopped off.

Mounted together with my wife on two chargers, we had already fought for the Cavaliers in the 'Battle of Powderham Castle', so I knew about the fervour raised by these events. The defence of Great Torrington had been enacted annually by another wild bunch of Cavaliers who had turned out in the main street to meet the Duke, armed to the teeth, wearing steel helmets and in full body armour. So not to leave them feeling disappointed, I ordered them to line up and be inspected. 'All those failing to pass my inspection please report to me after the parade!' I said. They did and, although I found pikes without spikes, I made such friends with them that they press ganged both Annette and myself to fight their next battle.

The Prime Minister
10 Downing Street, London

March 2001

Dear Prime Minister

Thank you for your enthusiastic letter of 2 January. Although I have just relinquished my position as High Sheriff of Devon, I am determined to pursue the idea of establishing 'Achievement Centres' throughout the Country in order to give children excluded from school the opportunity of becoming responsible citizens in due course, rather than expensive criminals. The American 'Pace' system provides them with a compelling way of learning any trade they wish on more tactile computers. The programme includes 'attractive; incentives, but excludes any 'unattractive' teachers. The first batch of computers are already sponsored.

Why is no government or local government support being provided?

Yours sincerely

RR

Comment: Is anyone out there? I should have realised that my efforts were going to get me nowhere now that my year serving the Queen was over. I would again be just a 'nobody' and there was nothing I could do about it. Hugely disappointed, I hoped that someone more important than myself would establish my idea of 'Achievement Centres' one day.

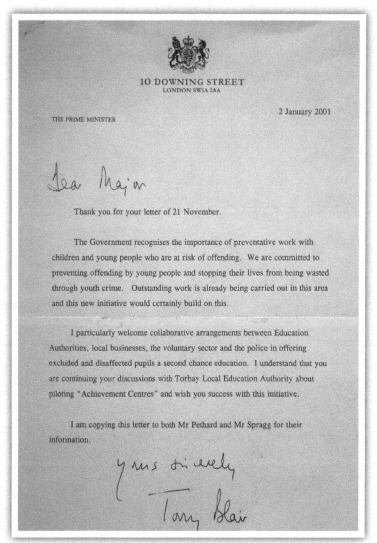

10 DOWNING STREET
LONDON SW1A 2AA

THE PRIME MINISTER

2 January 2001

Dear Major

Thank you for your letter of 21 November.

The Government recognises the importance of preventative work with children and young people who are at risk of offending. We are committed to preventing offending by young people and stopping their lives from being wasted through youth crime. Outstanding work is already being carried out in this area and this new initiative would certainly build on this.

I particularly welcome collaborative arrangements between Education Authorities, local businesses, the voluntary sector and the police in offering excluded and disaffected pupils a second chance education. I understand that you are continuing your discussions with Torbay Local Education Authority about piloting "Achievement Centres" and wish you success with this initiative.

I am copying this letter to both Mr Pethard and Mr Spragg for their information.

Yours sincerely

Tony Blair

Sadly I only received an acknowledgement from my second letter.

So, because I had been neglecting everything else meanwhile, I decided to return to my business life and continue trying to make a living.

Although Tim Thompson had previously completed a commission through me for a fellow called Tim Landon, who was presenting the painting to the Sultan of Oman, it had been followed by another of his motor yacht *Katalina* and subsequently by a painting of his second, much larger yacht, also named *Katalina* so as not to look too ostentatious. As the painting had just been delivered, I rang up the only person that I had ever liaised with, who helped Landon with his investments from his own London office. 'Peter' I said 'as I am in London, shall I bring it to you or take it to down to Hampshire as I will be driving past Tim's place on my way home?' But hardly had I turned into his long drive than two men jumped out of the hedge armed with Kalashnikovs demanding to know my business. I was then met by two liveried butlers wearing white gloves who, having mounted the painting on an easel they placed on a marble compass rose within some impressive pillars, asked 'Shall we fetch the brigadier, sir?' He had been a brigadier in the Sultan's army.

The Dhofar Rebellion, otherwise known as the Omani Civil War, which dragged on from 1962 to 1976, began at the time when Oman, ruled by Sultan Said bin Taimur, but under British control, was still totally undeveloped. The Dhofar Liberation Front (DLF) had been formed in the rugged hills of the Jebel Dhofar by a dissatisfied tribal leader to fight the Sultan's Armed Forces (SAF), aided in due course by Yemeni rebels when the British withdrew from Aden. Backed by the Chinese and heavily armed by the Russians, the Adoo, as their combined forces were known, were to become a dangerous Communist-led threat to the region, as shown when some desert sheikhs were pushed over a cliff and some other Sheikh families machine gunned. It was only due to Ranulph Fiennes, together with some other British officers, including Tim Landon, that British-led counterinsurgency units, aided by air cover, were, by 1976, finally able to defeat them. Oman had by then found oil, which at last enabled Sultan Qaboos, the old sultan's son, who, in 1970 had deposed his reluctant father in a bloodless coup, to carefully set about developing his country. When Landon, who had played a major part in the coup, was then asked if he would prefer a million pounds in thanks, or a tiny percentage of the country's future oil revenue, Landon, whom I had taught with Qaboos at Sandhurst, chose the latter, and although becoming unpopular with many Omanis, rapidly became loaded!

Letter

65

Baron Johnny Winterhalder
Beccar, Buenos Aires, Argentina.

June 2001

Dear Johnny

I cannot tell you how much Annette and I enjoyed Annabelle's wedding. It was a splendid occasion held in such a magnificent castle looking over the Danube. Nobody could have organised a ceremony for their daughter better.

Afterwards we had hoped to see the Spanish Riding School perform in Vienna, but we could not get hold of any tickets. While driving back to Salzburg, it occurred to me that we had failed to plan our annual challenge over a pretty girl, for there were plenty of them there. As you were holding the wedding ceremony in a castle once belonging to the Archduke Franz Ferdinand, why not invite his granddaughter, who inherited the castle, to Buenos Aires, while I attempt to get her to London?

Yours as always

R

Comment: Johnny, my old friend from Argentina, who I had once met while skiing in Chile, was obviously not enamoured with the idea, for the archduke's granddaughter was by now a crusty old lady aged eighty!

I hold up the photograph of The Duke of Windsor on our balcony at Wolfgangsee

The Duke and Duchess of Windsor meeting Hitler

Although offering her majestic castle with all its valuable treasures to her close relatives the Winterhalders for their daughter's wedding, she had refused to appear in public for a countless number of years. No wonder, for it was the asassination of her grandfather by a fanatic in Sarajevo, Yugoslavia, on 28 June 1941 that had triggered the outbreak of the First World War.

Our holiday in Austria had started with visiting Salzburg, the birthplace of the composer Mozart, and listening to his music. I had always had a passion for Mozart, and also for Austria from my days skiing there in St Anton - where I had met Prince Bernhard of the Netherlands, who had written the foreword in my skiing book - and also in Zurs. But particularly I remembered St Christoph, where we had once been treated to a holiday by a friend who had previously raced for Austria in their national ski team. It had been rumoured that the Hospice, where we stayed, was visited by Nazi sympathisers, which we thought was total nonsense while thoroughly enjoying our stay there plus some very hair-raising skiing. I had always been a man of the mountains and with my wife we continue to be, both in summer and in winter. The crystal clear air and the scenery were always to die for. As we drove that September through emerald green pastures full of fat cattle with snow-capped mountains rising behind, we felt like characters in *The Sound of Music*.

After a long drive, we came to the Wolfgangsee and beside the lake, a charming-looking hotel with green shutters and a welcoming green pine door. 'I am so sorry' said a man wearing a smart Austrian jacket, who looked a touch superior to the concierge sitting behind his desk, 'but we are, unfortunately, fully booked.' We must have looked very disappointed. Apart from the fact we had seen no other decent hotel for miles, Annette badly wanted to cool of by swimming in the icy lake beyond. Then, as I turned the car around, there was a tap on the window. 'I have not been telling you the whole truth' said the Austrian. 'We do, in fact, have one splendid suite available that we keep for our special guests. It was once occupied by your Duke of Windsor.'

On entering the suite we were immediately bowled over. Not only was there a large photograph of the Duke of Windsor, soon after his abdication, standing on the balcony directly in front of us, but with it we found a map of the surrounding area including Hitler's Berchtesgaden. The Duke had been accused of being a Nazi sympathiser and after the outbreak of WWII was appointed governor of the Bahamas just to keep him out of the way of Hitler, who some said wanted to entice him into his grip so that, when the Germans later conquered Great Britain, he could offer him the throne again. Therefore, when I discovered that the Duke of Windsor had stayed in the same room in early 1937, I surmised that he was not just there to enjoy the view. Because the British government were unhappy with the Duke's leanings towards the Nazis, although never substantiated, he had been followed everywhere. But not, surprisingly, to the Wolfgangsee. Therefore, as never recorded in history, the Duke had driven from the hotel to have a secret meeting with Hitler at his Berghof retreat high up in the nearby mountains at Berchtesgaden in order to arrange a further meeting with Hitler accompanied by Wallace Simpson, who was about to become his wife.

Letter 66

Peter Corder Esq. Nieuwedam Farms
Grabouw, South Africa.

December 2001

Dear Peter

We have returned to South Africa with a heavy heart after the appalling acts of terrorism in America. Such carnage must be stopped for ever.

You will remember that when we first travelled to see you South Africa in 1994 Apartheid was just coming to an end. This time President de Klerk arrived by helicopter in Tzaneen, where we were staying at the Coach House hotel - and then bagged our room! We have been over to see Giles, our youngest, on his gap year feeding Venda's starving people.

We are unable get hold of you. Is your apple business prospering again?

Yours ever

R

Comment: Peter's parents, who were friends of my own mother and father, had been part owners the famous Union Castle shipping line.

Giles 'tombstoning' on a day off in Venda

Apple lines

But rather than get too involved in his father's business, Peter and his German wife had started farming apples in the beautiful valley of Elgin some 70 miles east of Cape Town.

Apartheid had been a dirty word ever since the National Party had come to power in 1948 on a policy of racial segregation. So when in 1969 on my first visit to Johannesburg to see my brother Andrew, who was writing for South Africa's *Financial Mail*, I saw a bench with WHITES ONLY painted on it, I knew why. But with President de Klerk's intervention in 1990, who we had met at the Coach House before listening to one of his rousing speeches, by releasing Nelson Mandela from prison, where he had been incarcerated for no less than 27 years on Robin Island, a new stimulating era of co-operation between blacks and whites in South Africa was thought to be beginning. However, when government promises about better services and electricity for everyone were not fulfilled, unrest continued to disrupt many businesses as Peter had found out to his cost while growing apples.

His was a huge state-of-the-art enterprise that I had found fascinating. Every apple was watered by an individual, computer regulated, jet connected to pipelines that fed cool water from the nearby mountains over a vast area of orchards. Standing right in the middle of them was an impressive, fully automated packing station, were long conveyor belts carried many different varieties of apples to be sorted, cleaned and finally coated by robots with a fine spray of wax in order to preserve them while being shipped to other countries. But Peter, sadly, had told me that his was a dying industry plagued by endless industrial disputes and increasing competition from abroad, particularly from the South of France. Now, almost ten years after our first visit, I wanted to find out the latest.

But as I had received no reply from my letter, we decided differently and, rather than disturb the Corders, on travelling south we stayed at a comfortable hotel in Cape Town meeting up with some charming and sporty relations who took us climbing up Table Mountain. Then, suitably exhausted, we took to the road and headed east along the Garden Route, which every tourist has followed since it was created. Perhaps the route did not suit our love for wilder places, but when we stopped to swim at Plettenberg Bay on our way to fly from Port Elizabeth to Durban, we felt better as we dived into surf piling in from the Indian Ocean, greatly resembling the beaches in North Cornwall.

We never found out about our friends, the Corders, who had a holiday home there. It was rumoured that a few years before we returned, they had been diagnosed with cancer, and they may well not have received our Christmas cards or my letter because they had both, probably, died.

Letter 67

David Rattray. Rorke's Drift
Zululand, South Africa

February 2002

Dear David

We were thrilled to have been able to meet you when you flew back from your talk in England to personally recount the story of the British defence against an overwhelming number Zulus at Rorke's Drift.

With us were a smattering of generals who admitted that they had never faced any such a desperate situation, as none who come after them ever will. They talked among themselves as if you were the gallant Chard yourself.

Should you not have fallen foul of the Zulus, or been bitten by one of your pet venomous snakes, I wondered if you would ever give your talk to us ex-soldiers who have retired disgracefully to Devon?

Yours ever

RR

Comment: The Zulus, we discovered, were all around us when we were driving our miserable hired car from Durban to Rorke's Drift. We had been warned not to stop in Zululand; but when we were driving down a steep hill into a small village, we had to do just that when our brakes started to fail.

David Rattray standing by the ruins of the hospital at Rorkes Drift.

It was lucky that I managed to stop the car by steering it into a rock opposite a tiny decrepit-looking, garage. A Zulu mechanic approached us appearing frighteningly unfriendly; but when we told him about our problem, his face lit up and it became wreathed in smiles. He fetched a can of hydraulic oil, told us all was fixed, and thanking us for our tip sent us on our way as if we were old friends.

The mission station of Rorkes Drift, established by the British army some hundred miles to the north-east of Durban during the Anglo-Zulu war, had in January 1879 become famous throughout the world. The day before British forces had been soundly defeated after their camp at Isandlwana had been infiltrated by hordes of Zulus while many of them were still fast asleep in their tents. The Zulus had then turned on the garrison of just 150 British and colonial troops manning the hospital and its immediate surrounds only a few miles away across a river at Rorke's Drift. There Lt John Chard and Lt Gonville Bromhead, who later, received two of the eleven VCs awarded afterwards, successfully held off no less than 3,000 to 4,000 Zulu warriors in what was later to be considered the most epic defence of all time.

Ably told by David Rattray, a South African historian who ran a lodge close by, where he entertained countless visitors like ourselves, the story of Rorke's Drift, was stirring so many hearts again, that it was getting more attention than ever before. But once we had visited both battlefields and made friends with him, and because we were spending only on a brief winter's holiday in South Africa, we felt it was time to move on and see some big game.

Our guides tracking the lions

Completely 'whacked'!

We had chosen to visit a reserve called Phinda situated a farther hundred miles east on the coast just south of Swaziland. But first we had to negotiate many miles of unsurfaced roads and deeply pitted forestry tracks.

Phinda seemed to have everything we wished to see including the 'big five' plus hippos and many unfriendly crocodiles, as we discovered when one of them, which had scores of tiny babies, flew at us from the river bank and almost sank her teeth into the small boat we were watching from. 'No matter if she had lost them' explained our guide 'for crocodiles can replace any one of their eighty teeth some fifty times during their long lifetime. And as for all their babies' he continued 'if it was not for those huge, red necked, Marabou storks waiting to nosh them over there, crocodiles would take over the world. However' he said as we climbed back into our Land Rover 'we are now going to show you something completely different - a lion we found on the job with a lioness six days ago. He is now so worn out that we may be able to creep right up to him.' We did, very carefully, and I took one of my best pictures of a lion ever!

A few years later we heard that a lady at Phinda and been killed by a leopard on her way to have supper without an armed attendant, but, what was worse, that David Rattray, who had, obviously, not liked my reference to the Zulus in my letter, had been found savagely murdered by one.

Letter 68

Barclays Bank. Mortgages Department
Canary Wharf. London

March 2002.

Dear Sirs

I purchased a London flat ten years ago when you agreed to grant me a 75% mortgage. I have just had to redeem the mortgage to honour our agreement.

You have stated that I now owe you an additional £25,000 due to the decline in value of equities during the period, which annoys me.

My investment was in property, not in the stock market. Bricks and mortar have performed particularly well during the period.

What are you going to do about it?

Yours faithfully

RR

Comment: I had been invited by a noble earl in Devon to have lunch with him at the House of Lords at the time in order discuss a new project I had in mind, and it provided me with the ideal moment to take my 10-year old letter to Barclays Mortgage Department at Canary Wharf and confront them with it. 'I see' muttered a bespectacled, sallow-looking fellow wearing a dark suit 'then it looks as though we owe you £25,000 instead' he said looking, but not probably feeling, apologetic.

Letters are important to retain. The records could have vanished on my computer over such a long period. Also they were signed personally in ink. Without such hard evidence at that time I could well have lost my case. I had bought the new two-bedroomed flat for Giles, as it was a way of balancing all the cash I had been spending on the holiday cottages for our eldest son, Ralph. It looked south over the Thames and its own boat mooring, lawns running down to the river and a car park, and was convenient for driving home. My intention was that both sons would use it and by keeping a fast boat there would be able to travel to work without encountering the usual traffic problems. 'But dad' Ralph had pointed out 'although it may be a great investment, we have no friends around there and the pubs are hopeless. And as for keeping a fast boat on that mooring it would not work due to the speed limit on the Thames.' 'There isn't one' I replied.

I had long abandoned any idea of being a helpful father in London when, years later, I set off to the House of Lords with that extra money in my pocket and not a care in the world. 'So what is this new project about? my friend the earl asked me, trying hard, while at our lunch table, not to pinch the waitress's bottom. 'Well its about a major tourist attraction' you asked me to think up' I replied 'in order to stop all those people from driving through Devon to visit that damned Eden Project in Cornwall.'

I then described how, with co-operation from the Forestry Commission, I intended to develop the 14 miles of woodlands stretching across Haldon Moor to the west of Exeter, forming a natural barrier with just two major roads running through it, both heading for Cornwall. I have therefore thought of an exciting new 'grockle trap' which I have named Fantasy Forest. The earl looked puzzled 'What do you mean, a place were young girls may enjoy their fantasies?' 'No I replied 'Fantasy Forest will have four major attractions within it, such as high ropes, giant slides, bike trails and tree houses, all leading off those roads and all with very large car parks. But just at that moment, as the earl began to yawn, a speedboat shot past the window, being chased by a police launch. 'Forget it' I swore 'nothing that I suggest is ever going to work!'

Letter 69

Mrs Enid Scandrett. Blue Cottage
Sketchwith, Somerset

August 2002

Dear Mrs Scandrett

I was surprised by the letter you wrote to Madonna asking her to give up shooting. I must point out that, mistakenly, you sent your letter to the wrong address. We also have a pheasant shoot, just as Madonna has in Dorset, which are both run within the sport's very strict code of conduct.

Your threats to disrupt the coming Countryside March are being taken very seriously. If you step outside the law you will be in serious trouble.

What are your intentions?

Yours sincerely

RR Chairman Countryside Alliance South West.

Encouraged by the increasing hostility to country sports by the Socialist government then in office, most of whose members knew nothing about the land, protesters known as the Antis or the League Against Cruel Sports were growing increasingly militant. Mrs Skandrett, a known agitator, was obviously intending to mobilise as many of them as possible, supported by a large number of feisty university students, who would be paid for joining her on the day. Financial support was not a problem, for she was experienced at tapping into money from IFAW (the International Fund for Animal Welfare) plus other similar organisations.

The countryside march had been planned meticulously by former army officers to be the largest demonstration ever seen in London. Every village in the kingdom had been invited to send as many country sports enthusiasts as they could muster, most of whom had never been to the capital before in their lives. So 2,500 coaches and 30 trains were booked by individual groups of country people, all crammed to the roof with those eager to show their distaste for their largely urban-based, tormentors. It could have been a mighty battle, but all scythes and staves had been removed before passengers embarked, and those with the worst grudges had been banned from coming.

On the 9th of November 2002, 400,000 protesters were to descend on central London for the Liberty and Livelihood March, one of the largest demonstrations ever held there, costing the Countryside Alliance, Great Britain's country sports lobby, over a million pounds to stage.

There were many more than just one reason for the march!

Determined to force their message through to government, a number of forceful speeches were delivered both in parliament square, and in Hyde Park. At the same Tony Blair, the Prime Minister, was presented with a list of demands not only concerning fox hunting, shooting and fishing, but a plea for added protection for our farmers and legislation to prevent any of the unjust measures under consideration at the time from being implemented. Several of the speakers threatened that the countryside would erupt in fury should fox hunting be banned. But although temporally placed by Blair on the back-burner it was probably due to his wife that he soon allowed it to happen. Fortunately the march remained remarkably peaceful, and the force that Mrs Scandrett had threatened to bring, mercifully, stayed at home, fearful of the 1,600 policemen that had been drafted in for the day. Previously many people in the West Country had been growing increasingly concerned that the British Field Sports Society were lobbying too much for fox hunting and not enough for our other field sports including angling. Having been chosen as their chairman for a time, I had told the BFSS that we would break away unless they became more representative. So the Countryside Alliance had been born.

Rounding up our villagers from the pubs afterwards was stimulating, but not as much as our journey home. Our man proceeded to overtake every other coach on the road by using the hard shoulder. So having collected a donation for the Countryside Alliance we gave it all, instead, to our very sporting driver!

Letter 70

The Harbour Master. Dartmouth
South Devon, England

September 2002

Dear Sir

Although I can understand why you wish to control traffic on the River Dart during
your end of August annual flying display by the Red Arrows, I was amazed by the
'strong arm' tactics being used on this last occasion by some of your employees. On
approaching Dartmouth harbour from up river on Friday, my RIB was charged at
by two of your boats clearly marked as Harbour Master, and we were lucky not to
be punctured, or indeed sunk, when we were shoved onto some sharp rocks under
the river bank.

Please tell me what right you have to close off a river belonging to Her Majesty The
Queen?

Yours faithfully

RR

Comment: I had bought the 25ft RIB (Rigid Inflatable Boat) the year previously. It was not only good for going places, as it could achieve over 70 mph, but also, I thought at the time, the ideal fast ferry for our two sons in London. So when they rejected the idea, I decided that it was far better for their dad to play with it as a Boys Toy back at the ranch. A RIB makes very little wash when travelling at speed, and I had no concerns about taking her down the river Dart much faster than allowed. But on every occasion I had done so some nasty person living in a riverside cottage had, while using binoculars, reported us to the harbour master. No matter, as the RIB had no identification and because I always gave a false name when caught, the harbour master's ruffians never had a clue who I was or where the boat had suddenly arrived from.

I would not have written to the harbour master and given away my address so easily, which may cause problems when putting pen to paper, but we were destined to take our RIB elsewhere for a number of years, having towed it three times down to the South of France to see the classic yachts racing there, and once, during the winter, to North Cornwall in order to surf over some huge Atlantic rollers, while followed by seals and dolphins plus a leather backed turtle. In Devon you just had to enjoy the sea, which lapped against shores on both sides of the county, and it saddened me when friends refused to come for an exhilarating ride with me. Although I had completed an intensive handling course, my reputation as a 'loose cannon', it seemed, was never to leave me!

Launching the RIB at Port Grimaud

The Red Arrows over Dartmouth

It was particular fun watching the summer air displays, always held over water. And none was more spectacular than the Red Arrows arriving at precisely six o clock in the evening, after flying low into the Dart estuary without being seen, to erupt in a bomb burst over the harbour. How, many years later, the event could be banned by the town council because of the possibility of an aircraft dropping onto someone's boat, or disturbing another person's siesta, we will never understand.

Such a feeble argument directed at nine reasonably new aircraft maintained by the RAF to the highest standards of airworthiness and flown by pilots renowned to be the best anywhere in the world, was not good enough, nor was the pathetic attitude adopted by the British CAA (Civil Aviation Authority) when, after the crash in August 2015 of a classic Hawker Hunter jet fighter over dry land at the Shoreham Air Show, a town on the south coast of England, they banned most air shows in the Country. I was amazed that it was precisely the same aircraft, once known as 'The Captain's Barge', that I had almost ejected from when being flown by the Royal Navy in 1964. They had looked after it immaculately, as had been the case ever since. For we prided ourselves on all our old fighter aircraft, and that Hunter may well have been worth a quarter of a million pounds while a decent WWII Spitfire could fetch two million. Different from the £700 we had been lucky to get eventually for our Auster, the same money we had paid for it many years earlier!

Letter 71

The Manager. Hotel Michelangelo
Calafate, Patagonia, Argentina

February 2003

Dear Sir

We much enjoyed our stay with you, amazed by the calving glaciers, shedding such large chunks of ice that they made our passenger boat behave like a bucking bronco. Also by the views of your icy wilderness stretching north to the Andes and south towards Cape Horn.

You may remember that one of your excursions was to a sheep station. While we were there watching the shearing, my wife lost her camera, a small Minolta.

Has anyone handed it in?

Yours truly

RR

Comment: The Tierra del Fuego forms the southern tip of South America. It is known for shipwrecks and whales and some of the most desolate land on earth. For ending at Cape Horn, with its raging Southern Ocean, lies only Antarctica.

The group of tourists we were with were a mixed bunch from all over the world; and although most were nice enough, some looked remarkably disinterested. We had been the only passengers brave enough to stay on deck in the icy wind while the remainder huddled below without seeing the astonishingly blue glaciers.

The flight to that desolate region had been arranged by our friend the baron, who had subsequently agreed to meet us at the airport in Bariloche, Argentina's beautiful Lake District. There we caught up with his daughter Annabelle and her polo-playing, Belgian husband, whose wedding we had attended before enjoying their hospitality in the magnificent castle overlooking the Danube. Hubert, son of a property magnate, owned a lodge near Bariloche with polo grounds long views towards the snow capped mountains. 'We are looking for land throughout Patagonia to establish cattle ranches, largely for those well heeled Yanks who wish to get away from America after 9/11. Some believe that buying a ranch so far south, they won't be seeing the next world any time soon!'

Annette in Patagonia

Calving glaciers

The following day three Land Rovers arrived at the door and after packing just a few necessary belongings into some sailing bags, we piled into them.

'We are now going to drive 300 miles south into Patagonia' he announced 'to visit the first of our few ranches that have not yet been sold, but each of which has recently been furnished to perfection by Annabelle.' The first ranch certainly was, with its colourful ponchos and saddle cloths; but what was more, apart from helping to round up the cattle to be branded or castrated by the gauchos, we were soon led down to the river running through it, alive with brown trout. So we fished for our supper and ate barbecued steaks fresh off the farm followed by delicious plates of lychees grown there from seeds imported from Brazil. We were, therefore, unhappy when we were told that we were about to move on, not knowing about the excitements to come.

Hubert and Annabelle had also been arranging hell-skiing expeditions in the Andes during the southern winter; and it was hardly a surprise to find a helicopter waiting for us, after driving west across the Chilean border. 'We will leave two of our 4x4s here' Hubert directed 'and then fly to the next ranch El Yunge at Coyhaique, before continuing on to Bahia Mala, the wicked bay, where we have another interesting place we are developing amidst the sand dunes. 'A great idea? we thought, for El Yunge had been interesting enough when we found out that, in 1972, after General Pinochet had completed that section of the coastal highway, some soldiers had shot three people there - in our bedroom!

Wild strawberries growing on the black sand. on a rare calm day at Bahia Mala.

The third Land Rover was to be employed for refuelling; and as we flew on in the Robinson 44 helicopter, the driver managed to follow us down tiny tracks snaking through the mountains and glaciers just a day later.

As there was insufficient room for the five of us plus our bags in the chopper, the pilot always had to fly us to a new location in two separate trips, which was fine until we arrived at Bahia Mala to find ourselves being dropped off alone in a blanket of wild strawberries, all growing on black volcanic sand stretching as far as the eye could see. 'This is extraordinary' I said to Annette with no one yet there to show us to the deserted ranch house. 'Just look at those colonies of sea lions beyond the surf and then back again to where the glaciers fall off the mountains directly into the Pacific ocean!'

The Bahia Mala was to feature in my life in a different way ten years later, but now we were there to enjoy ourselves by galloping gaucho horses along the line of the sand dunes and taking the RIB, which was kept there, to explore more of the bay's savage coastline and seek out the abundance of wild life to be seen everywhere. It all seemed so remote from the world we knew, and was to become the experience of a lifetime. Apart from the sea lions, just a few of the two hundred thousand inhabiting the coast of Chile, once we had finished looking at them adorning their rocky islets, while enduring their dreadful stench, there were huge whale sharks to be seen, some with calves, which they, apparently, gave berth to regularly there. As the largest living vertebrates, some were nearly a hundred years old, while reaching over forty feet in length.

Sea lions at Bahia Mala

Going for a ride at Bahia Mala with Johnny and Annabelle

Their mouths, set far more to the front of their gloriously spotted bodies than the jaws of their carnivorous cousins, were almost five feet wide and large enough to consume millions of tiny plankton their staple menu.

It was still summer in South America and flying west to the coast of Chile through the mighty Andes had been an extraordinary and thrilling experience. Extraordinary because we also had an experienced Argentine fisherman with us who was constantly exploring the mountains for rivers yet free of ice snaking their way towards the sea. It was part of Hubert's quest to find land for Americans, sometimes complete with fishing.

One day we took the RIB into a quiet lagoon, only disturbed by nesting albatross, where Hubert was intending to moor his 70 foot sailing yacht when it was launched. At one end stood what appeared to be a small corrugated iron hut, largely obscured by undergrowth. 'Please wait here for a few minutes instructed Hubert, but the minutes turned into an hour and when Hubert failed to reappear from the hut, we began to worry about what had happened to him. 'Sorry' he said 'my negotiations took longer than expected. The man I was talking to there, because he is the only person living permanently in this remote place, holds the title deeds to all of it.' We could hardly believe what he was saying until, while flying back to Bariloche in the helicopter, he concluded 'By offering to build that old peasant a house in the nearest village, I now own all of his twenty thousand hectares.'

Letter 72

Captain Charles Perry, Cavalry Club
Piccadilly, London

April 2005

Dear Charles

Just before you leave for Venezuela, I want to tell you how unhappy we are about being your 'mules' and carrying all those dollars for you.

You will have read that president Chavez, like Robin Hood, has instructed the growing number of poor people in his country to rob the rich and give the money to the poor, so we shall be sitting ducks.

You say that your crew of six have not been paid for five weeks, which amounts to a considerable amount of cash.

Have you insured the money, and more importantly, ourselves with it?

Your ever

R

Comment: He had probably already left. But receiving no reply had placed us in an awkward situation. The 90-foot yacht, apparently, was going to set out to sea from a small harbour on the southern Caribbean coast directly following our arrival, which was the day after her joint owners boarded her from England. If we failed to carry out Charles's instructions, anything could happen, from getting nothing to eat for ten days, or maybe the Swedish crew jump ship, then having to resort to a boat manned by pelicans!

So I rang up our son's brother-in-law who had worked for Goldman Sachs in South America. I asked 'Do you know of a decent hotel in Caracas?' He replied 'Yes, there is a five-star hotel, but when I stayed there last time there was blood running out from under the door of the next bedroom.' So we decided to book by Air France instead of British Airways. We could then avoid a night spent waiting to be murdered, but transfer by small plane instead and join the yacht by taxi the same day.

Only four years previously Sir Peter Blake, who had been the power behind New Zealand winning the America's Cup both in 1995 and in 2000, and many considered to be the greatest competitive sailor ever, was shot dead by pirates while on his yacht Seamaster studying the environment at the mouth of the Amazon. The pirates were increasing in numbers, armed with assault rifles, VHF radios, and high-powered binoculars; so they were becoming a dangerous threat to the whole region including Brazil, Peru and Venezuela. After a night spent in harbour amongst some stinking sewage, we sailed out into the blue Caribbean the following morning, feeling relieved that the crew had been paid, although it had meant stitching the dollars into our underclothes.

The final part of the journey had ultimately been surprisingly uneventful, apart from the taxi ride. Despite Venezuela having the largest oil reserves in the world, partly due to a strike by their workers in 2002, when oil production had been temporarily halted, president Chavez and his semi-authoritarian populist government had been incapable of getting their economy going again. Not only was there a growing shortage of food but their rate of inflation was climbing to new heights every day. So when our taxi driver stopped to repair a puncture, we were scared that we were now those sitting ducks - about to be robbed.

Swedish crew

Pelican crew

The sail that second night was one we shall never forget. The pirates operating from our part of the coast were known to be driving fast 'cigarette'-hulled boats, and so we were constantly searching the horizon behind us. But on our midnight watch, all we could see behind, as we glided over calm seas driven by a 12-knot breeze, was our phosphorescent wake, brighter than believable, while ahead lay the pink coral Islands of Los Roques and some brilliant diving.

We only just caught the Air France flight to Paris and our baggage was left behind. So we were each given a sponge bag with a condom inside!

Letter 73

The Editor. The Daily Telegraph
Fleet Street, London.

June 2006

Sir

'A nation that destroys its soils destroys itself'. Franklin D. Roosevelt

Only some 70% of the land in the United Kingdom is suitable for growing food, so there remain vast areas available for developers, who often refuse to build on any site more difficult than flat agricultural land.

Why does this government, while ignoring our green belt which was once never allowed to be built on, not specify the land which may be built on?

RR

Devon

Comment: Sadly planning permission is now more up to the whim of local councils, many of whom including, perhaps, the letters editor of the *Daily Telegraph*, care little about farming for food or preserving the beauty of our countryside. We are already one of the most overcrowded countries on earth, and it seems crazy that there is not enough of an outcry over building land, which some farmers are only too willing to sell for decent money. It is not decent, for when we run short of food, they will be out of a job, too much of our agricultural land being under concrete.

Many pundits think of our land policy only as a matter of statistics. Yet they fail to understand that under 70% of our remaining land may be suitable for food production, and why it is so important to retain all of it. Probably the greatest asset we have in England, apart from some of the best soil anywhere, is a plentiful supply of water. In India, for example, due to their exploding population, the water table has sunk so fast that in many areas growing rice and arable crops is no longer possible. We may soon have to feed those countries as well as our own if the world population doubles again as it had done in the last fifty years. But as we continue to import so much food, those frightening statistics have never been included in the equation.

Being a nobody gets one nowhere. But I shall continue to pursue the subject of land use as politicians in their selfish quest for votes continue talking about building thousands more houses without thinking about the consequences. Houses are necessary where there is work to be had and where it bolsters the economy, but there are also too many single parent families having babies in order to get a home of their own, an issue which must be addressed sooner than later.

In 2014 a BBC environmental survey pointed out that despite increasing our arable yields and reducing our meat consumption, by 2030 growth in our population will mean that we must, somehow, find, not lose, an additional 2,000,000 hectares, or nearly 5,000,000 acres of agricultural land in the United Kingdom. So when it was pointed out to me that an organisation calling themselves the UK National Ecosystem Assessment (NEA) had worked out that only two per cent of our land has by now been built over, it made me furious. No more than the man who accosted me in the lanes said one day. 'Major you know you are talking so much nonsense. Very little land in this country has been used for housing as you can see looking out over the countryside from here. Just compare us with countries like Monte Carlo for example.'

Letter 74

The owner. Restaurant Miniskar
Hvar, Croatia

September 2007

Dear restaurant owner

You may remember us as the 'rabble' you despaired of when we were unable to take up your mooring while trying to secure our 50-foot yacht in front of your restaurant a week ago.

The mooring, a large plastic bottle serving as a buoy, was difficult to pick up in the fast-running current, and no wonder. When grabbed with a boathook it shattered and its rope sank to the bottom.

On reaching Dubrovnik and examining your bill, we were surprised that, without asking us, you had added an excessive amount of money for replacing your decrepit mooring.

You have my business card. What are you going to do about it?

RR Yacht Libertas.

Comment: The Bosnian restauranteur, who spoke English, had been so abusive to us before seeing the colour of our money, that we were thinking of calling in again on our way back to Split. Most people we had found were charming.

Korcula

Libertas at rest in Hvar

Although, by then, we were enjoying the attractive city of Dubrovnik, where we had left *Libertas* in the harbour, we had not forgiven the fellow's attitude. He was responsible not only for the wretched state of his mooring but also for what he had said to us at the time about the 'interference' by British troops during the Bosnian War, which had ended more than ten years previously.

The war had been a frightening example of what is since described in the English dictionary as *ethnic cleansing*. Even those from other countries involved in trying to stop the fighting, including the British, found it hard to work out the complexities of the war not expecting it to be so horribly barbaric. When in October 1991, Dubrovnik was laid siege to by the JNA, or Yugoslavian Regular Army, supported by a naval blockade, who then proceeded to bomb the city, so many civilian casualties were caused and so much damage to the city's historic buildings, including those of its UNESCO World Heritage Site, that the whole world was scandalised. But so would they have been if they had known about the many unreported murders that had taken place within the walls of the castle overlooking Dubrovnik, before Croatian forces had finally managed to join the defenders and drive out the JNA from the area that December. In Bosnia, even those who had experienced untold butchery during WWII continued to be shocked by the savagery being shown by all sides struggling to gain supremacy in Croatia, culminating at Srebrenica in 1995, when the Bosnian Serb army under the command of Ratko Mladic, massacred over 8,000 men and boys, in a final terrible act of ethnic cleansing under the very noses of the United Nations.

It was difficult while sailing along the beautiful coast of the Adriatic, and then walking among the recently restored old buildings in that lovely city, not to cast one's mind back to those violent times, knowing that such deep-rooted hatred between fellowmen does not get snuffed out overnight. Indeed we had all been careful to keep off the subject of war wherever we went and whoever we talked to every time we landed ashore. There was so much to see on so many Islands. They totalled over a thousand according to the guide books, which, presumably, included many uninhabited grass-covered rocks, although it was clear that mass tourism would soon swamp everything on the map. I had first travelled there with my father on one of his political visits soon after WWII and remembered how, even then, he had arranged to have a pocket built under the dashboard of his car in order to conceal his Smith & Wesson .45 calibre revolver. Had times, I asked myself, changed that much?

What we had discovered, wherever we sailed, was that restaurants and shops on the waterfront of any Island we visited were remarkably expensive after such a long time without customers. However, being of a more inquisitive nature, we soon discovered that by delving deeper along the narrow streets, it was possible to find far more reasonable places to eat, with bars full of friendly locals, some of whom sang for us in deep bass voices.

Letter 75

Chairman of Exeter (Haldon) Race Course.
Exeter. Devon

October 2007

Tony

I have just been having dinner with racehorse trainer Keith Bradley in the South of France and he has told me that you may be negotiating to sell our racecourse to Northern Racing.

Before you removed me from the board for disagreeing with your intention of changing our historic racecourse from its charitable status into a limited company, you agreed to sign a declaration that none of the directors would benefit financially should the racecourse ever be sold. But Keith believes that if the racecourse is now purchased by Northern Racing, they may award each of the directors with a substantial sum of money.

Is that true?

R

Comment: My family had been involved with the Devon & Exeter Racecourse, later abbreviated to just Exeter, high up in the Haldon Hills, for over 70 years. It was one of the best courses for novice racehorses in England.

Haldon Gold Cup

Annette presenting a trophy with Prince Michael of Kent

My father, during his second time as chairman in August 1977, on the day before he died, had arranged for the Queen to visit the course, now famous for his Haldon Gold Cup. Having saved the course from closure he wanted to show her the new stand he had arranged to have built.

I had followed him onto the board while also being a steward there for thirty years and was astonished that the current directors should be rewarded with a single penny for selling the course. The thought of them raking in many thousands of pounds, in contravention to my agreement with the chairman, made me livid.

I was so angry that I flew home, immediately joining a hunting party on Exmoor where I explained the problem to an important member of the British Jockey Club.

'You know' Charles told me 'the Jockey Club once thought about acquiring Haldon Racecourse, but somehow nothing was ever done about it. I think we should meet there to discuss the various options right away. Is the course solvent?' I replied 'Yes' I replied 'very much so and, sadly, the reasons for selling it may not be just to secure its future but, possibly, for the directors to line their pockets. But the threat of it being sold is imminent' I warned him 'enough to make it imperative that we act fast if Northern Racing is to be seen off before writing out their cheque.' However I remained puzzled on how the chairman had got around our agreement, so I decided to find out.

Haldon, shared with Newmarket, the distinction of being the oldest racecourse in the Country. For during King Charles II's reign in the middle of the seventeenth century, horse racing had become fashionable largely due to the King's love of the sport. The rules were subsequently established in 1750 after the Jockey Club was formed. Before then the lust for gambling had taken many other directions, amongst them the noble sport of spider racing as once practiced once in the tower onto which my parents built our house in 1935. The largest spiders possible were brought in tinder boxes to be released on heated metal plates placed one at a time in the centre of the floor. The fastest spider to hit the wall won the wager, the skill being not to heat a plate too hot, or too little, which just made the spiders go to sleep!

There was nothing sleepy, about many who raced at Haldon, however, and on one occasion the irate jockey who I had reprimanded for failing to finish, told me to meet him behind the stands. There was also nothing sleepy about my former friend the chairman either, who I soon discovered had solved his problem of encouraging the board to sell the racecourse, by issuing each of the directors with a one pound share. Thus it was to be the shareholders, not the directors, who benefited.

Letter 76

Lord Coe. British Olympic Organising Committee
I Churchill Place, Canary Wharf, London

January 2008

Dear Lord Coe

Together with my son Giles I design water sculptures, which we now install all over the world. We would like to show you our proposed 'Coubertin Fountain' design for the London Olympics. I enclose two photographs of the maquette we have built plus some details.

The design of these Olympic rings is totally unique in that they slowly revolve. This is made clear in the second photograph. The details of each event and those taking part, are projected onto a curtain of water, created across the width of the sculpture with fan jets.

Shall I bring the working maquette to show you in London?

Yours sincerely

RR Dashcombe Sculpture.

Comment: I was unimpressed that Sebastian Coe had not to even bothered to acknowledge my letter. Then, having telephoned an assistant without receiving a satisfactory reply, it annoyed me greatly.

The Coubertin Fountain   The Olympic rings slowly revolve

Perhaps I should have taken the train to London and left the maquette in Coe's office; for if he was too busy to see me, at least he could play with it by turning the Olympic rings with a small handle. I had named it the 'Coubertin Fountain' after the enterprising Frenchman who, in 1892, had founded the modern Olympic Games. I had sent Coe this description:

THE COUBERTIN FOUNTAIN

The Olympic rings

Each ring is 20 feet in internal diameter. The circular faces are 5 feet wide. The top of each ring stands 30 feet above the ground. The rings are constructed from 10-millimetre-thick stainless steel sheet and are supported by 10-inch-diameter stainless steel tubes, each of them connected to hidden synchronised water driven mechanisms, which we have developed over a period time with help from some of our leading engineers. The polished rings are in Olympic colours using a translucent paint obtained from America. Each ring acts as an oil reservoir. They may be lit simultaneously to form the Olympic Flame. As the rings rotate, at one revolution per minute, they flash in the sunlight and at night create extraordinary moving images of fire and water.

No electricity is used and the fountain is entirely operated by water.

The stems

Ten inches in diameter, the 10-millimetre-thick walls of the five tubes are fitted internally with stainless steel drive rods of slightly less diameter. These are lubricated by water, which is pumped up within the sides of each tube, exiting under pressure from a large number of fan nozzles directed to form an uninterrupted projection screen between the stems.

The basin

The stems are mounted in a hundred foot long by thirty foot wide basin, positioned to capture and then recirculate the water.

Maybe our 'Coubertin Fountain' was too complicated for Coe or perhaps he was just not artistic. But having dropped the idea, I was never going to find out. I would have been more disappointed if our design had been rejected, but I doubt Coe had even looked at it. Instead I considered lobbying the Brazilian Olympic Organising Committee in Rio for their own summer games. No, I thought, I will give the maquette to our grandson should the Olympics return to England one day without Coe.

Letter 77

The Director. The Nature Conservancy
Thompson Bvld, Nassau, Bahamas

February 2008

Dear Sir

A short time ago my wife and myself were invited to spend a holiday in South Eleuthera. It has some of the most beautiful beaches anywhere but the ones on the south eastern tip of the island were so covered with plastic garbage that we were unable to swim there.

One local reporter during our stay wrote, totally ignoring the danger posed to marine life, that he had found a full bottle of scotch among the debris. What about all the dead fish and those turtles and other creatures dying because of plastic out there in the ocean!

I would be interested to hear what you are doing about it?

Yours faithfully

RR

Comment: We had been out deep sea fishing in the boat belonging to the American friends we were staying with. Among the catch we had landed, were several sheets, bags and bottles of plastic. It seemed that the Atlantic coast was worst for trash but best for the fish like wahoo, bonita and the black fin tuna we were trying to catch. We pitied all of them.

Plastic on our beach in Eleuthera

Reeling in a Tuna

Spanish Greenhouses

The wife of the boat's owner, unimpressed with my rod handling when I hooked a tuna, had rushed to my assistance. 'Reel in, reel in faster -much faster' she yelled, grabbing my rod and winding in the line like a dervish. 'If you want a whole fish here it comes, if you don't, then just relax and allow a shark to take half of it.' It made me think about the dreadful plastic, for no one seemed to doing anything very fast about that. If action was not taken by those who cared about the environment, fish like my tuna, which are known to consume hundreds of small fragments of disintegrating plastic, may no longer be food for sharks, for they will no longer exist.

It was said that the production of plastic, a process now consuming 10 per cent of the world's annual supply of oil, had risen more in the past decade than in the past 50 years and was accelerating. Also that as a direct result of human irresponsibility and laziness, annual plastic waste would soon weigh as much as the whole of the world's population. The figures were frightening, particularly as so much plastic was being manufactured for single use only. For instance, no less than a million plastic bottles are calculated to be purchased in the world every minute and at the moment, some 5 trillion plastic bags are sold every year. So what action could the the Nature Conservancy in the Bahamas or any other country take to save us from such a growing disaster, unless a sensible policy could be adopted by the whole world in general.

Plastic was relatively cheap both to produce and to buy, it was clean, easy to handle and had a multitude of uses including packaging. But there were many alternatives for packaging, for example, paper and other low cost materials based on wood pulp and other natural fibres. Such packaging is already proving to be just as efficient. Many agree, however, that the main thrust by all countries should be to re-educate their 'throw away' society so that, instead of so much of plastic waste being washed into the ocean, it should be disposed of better by themselves. Alternatively they should be encouraged to pass it on to professionals more able to bury, burn, or recycle it. But the problem with plastic sheeting or polythene tunnels as used by farmers the world over such as at Almeria in Spain, needs an even more determined solution.

Many people think that governments such as our own, through legislation, must impose hefty fines on all those who both produce and throw away plastics that are not bio-degradable. But even those, at the moment, are subject to concerns over the process in making them. For they must no longer have to rely on the elements to break them down, before a creature, like a fish, finally devours them. That really matters if by 2050, as calculated, there may be more plastic in the ocean than fish!

Letter 78

The Very Reverend Jonathan Thorn
The Dean, Exeter Cathedral, Devon

June 2009

Dear Jonathan

We understand that you are considering how the Cathedral Green could be enhanced with work by local artists.

Giles and myself have been designing and implementing water sculptures for over ten years since Giles left Exeter University. Our proposed three-winged 'Angel Fountain' will suit the times we live in.

Angels are known to every religion in the world for bringing messages from God. Our angel brings the message: 'May all religions of the world unite'.

Would you be interested if we showed you a maquette of our design?

Yours sincerely

RR

Comment: As a result Giles and myself did not receive a call inviting us to meet the Dean until a year later, after he had been prodded by the Bishop of Exeter, who liked the concept.

Exeter Cathedral   The proposed *Angel Fountain*

We duly took the maquette of the proposed angel along to confront the dean and his gathering of monk-like worthies known as The Chapter. Neither of us had sat on such a hard wooden bench in such austere circumstances since waiting to be beaten at school, and it made both of us look at each other as though that was, again, just about to happen.

'Thank you for your suggestion' said the dean, after we had described our concept with the maquette, which we then gave him. 'That will be all.' Acting without a commission and putting our water sculpture forward to the church in such a determined manner may have been pushing our luck too far; but on the other hand, we were offering Exeter Cathedral a unique opportunity of installing a sculpture which would, we hoped, attract people of every creed and every nation to visit Exeter just to see it. Also we hoped to have the angel financed entirely by others.

The reason for the three wings was straightforward but again may have been frowned on by the clergy. Apart from their fear of involving themselves in anything controversial, were probably not going to stick their necks out for many other reasons. 'A three-winged angel' they must have muttered amongst themselves 'surely no one had ever heard of such a holy being.' Having been let down over our concept for an Olympic fountain, it was the probably the next best thing we had in our locker, but persuading the Church would be even more difficult.

The Angel Fountain had been designed to be cast in bronze and stand 10 feet high to its wing tips, while the Angel's somewhat contemporary body was to be 7 feet tall with water directed from each of the wings to form a halo above its head. We hoped that it would be chosen by the dean, who was responsible for all such cathedral business matters, to stand in the cloisters close to the walls of the cathedral, but preferably where the sun would catch the halo. It would, we told him, give the Angel such an ethereal feeling that even his Chapter, who had first looked totally uninspired and half asleep, would, perhaps, be lit up by it.

I had met the Prince of Wales long ago on the polo field. He was a substantial landowner in South West England, and the Aga Khan, who leads some 15 million Ismaili Muslims, while competing in the British Ski Championships in the Swiss Alps. The two of them were passionate about bringing the religions of the world together and I had hoped they would sponsor two of the wings. A leading member of the Sainsbury family had already agreed to sponsor the third Jewish wing. Then, as the Torquay hotels were empty during the winter, we thought of an annual gathering of all religious leaders influenced by the fountain, which we also put to the dean. But he did nothing about any of it.

Letter 79

Giles, Farmhill House Studio,
Avening, Gloucestershire, England

September 2010

Dear Giles

I am only putting this on paper as it is over ten years since we started the water
sculpture business together.

Now that you have accomplished so much, I believe that it is the right moment for
launching into the Arab world, which we have so far neglected. Tim Landon, who
commissioned those three paintings from me, sadly died three years ago but you will
remember me talking to Peter, his right hand man in London, at the time.

Why don't we get hold of Peter again to ask him if he will give you a leg up in Oman?

Best love

Dad

Comment: I never really expected one as Giles, like many of his age, only answers emails. So a month passed by before I finally decided to ring Peter just the same.

Giles and the stainless steel Maquette he had just completed for *Arches*

'Yes' Peter replied. 'I would certainly like to give your son Giles a hand as I have already been told about his work. But I am leaving for Oman tomorrow. If he wants me to help him, he had better fly out and join me there immediately'.

Giles was dubious at first, for he had arranged to see two fountain prospects in Yorkshire, but he rang back later that evening saying that he had managed to fix it. 'What is more Dad, you simply won't believe this. The son of the your friend the Earl of Suffolk, who you met in Cambodia in 1969, rang me just five minutes ago to ask me, as I know him quite well, to fly with him and his party to Oman for the weekend, all paid for, leaving tomorrow morning!' I took a deep breath. 'Good heavens what an amazing coincidence' I said 'it must be an omen. *Oman* with an *e* for *enterprise* - what an opportunity!'

On arriving at London airport, Giles had told me he was ushered straight though passport control, where there was a notice saying Viscount Andover's party. He was then driven out to an unmarked aeroplane, where he was met by his friend Alexander, better known as Ali, being surprised when a line of trucks drew up alongside the aircraft. Ali had then put them all, at last, in the picture. Apparently the wooden boxes being loaded onto the plane contained the latest American M16 rifles. They were being taken to Oman by Ali in order to fight the then-rampant Somali pirates. Giles and his other guests were included as import regulations stated that each had to vouch for a share of the ammunition.

The hotel Ali had put him up in was excellent, but when Peter rang and told him to meet him at another hotel, it was even more magnificent.

Qaboos in earlier years   An Oman street scene. Photo by Giles

There Giles was introduced to the owner who said that although he would like to have one of his sculptures, he should talk to his son-in-law about them, who was coming for tea. He was about the same age as Giles and was the minister for municipal affairs in Muscat. It was a dream come true.

Giles was then invited to accompany the young minister in his limousine to look at suitable sites for a water sculpture, the first of which was on bare ground facing the new Royal Opera House. Giles thanked him immediately, saying that there was no need to look any farther. And so his *Arches* concept was born, without any of the usual constraints or competitions, on the very first day of his arrival in Oman. With more days left to think about the project, Giles then decided to spend the remainder of his time in that beautiful country first taking photographs of the villages and the mountainous Jebel, followed by studies of different aspects of their inspiring Arab architecture. For he was determined to build something hugely impressive not to compete with the solidarity or texture of the Royal Opera House but to replicate and complement the building's many superb arches with water doing the same for its music. 'It will be fantastic' Giles told me on the telephone.

It was some time after returning to England that I was summoned to Giles's studio in Gloucestershire, to see the first clay model of what he had in mind. 'That is outstanding' I said without any hesitation. 'It will rank among the best contemporary sculptures ever. How did you think of the design?' Giles gave me a wry smile. 'It was your word enterprise that sparked it off dad.' I just knew that I had to be more enterprising than I had ever been in my life and although the design, which looks a little like an Arab letter, may look straightforward at first sight, it is not for it will change in shape dramatically according to every angle you look at it from.' I wished Giles well and returned home to Devon to help him perfect the fountain's spectacular water effects.

Then came the difficult bit. We now had to persuade His Majesty Qaboos bin Said, the Sultan, who had been solely responsible for the city of Muscat's remarkable profile, to agree to *Arches*. So with help from Peter, who had stayed with the Sultan several times in one of his royal palaces, we set about creating an album of Giles's work and a video to show the proposed water sculpture when it was up and running.

At first I had an A3-sized album made up and bound in pink moroccan leather, the Sultan's favourite colour. Giles then filled it not only with many of his previous designs but also with the superb photographs he had taken of the country and its buildings during his stay. Finally, before being sent off in a diplomatic bag to Oman, the album was inserted into a similar-coloured case complete with the royal crest.

The video would have been more difficult if it had not been for the scale model of *Arches* Giles had already constructed by then in stainless steel. We took this with us to see a geek who lived in an attic in Leamington Spa. I had been told that he produced the finest animated videos in England. The result was astonishing. Not only had he placed the sculpture standing realistically facing the Royal Opera House backed by beautiful gardens with a fringe of palm trees, but he had also demonstrated its ever changing water effects both by day and lit up by night. It could not have been more impressive and gave all of us increasing confidence.

I had asked Giles what he thought we should charge the Sultanate for the water sculpture and when he gave me his estimate, as I knew from experience, that it was too much on the low side. As I had no idea of either the building or implementation costs, let alone the time it would take to install, after doing a few crude calculations, I doubled the figure. So there followed, as with all our projects, a nail biting time waiting for the Sultanate to agree the quotation which had to be passed by a multitude of officials at many levels of their vertically integrated council. But Arches was to cost us far more than I had first estimated as readers will find out, for it was not to be installed for a further six years!

Letter
80

The Right Honourable Jim Paice DL MP
Minister of State for the Environment, Food and Rural Affairs
The House of Commons, Westminster

June 2011

Dear Mr Paice

We were disappointed that you did not attend our Devon County Show this year, nor had delegated a colleague to stand in for you. Instead I tackled you at the Royal Cornwall Show to ask about problems facing our farmers including the need to attract more young into the industry.

In 2007 David Cameron, on attending the Oxford Farming Conference, had complained about the delays in tackling the problem of badgers and TB, which is decimating many West Country dairy farms. So, apart from the other problems, four years later I wanted to know what is being done about it?

Yours sincerely

RR President Devon County Show 2011.

Comment: When I was elected to be president of the Devon County Show, I felt it was the moment to air the frustrations we have about some of the problems facing all of us in the countryside. Ralph, our eldest son, who had meanwhile taken over running our agricultural estate, while starting to put right everything that his father had got wrong, thought the same.

The average age of practicing farmers in Great Britain had risen by 2011 to sixty-two, an escalating figure that should have shaken politicians to the core; however it continued to be totally overlooked by all of them. I had just appointed a 23-year-old youngster to manage our farm at Dashcombe, who, like myself, had attended agricultural college. But now my college, Seale Hayne, had been stupidly closed and those few colleges left seem to be moving to more esoteric subjects. Why?

With all the new technology arriving on farm such as satellite guided seed and fertiliser application, the future of farming surely depends on these colleges. Worse still, while the country climbs towards full employment, most of those in farming, particular in the dairy sector, are making so little money that, unless they are true sons of the soil, young people now find farming no longer attractive. Without plenty of professional young farmers the industry is going nowhere, so I wanted to discuss two proposed schemes with Paice I had in mind to entice them.

Our parish of Dashcombe had once been home to six dairy farmers, each within herds varying from 10 to 100 cows. But due to the low price of milk and the high cost of labour, not one of them has survived.

Our eldest son Ralph now running Dashcombe after a successful business career.

Local press report

South Devon cattle at the show.

European competition from better subsidised dairy farms and from supermarkets who sometimes regarded milk as a 'loss leader', had resulted in some milk being sold for less than the price of bottled water.

So instead of dairy cows our fields were being grazed by sheep and beef cattle, all now being condemned for contributing to global warming!

The only other way for labour-intensive dairy farms to survive, other than greatly increasing the size of their herds, was to concentrate more on milk processing in order to cover their overheads. Quickes, a local Devon dairy farm now famous for their cheese making, had improved their profits by exporting their produce all over the world, while reducing their overheads by introducing smaller cows from New Zealand which were happy to remain outside over the winter and did not 'poach' or wreck the ground. Their vision was an example to most other dairy farmers.

The government had a duty, I told Jim Paice, to encourage all farmers to do just that. As we were leaving Europe, surely Great Britain's largest industry should now embark on exporting far more 'long life' and processed farm products, which would also provide employment, to the rest of the world. He had been too busy to listen to me, but what annoyed me most was his apology to our show chairman for being absent due to other commitments. He had added 'Nor will I attend the Devon County Show in future until your current president is well out of the system.'

Letter 81

Sir David Hoare Bt. Messrs C Hoare & Co
Fleet Street, London

October 2012

Dear David

I realise how much you and many other neighbours may object to the 70 acres of solar panels we have recently installed at Dashcombe.

The Mail on Sunday by viewing them from a helicopter, while pointing out that a director of the company installing them had links with the royal family, failed to admit just how well they are concealed. That is not possible to illustrate from an aerial photograph!

I wondered why you were objecting so strongly when, we understand, you are pouring concrete for those houses being built on your land?

Yours ever

R

Comment: Solar panels, which are considered by many to be a blight on our countryside, now provide almost 4% of Great Britain's electricity. During the summer of 2018, for the first time, they overtook the electricity generated by coal. However should England, for example, wish to become entirely reliant on energy from the sun, which is not always so available during winter, they would have to sacrifice 1% of the entire Country to solar panels.

A small array of solar panels at Dashcombe

The future is therefore more dependant on advances in technology, not only to make the panels increasingly more efficient but also to ensure that the storage of the electricity they generate improves likewise. That is one of the greatest challenges facing our world today.

David was a great friend of mine and it was a pity he had not replied with a strong riposte, which I would have enjoyed. However, his objection had emphasised the problems of using our green and pleasant land for other uses than agriculture. Even for alternative energy.

So when later I was able to discuss with him the merits of solar farms, as they have become known, it was also necessary to compare them to the miles of plastic sheeting being rolled out by farmers like snowscapes. No one can deny their enthusiasm for growing crops beyond their normal seasons, or for competing against foreign imports of fruit and vegetables, which should be encouraged, but the downside comes when the sheets have to be disposed of.

Solar panels. it is true, also spoil the look of our countryside, but placed sympathetically where they do not cause too great a blot on the landscape. The installers, apart from being generous to the landowner if not installed by him, always include an annual contribution to the local community. In our case this financed a fast broadband mast and better mobile telephone communications. When professionally removed after 25 years, the bare land is left more fertile than ever.

The Manager. Mystere Boat Rentals
Port de Sainte Maxime, Provence, France

October 2013

Sir

Together with a friend of mine I hired a 7m RIB from you two weeks ago in order to photograph the yachts racing out in the bay. On our return I dropped my friend off in St Tropez, and, because I have a serious leg injury, left the boat at the Capitainerie, where I was told to leave it close to where my car was parked.

Although I had tied up the RIB up, to be clearly visible from your office, I have since received a statement from my credit card provider saying that you have charged me the sum of 7,000 euros for failing to return the boat on time. That is nothing short of daylight robbery plus nighttime robbery. For I notice that you are claiming for loss of hire over twenty four hours!

Do you, against all local regulations, hire your RIBs out at night?

RR

Comment: My friend had originally hired the RIB using my credit card, while I parked the car. So I had not met anyone at Mystere and was surprised that, knowing about my injury, and where I was going to leave the boat, they had behaved so dishonestly.

Photographing the classic yachts   Photographing a charging yacht

I therefore rang up the credit card company to ask them how it was possible for them to use my card number a second time without my permission. On three previous occasions we had towed our own RIB down to photograph the yacht racing during October, which was a lovely uncrowded month to be enjoying the delights of the South of France. Now I realised that hiring a boat instead was a mistake.

As there was little business with winter approaching, companies such as Mystere were out for every euro they could get. It was only as we entered Paris later on our way home, that my mobile telephone started ringing. 'Is that you Mr Major?' said a fierce French voice. 'This is the Sauvetage calling. We have been searching all last night and today for you. We thought you had drowned. Having got hold of you are you OK?'

Then I twigged what had happened. The man on duty at the time my friend had hired the RIB had obviously gone home for the weekend without telling the man who followed him on duty, what our special arrangement was. But I remained most suspicious. Why, before calling the Sauvetage, had not bothered to look for the boat themselves?

I had always felt that I was a 'Jonah', or a sailor who brings bad luck to others on the briny, and nothing could have been more true when ten days before, I had been invited to crew on a 100-foot classic yacht during the famous Les Voiles de St Tropez. We had set out late for the start as the yacht's bosun had woken up too late to buy all the drink for the following night's piss up, so the helmsman instead of joining the fleet where they were limbering up behind the start, aimed straight for it.

Joining in front of speeding yachts when barely travelling at five knots is not a good idea, and as we rounded the start buoy I noticed a two masted yacht, which was one of the fastest modern yachts racing around the Mediterranean, charging straight at us. 'Look out' yelled the helmsman from his position just forward of the cockpit where we were sitting. 'Look out, get below fast, for if she hits us the rig will come down!' She hit us hard, driving a huge wedge into our stern, and as I continued to take a sequence of photographs, I could hear one of her two backstays part and her tall mast creak ominously, threatening to crash down on both the helmsman's and my head. Then my attention quickly turned to our aggressor as she screwed sideways and continued to plunge closely past with her gashed bow looking like the jaws of a shark ready to devour us.

All hell then broke loose, with accusations being shouted across the water from every direction. But I knew that my photographs would show that two masted yacht was to blame for not avoiding us, as was later agreed in Court. But the French owners appealed behind our British backs and overturned the decision, saying that we should not have been there in the first place, while, on the brighter side, the credit card company, I found out later, had refunded my payment to Mystere in full!

Letter
83

Licensing Department. *The Civil Aviation Authority (CAA)*
Aviation House, Gatwick Airport, London

May 2014

Sirs

I wrote to you in early 2010 asking you for your documents in order to licence a small air show I was intending to hold at the end of June in South Devon. Receiving no reply from your department caused great anxiety among all the pilots waiting to be briefed.

Two years ago in 2012 the same happened again and although our event on that occasion only involved a small number of parachutists and one helicopter, we again only received your permission at the last minute. Now, once again, you have left us in limbo.

Why is it taking you so long to process our applications?

Yours faithfully

Major RR

Comment: I had hoped by stating my military rank, however humble, that I would be able to get the CAA motivated. I had constant visions of them sitting in a Nissen hut at the end of the runway at Gatwick drinking tea.

The Sea Picnic at Anstey's Cove

Auction

But maybe they were ex RAF staff and applications from a pongo were answered last. Or just that they were the most inefficient outfit ever!

I had initiated the Sea Picnics in 2006 as a result of our catastrophic shipwreck mentioned earlier in the book. The Brixham trawler *Scaldis* which had rescued us, had subsequently been lost with all hands in another violent storm; and as they had never claimed salvage or asked for any remuneration, I felt that it was time to support an associated Brixham charity which had been started in the millennium year and named the Trinity Sailing Trust. The trust owned four Brixham sailing- trawlers, which had once joined another thousand of them fishing off our South Devon coast before WWII. They were magnificent craft, the oldest built in 1892; and the trust kept them busy by taking more than 600 disadvantaged young people to sea for a week every year.

The aim of the picnics was to raise money for the charity. On one occasion in 2010 the event took £70,000 in one day. Although the CAA had not given me permission to hold the air show until the very last moment, I had arranged for several types of British WWII naval aircraft to participate including the Fairy Swordfish from Yeovileton, a Sea Harrier, a Sea Vixen and a Seafire, the carrier-born version of the Spitfire with a more powerful and wonderful sounding Merlin engine. Between 2006 and 2014 I was to organise five Sea Picnics.

After an initial rum punch, we always served a delicious mix of marinated scallops and freshly caught Brixham fish, followed by a succulent trinity tart full of blueberries and wild strawberries laced with rum and topped with lashings of Devonshire clotted cream.

Pirates!

James Bond preparing to drop his bombs

That second year the picnic was also memorable for a dramatic raid by pirates on our four trawlers anchored directly below the 1,000 onlookers.

I was going bananas on the blower when the eighty or so modern pirates dressed for the part with red bandanas and armed with rifles failed to attack on time. 'They must have found a cask of our rum or something better' I announced. Indeed they had, for when I had asked them earlier to hide on their assault craft behind a distant bluff of cliff, I had not realised that it also concealed a flourishing nudist colony!

The best of all my Sea Picnics, however, was the last. After an introduction by some ruffians singing sea shanties and the usual spread of seafood followed by another magnificent tart, an auction of marine paintings and sea-born opportunities was held, with more punch flowing liberally while a jazz band played wild music. We had returned to our original site with marquees erected on an ancient 1920s concrete bathing platform standing just above the high water mark with below a pontoon hired by us for tying up the tenders of the visiting yachts.

On arrival, the stunning scene with the four sailing trawlers anchored below in a horseshoe cove fringed by steeply wooded cliffs was a sight none of the 300 guests are ever likely to forget. Neither will they forget the *James Bond* extravaganza they were to enjoy before departing.

The trawlers under attack!

I had found a willing Bond and a Blofeld, but at first lacked an Oddjob and, until a beautiful blonde volunteered, a Pussy Galore. Finally, I managed to find a willing South African timber stacker in our agricultural merchants, who, being squat and well rounded, fitted the role perfectly.

All we needed then were the props to include a number of paramotors, or men on parachutes with propellers strapped to their backs; a high- speed motor launch, a black helicopter and a pile of flour bombs plus some mines packed with high explosive. The paramotorists and helicopter pilot had performed miracles for me on all four previous picnics. But the first motor launch broke down and although it was substituted by a friend with a faster one, the owner did not have time to attend the briefing. So everything then went horribly wrong!

The skipper was supposed to pick up Blofeld and Pussy Galore and then, rounding the rocky headland where he was waiting, head fast for the trawlers. Again I had to announce a hiccup over the tannoy when he failed to appear 'I think Blofeld must have lost his cat overboard!' Later he explained that it was indeed a pussy that had held him up. 'You have no idea how difficult it was getting her into her golden cat suit!'

My agitation got worse when the fellow manning the radio said he had lost communications with both the paramotors and the helicopter. So by the time the launch came creaming towards us, because the trawlers had not yet been boarded, the paramoters dropped their flower bags on the trawler crews, followed by the helicopter with its bombs, while Blofeld, trying his best to look aggressive as the launch sped towards us, knew that his attack had failed miserably as he would never get there.

All would have been OK except for the minefield. Several powerful explosives had been lain directly behind the trawlers in order to make the helicopter bombing look more realistic. The pilot had been instructed then to drop off Bond, who had been throwing the bombs out of his door, onto the pontoon. But his part came abruptly to an end when he had to dive into the sea to rescue a terrified Pussy Galore, who had jumped off the launch and made for the shore as fast as she could swim. Terrified because the driver, failing to understand where he was to stop, instead, as we all held our breaths, steered his boat straight into the minefield. There were some mighty explosions, with water shooting 60 feet into the air; but when the smoke cleared, apart from the missing Pussy, the launch, the driver and Blofeld all reappeared surprisingly intact!

Those interested in the Major's charity see www.trinitysailing.org

Leader of the Town Council. Council Offices
Dawlish, Devon

July 2014

Dear Sir

Recently while on holiday in Argentina we saw the Dawlish railway disaster reported
in the Buenos Aires daily press. I cannot emphasise enough that no small seaside
town in England has probably ever received such extraordinary publicity.

As Dawlish seems to have a declining number of shops and visitors I have suggested
a sensible way of cashing in on the disaster is to build a pavilion in order to illustrate
the effects of climate change and everything about Brunel's famous atmospheric
railway. If I raise the necessary funding, will Dawlish be interested?

Yours faithfully

RR

Comment: Dawlish, possibly the finest example of a Victorian seaside town anywhere seemed so determined to drift into obscurity that, as it had been a town I had visited throughout my life, I was determined to help them.

Dawlish railway disaster photographed by our son Ralph

With miserable parking and too many charity shops lining the Green, they seemed blinkered to any suggestions from outsiders like me.

Bam Nuttall, the company which had been instrumental in building the Channel tunnel, had repaired the railway in record time, so when I approached them about sponsoring a Dawlish Pavilion in which they would feature, they seemed very willing to consider it. Armed with that knowledge I felt rewarded when the mayor of Dawlish and the leader of council agreed to accompany me to see the local planning authority.

The planners were receptive. 'As long as you can raise the cash Major, then, in principle, we can see no immediate objections.' So on our way back to

Dawlish, I asked my passengers if they knew all about Isambard Kingdom Brunel, which they probably did not. 'One of his greatest inventions was the *Atmospheric Railway* completed by him past Dawlish in 1846 after the first line from London to Exeter had been inaugurated by the Great Western Railway just two years earlier. The trains hired from the GWR at the cost of only two shillings and sixpence, were adapted to be sucked along by a vacuum pipe connected to two pumping stations, but when rats gnawed through some of the leather valve flaps, the idea was abandoned. However, Brunel, whose double performed at the opening ceremony of our 2012 Olympic Games, went on to do greater things, and today is heralded as the most ingenious and prolific engineer in our country's history.'

I told them that most of the great British public don't know much about Brunel because, apart from a few minor attempts to commemorate his work, he is only properly remembered under an archway in London and in Bristol, where his innovative ship the *SS Great Britain* is on show.

'So my idea is as follows.' I told them. 'We build a pavilion on the Green at Dawlish not just to celebrate Brunel for building the railway, but also the company Bam Nuttall for repairing it so swiftly, thus saving half the population of Devon and most of that of Cornwall from being prevented from going to work for too many days. They would like us to do that by giving them the whole of the ground floor of the proposed pavilion and, in return, I am hoping that they will sponsor the whole building.'

'So what else do you have in mind for the pavilion, Major? We were going to use that area for a children's playground.' So I told them that as climate change was responsible for not just raising sea levels but also for wrecking their railway, I intended to set up the first exhibition ever attempting to explain it with help from the British weather centre in Exeter. 'The pavilion will attract a large number of new visitors and new business. Please then let's go for it.' But they built the playground!

Colonel John Blashford-Snell OBE
Expedition Headquarters
Stockbridge, Hants, England

October 2014

Dear John

I am writing to tell you the dreadful news, which I have just heard, that my great friend the Baron, Johnny Winterhalder has been shot dead.

Also that Hubert is going through a divorce with Annabelle, Johnny's daughter, and will be unable to provide us with his yacht and helicopter.

The expedition was a great idea but now it will be difficult to carry on without the support we were hoping for. Maybe the cave will just have to wait, or have you any other ideas for completing our mission?

Yours ever

R

Comment: I then discovered that John was by then away on another expedition looking for the world's largest elephant somewhere in India.

John Blashford-Snell   *HMS Wager*

During the millenium he had taken a baby grand piano up the Essequibo River in Brazil, balanced on a dugout canoe, to deliver it to villagers he had met previously in a jungle village called Masakemari.

Our proposed mission was to look for the important remains some Indian chiefs which had been buried in a cave on one of the wildest and most dangerous shores on earth. The last person to have seen them, John had told me, was the only survivor from a shipwreck.

Planning the expedition would all have been possible, as far as I was concerned, had not my great friend Johnny Winterhalder been shot dead by robbers on his way home from a bank in Buenos Aires, carrying a suitcase full of dollars. Now that he was dead all the logistics seemed to have fallen apart. Apart from planning the expedition I had spent more hours of fun with Johnny than anyone else in my life and even during those long periods when we were not staying with Johnny and his wife Lucy in Argentina or they with us in Devon, we used to talk for hours on the teleohone as he berated me about our useless football team, our hopeless tennis players, or the scandal of British troops still occupying las Malvinas, their treasured Falklands Islands. Now both my long friendship with Johnny, and my excitement in helping to organise the expedition with him, were all over.

After I had first met Johnny skiing in Chile, and when subsequently flying with him in his twin-engine aeroplane to tour his vast cattle ranches, I realised that he was one of the largest cattle farmers in the Argentine.

I had once stayed with him, before succumbing to married life, in the magnificent baroque mansion his father had built near the yacht club in Buenos Aires. He had even lent me his new Ford Mustang to take a bird out one evening to a nightclub. His father had managed the von Thyssen steel empire in South America and it was for that reason that, sadly, Johnny's life was soon to go into the steepest decline of anyone I have ever known. The problem began when he discovered that no steel ball bearings were being manufactured in South America and because they were all being imported, he had persuaded the Argentine government to loan him a large amount of money to build a factory.

It was unfortunate timing, for just five years later, Argentina was to reach an all-time high in their galloping inflation rate, by 1990 reaching the astonishing figure of 2,000 per cent. All would have been well ultimately if the government had not called in the money Johnny had meanwhile spent on the factory. For it meant him having to pay them back a million dollars in cash every month!

Slowly the great cattle ranches had to go, even the one in Mendoza, where, in the foothills of the Andes, Johnny used to feed his cows on the vast acres of thorn bushes to get them leaner for the bull. I slept on the floor of in his barn there, where, because there were no eggs or vegetables, I was fed morning, noon and night only on barbecued steak eaten in one's fingers. It was therefore necessary to drink mate tea sucked though a silver straw from a gourd in order to provide the rest of one's body's needs. But I remember the ranch most for my contest in a small coral with the fierce cow mentioned earlier, while, as I dodged it around a hitching post, the toothless gauchos cheered me on.

Sadly once all the ranches had gone, matters became even worse for Johhny and on returning to Buenos Aires with Annette in 2003 we found to our horror that if it had not been for their daughter Annabelle, and her husband Hubert, who had bought their house from the Argentine government, both Johnny and his wife would have been left with nowhere to stay.

Johnny had been as intrigued as I had been by Blasher's idea, as everyone called him, to look for the remains of the Indian chiefs. He told us how during the winter of 1741, a naval square rigger *HMS Wager*, which was part of Commodore, later Admiral, Anson's fleet of six ships rounding Cape Horn, had been wrecked on a desolate island in southern Patagonia. In those days the loss of a ship also meant the loss of all naval authority; and most of her crew, unlike those gallant men wrecked on Ernest Shackleton's ship *Discovery* in 1874, mutinied, with many scattering inland to join the Indians living there. The conditions on Wager Island, as it became known, were almost as atrocious as those that Shackleton had endured in the Antarctic, so although one of the ship's pinnaces had been adapted by the carpenter to carry the remaining twenty men south, when only four starving men eventually survived, they traded the pinnace in for help from some local Indians. The Indians instead of continuing south then agreed to guide the party, including their dying leader Captain Cheap and Lieutenant John Byron, grandfather of the famous poet George Byron, north through the mountains and glaciers of the savage coast of Patagonia, finally reaching the bay of Bahia Mala, where I had flown in Hubert's helicopter.

'What happened next' said Blashers 'as far as we know, is that only three of them made it that far and when they sheltered in a cave the Indians had shown them, they discovered these remains of some ancient Indian chiefs of great anthropological importance. We would never have known about them but for Lieutenant Byron, who eventually made it back to England, having been the only one to survive a further journey north by canoe to Puerto del Monte. So it was his account that sparked off my previous expedition to find the wreck of the Wager and substantiate the evidence. But instead of finding her underwater, her 'bones' were high up in a creek due to a massive earthquake that had raised the shore line.' But when I asked him if he had an alternative plan for finding the cave and he suggested we hired the only fishing boat from a remote village on that wild Pacific coast, I replied 'No bloody fear!'

Letter 86

Herr Luggen. Director Zermatt Tourism
Bahnhof Platz, Zermatt, Switzerland

March 2014

Dear Herr Luggen

The tragic death of little Daisy Neale last week, run over in front of your office by an electric taxi while being delivered with her family to the station, illustrates the town's complacency about these vehicles.

Surely Zermatt cannot be called car free. Cars, agreed, produce toxic fumes but electric taxis driven silently at speed are far more dangerous. Daisy was run over twice when she walked to the back of a taxi.

Why not fit your profusion of taxis with cameras, or other devices to warn both the driver and pedestrians when reversing?

Yours faithfully

RR

Comment: It was really none of my business but I had only been bouncing 18-month-old Daisy on my lap the evening before, when we were having a drink with her parents after skiing .

Electric taxis   A better form of transport?

I never received back a reply to my letter to the director of tourism or to the letter I wrote to the Kanton police, so I believed that nothing would ever be done about it. However, always an optimist, I hoped that they were at least aware of the problem.

Zermatt in the old days had always been my favourite place in the Alps. I had skied and climbed there many times, returning in my dotage to take in the superb mountain scenery again and to ski with Annette down some of the more gentle runs although still more challenging than those in most other ski resorts. When we were young and impecunious we always thought the Gornergrat railway there a 'swizz', as it climbed the mountain too slowly. Then one day my brother Nicholas was caught holding only half a ticket, while I had the other half in my pocket. He had been thrown out at the top station by the guard without his skis and would have died trying to walk down that evening but for a sympathetic American, who kindly came to his rescue. Now, on returning to Zermatt, I wondered if the town was no longer concerned about its reputation, for it seemed that it was so full of new hotels and chalets that all the families I had once known were getting far too rich.

My biggest quarrel with Zermatt, apart from the plethora of silent electric vehicles, which were now making walking the streets more dangerous than skiing, had happened many years previously. First when we were skiing off piste down a particularly sharp incline, and secondly when we were in Zermatt seeking out the spring snow and were loaded into a cable car with electric cattle prodders.

On that first occasion we had hired a registered, but not a Zermatt guide, to take us safely down the mountain. It was not a known avalanche slope but the weather was warm and we had to descend most carefully. When we reached the deep valley below the guide stopped and opening his rucksack took out some chocolate bars to give us. I could not help but look into his rucksack and having already noticed that it did not have the usual snow shovel strapped to its rear, I found that it was totally empty.

On returning to Zermatt I complained in the guides office that the man was a danger not only to us but also to himself for not carrying either a shovel or any avalanche bleepers. They shrugged and said he was probably an interloper. The second incident had annoyed me more. During April you don't expect many of the Zermatt ski lifts to be shut, and the remaining cable cars, which failed to reach the slopes we were looking for, then filled to capacity without mercy. So I went to see my former ski guide, Erwin Aufdenblatten, who was by then head of the Kurverein. 'If you look at those old cow sheds up the mountain' he pointed out 'you will notice that they now all have windows, so we had to employ the cow herds somewhere else.' But when I said that we would not be back, he replied 'Macht nicht, we have the Matterhorn.'

Larry Ellison. The Golden Gate Yacht Club
Yacht Road, San Francisco, USA

February 2015

Dear Mr Ellison

I have sent some posters to your yacht club of my painting of the 2013 contest for the America's Cup, which I congratulate you on winning.

The event was marred by the unfortunate accident to Bart Simpson, one of our leading British sailors, so with the prints from my painting of the final race, showing the Golden Gate bridge in the background, I am hoping to raise funds for the 'Bart Simpson Foundation' set up by Sir Ben Ainslie to encourage the young to go competitive sailing.

The Bart Simpson Charity is well advertised on the internet. Would you ever consider buying my original painting with all proceeds going to the charity?

Yours sincerely

RR

Comment: I could not be certain if the secretary of the yacht club had ever forwarded my letter to Ellison, or my book which I had sent with it.

My painting of the final race of the America's Cup in 2013

Ellison was becoming central to the cup's future and in particular the 2017 match, which he had chosen to take place in Bermuda where I was hoping to provide a water sculpture resembling a wingsail.

Larry Ellison, a multi billionaire and an accomplished helmsman, had previously thrown himself and his money into the 2010 America's Cup with more vigour than most, and by beating *Alinghi* the defending Swiss catamaran with a trimaran (or three-hulled yacht) fitted with a wingsail, he had secured his place for the 2013 match in San Francisco as the new defender. But many yachtsmen felt that he had only got there by shutting the rule book, which stated categorically that the challenger had to compete with a yacht of similar design to that of the defender. It had all led to the inevitable court case, which Ellison had managed to win.

Now that he was the defender, Ellison was to embark on such a radical new design of catamaran that most of those wanting to take him on in San

Francisco - apart from the Swedish entry *Artemis*, Team New Zealand's entry *Aoteorea*, and the Italian entry *Luna Rossa* - simply could not afford the costs estimated to reach as much as $200,000 an entry. It was the first time that racing yachts such as Ellison's new AC72 class, had been equipped not only with expensive wingsails, but also with radical new foils to raise them out of the water. These had been developed by the Kiwis, with insufficient secrecy, a few months earlier.

The trials beforehand had been hit by tragedy when the Swedish yacht *Artemis* pitch-poled when turning fast down wind and Bart Simpson, an accomplished British yachtsman, had been trapped underneath and drowned. It was a wake-up call for the new catamarans were more powerful than any yachts ever seen before with their instigator Larry Ellison, armed with all the latest technology, expected to win.

However as the 2013 contest was reaching its conclusion Ellison began biting his finger nails. The finals had been staged inside the Golden Gate bridge on a stretch of water close to the former prison of Alcatraz and the large crowd of spectators gathered to watch the racing closer than ever before, were devastated to see Ellison's Yacht *Oracle* dropping further and further behind the Kiwis until their skipper Jimmy Spithill asked for a lay day. Having been soundly defeated in five races he admitted then that his position in the boat could change from being 'a cockerel to a feather duster' with a flick of Larry's fingers. However, after the layday, when the British sailor Sir Ben Ainslie joined *Oracle's* crew, Spithill and his American yacht were seldom to lose, beating *Aoteorea* by the incredible score of nine wins to eight in one of the most dramatic sporting comebacks in history.

Ted Turner. CNN
Atlanta, Georgia, USA

March 2015

Dear Ted

You must be fed up with me bothering you about supporting various British enterprises, the last being the Duchess of Northumberland's Alnwick Garden project, where we we hoping to build the fountains she had asked us to design for her. My next request, which may be closer to your heart, is to help the British win the 2017 America's Cup.

I deplore Larry Ellison's move into catamarans, as I am sure you do. By supporting the British challenge it may encourage a change of direction back to monohulls, for if equipped with foils, they will sail even faster.

Would CNN be willing to help sponsor Ben?

My very best wishes

R

Comment: For Ellison the race in 2013 had been a triumph. But because of the colossal power being generated by his new catamarans it had sensibly been decided that the 2017 match would be held with yachts reduced from 72 feet in length to a more manageable 50 feet.

Presentation of my maquette to the winners of the Junior America's Cup.

CNN told me that Ted was in Moscow, when I wrote to him, but I was getting the gut feeling that, although he had kindly written the foreword to my book about the race, I should not have approached him again. Maybe, I thought, I should give up writing to tycoons altogether.

One of my last attempts to do something worthwhile, as I struggled with retirement, was to design a 60-foot-high wingsail sculpture for Bermuda, which was to turn, flashing in the sun, from a prominent point near their old naval dockyard. So I built a 3-foot-high maquette of it and flew with it to Bermuda where an evening's occasion had been laid on to show it off. But although my presentation attracted a full house, not one of the island's decision makers bothered to turn up.

Luckily, however, the racing had gone, at least for myself, in the right direction. Although the British entry did not excel in the preliminary rounds, the other boats faired similarly. However, one entry was missing, and when Team New Zealand arrived with the most advanced catamaran that had ever been seen, none of the rest of the fleet, including Ellison's *Oracle*, stood a chance. Better still it had prevented Russell Coutts, who had once been accused of abandoning his New Zealand cup winning team by joining the Swiss, from further commercialising the race through his 'Americas Cup Events Authority'. As that plus his 'cats' were now dead, it gave the Kiwis, who still refused to have anything to do with him, the opportunity of designing a monohull instead. Great, I thought, but for a moment things became even better when I heard that my maquette had been presented as the perpetual challenge trophy for the Junior America's Cup.

Letter 89

The Most Rev The Archbishop of Canterbury
Lambeth Palace, Lambeth, London

May 2015

Dear Archbishop

Both our religion and and our country churches are suffering from serious fallout in congregations due to an increasing number of marriages taking place in every other place imaginable.

As the law stands, there are not many young people left in most parishes who qualify to get married in their village church. Although it is possible for couples to get a license, it remains both difficult and time consuming.

Should not marriages in country churches be made more attractive?

Yours sincerely

RR Dashcombe PCC.

Comment: I had marked the envelope, which I had addressed to the archbishop as personal, because he knew some members of of my mother's family. I had also added a note about that on the back of the envelope. So It had annoyed me when the letter was eventually answered by someone else. But not as much as their reply. As far as I can remember before tearing it up, it stated 'The archbishop thanks you for your letter, but it is my duty to point out that should you be suggesting that country vicars marry more couples in their churches you are being unrealistic. The demands on our clergy are onerous enough already.'

I should have sent the person's letter winging back to the archbishop but such was the level of censorship at Lambeth Palace, it seemed, that my second letter would not have reached the archbishop either. How, I thought, could a member of the archbishop's staff be so insensitive to the decline of the Church of England as we remembered it, when services were held every Sunday morning and marriages, with consequent baptisms and confirmations, were considered to be the highlights of the church calendar. Without church marriages, children are less likely to attend, and instead of vicars being pillars of their local communities, they must continually take on more parishes and become increasing strangers.

Our own village was lucky to have one of the most beautiful twelfth century Norman churches in the kingdom, with all the facilities nearby that anyone getting married could wish for.

Dashcombe village church

It was true that an engaged couple could get around the law by taking out a special marriage licence, but the vicar had to agree a long and tedious process, which often involved many hours of travelling if they did not live close by. Thus church marriages are now at their lowest figure ever.

To me the whole system dated back to the Middle Ages and although it would be difficult to change the law in a hurry, it was high time that the head of our Church of England did something sensible about making the process of obtaining a marriage license much easier. Due to townies taking over from retiring farming families in many parishes, such as my own, not only were country churches losing their congregations but with them all their financial support. Various attempts to save them from being closed down remind me of that time I had arrived on a sheep station in Australia to be taken first to their chapel to pray for rain, only to find, having removed my hat, that it was a part time casino. So because of depleted churches and fewer vicars, new innovative methods of fund raising, which often have nothing to do with the church, must be found.

One of the least holy is a four wheel drive course set up by our eldest son Ralph in the Dashcombe woodlands. On three weekends during the winter rogues from all over the South West will arrive in every type of cross country vehicle imaginable, some with larger tyres than those fitted to tractors, to attempt the course. Although I once offered a £100 reward for the first to get round the steep, muddy inclines without a winch, no one has yet claimed it! Many of these ruffians may not have thought about God in their lives, but the money they pay into our church funds is invaluable.

Letter 90

President. The Royal Horticultural Society
80 Vincent Square, London SW1

June 2015.

Dear Sir

Last month we were fortunate to have been given a stand again at the Chelsea Flower Show. But we continue to be most disappointed in it. Despite the fact that we have exhibited at Chelsea every year since 1998, we are never given the position that we have always requested.

The stand costs us much the same on either side of the marquee but every year we ask to be in the sunshine, either your staff do not understand why, or they are indifferent to the eighteen years that we have been supporting the show. It remains our only form of advertising.

May we be given a better stand on the sunny side next year?

Yours sincerely

RR

Comment: Both Giles and I were surprised that we were not being looked after better by the RHS, particularly as Giles had installed several of his water sculptures in their major show gardens on different occasions and also fronted two of their TV programmes without his name ever being mentioned. Because flowers, probably, came first, I had never received a reply!

The Chelsea Flower Show, renowned to be the most important anywhere, had always been an ordeal not only because of the preparations that were needed beforehand. On one occasion my poor wife, Annette was left washing piles of gravel just as the doors opened. Then there were the difficulties of delivering the stand and our exhibits to the site. I remember waiting for hours until we were allowed to offload and then for many more hours afterwards, when we had to remove everything and make the ground good again. Because Giles was so busy building and installing fountains, he, as my boss, had asked me to help him construct the stands that year, which I did within our old fire engine shed back at the ranch in Devon. All was fine if I was left alone to get on with it, but there was a time when a girl, out to make a name for herself as a garden designer had been seconded by her firm to help us. We should have sent her packing immediately.

We landed up with an expensive forest of plants, which later we had to find room for in our respective gardens.

Annette washing gravel for the stand.

The stand completed.

Exhibiting our fountains was always fun when it was not raining, and often worthwhile, but there was no sun to make them sparkle. In many ways the number water sculptures that we were selling to the owners of British country houses were diminishing, but foreign buyers were taking their place. So Giles began travelling abroad, particularly to America. One year, we met a delegation from the University of Illinois at Chelsea, who chose a design we had called *Aspiration*. Illinois was not far from Chicago and so the pump could only be switched on for six months of the year. During the other six months the water was frozen solid!

From the outset we had also been fortunate to be invited to join the renowned Cornishman, Charles Williams, on his gold-winning Burncoose Nursery's stand. After a good lunch we always tried to stop him meeting the press. On one occasion when we failed, Charlie had let rip at the RHS, landing him the next year with only a bronze. 'Tell me about that plant, is it hardy?' was a typical question people asked me as I stood there flogging our fountains from his stand. 'Madam' I would reply with my meagre knowledge of gardening. 'It would grow at the North Pole.'

Sometimes people were unable to fathom out how our fountains worked and one year a fellow asked me on our stand 'How the hell do you get that whirlpool effect?' Not wanting to give any secrets away I replied 'Simple, but you need a man down in Australia sucking through a straw!'

Letter 91

The Director. Museum of Telephony Inc.
Emsworth, Maryland. USA

June 2016

Dear Sir

I was the owner of Hitler's red Hotline Telephone sold recently by Alexander Auctions in Maryland.

The auction house, which is regarded as the world leader in Hitler memorabilia, accepted the telephone only after agreeing that it had **cast iron** provenance. I had also signed an affidavit that I had witnessed my father bringing the telephone back from Hitler's Bunker on 30 May 1945.

When calling it a fake with an English handset, why did your museum not know, or bother to find out, that Siemens had a factory in England throughout the 1930s?

Yours faithfully

RR

Comment: 'Is anyone out there?' I had shouted down the telephone when my father returned with it from Germany. But there came no reply because Hitler and over four million Germans, who had fought for his Third Reich, were all dead.

My father had served as Field Marshal Montgomery's deputy head of communications in his 21st Army Group throughout their advance into Germany and had been present when Monty took the German surrender at Forward Tac HQ on Luneburg Heath, not far from Berlin, on 4 May 1945, four days after Hitler had committed suicide in his bunker there.

The Russians, my father told us on his return, were still fighting their way into the city, when Monty had asked him to get hold of an interpreter and get to Berlin as fast as possible in order to find his opposite number and arrange through him to meet the Russian general in charge as soon as possible. So driven by Mustard his driver, they set out through the crowds of refugees fleeing the Russians, fallen telephone wires and shell craters, to enter the Berlin that evening to the sound of gunfire. How he found his Russian counterpart is a mystery; but when he did, he told us that he was wearing a smart newly pressed officers uniform.

Then, having arranged for Monty to meet Marshall Ivan Konev, my father was immediately invited by the Russian communications officer to see the bunker where Hitler had just committed suicide.

Hitler's red hotline, portable, telephone. The cable plugged in anywhere

Possibly the only Hitler memorabilia with the Fuhrer's name engraved on it.

So my father became the first person, other than a Russian, to descend into its damp and gloomy corridors, where on entering Eva Hitler's bedroom he was offered her black telephone as a suitable trophy of war.

My father had said 'Niet' as he did not want to purloin anything on seeing that all her Paris-acquired undies were being nicked by Soviet woman orderlies. But when on entering Hitler's bedroom, on stating that red was his favourite colour, the Russians had been so chuffed that they had then presented him with the red telephone off Hitler's bedside table. He was lucky, for just over a week later a number of drunken Soviet soldiers forced their way into the bunker, trashing everything in sight and destroying all remaining records held there.

But, fearing that he would be accused of looting, as Monty had just issued an order saying that anyone found doing so would be court-marshalled, my father had to smuggle his trophies, including a porcelain Alsatian, out of Germany in a suitcase, before locking the telephone away for years in his safe. So it was only after we had laid on a party for him on his eightieth birthday, attended by many of his old army and political friends, that he told the whole story, which I then passed on to Bill, the owner of Alexander auctions in Maryland, whom we had chosen to sell it. Possibly because of possible reprisals, I had discovered that none of the other major auction houses would touch it. When the telephone arrived by carrier Bill rang me immediately. 'This is the most important item of Hitler memorabilia that we have ever seen!'

The auction house, who were said to be the specialists in Hitler memorabilia, then told me that they would do everything they could to promote the telephone throughout the world.

Hitler's bedroom. The scorch marks on the table show the telephone's position.

And they did, for it then appeared as headlines in leading newspapers including the *Shanghai Daily*, *Moscow Times*, *Indian Express* and the *Arab News*, to name just a few, in countries around the globe.

I had decided to sell the telephone, because my father had written a letter to me directly after the military concert, to thank me saying that he hoped, one day, I would share the telephone with our two sons. Now, because we were moving house, there was no option other than to sell it, as it was not possible to cut it into three pieces! So we asked the auctioneers to set a very high reserve and hoped for the best. As the day of the sale approached, we all became increasingly excited. Bill told us that they were taking calls from everywhere, including a one from from the Sheikh who had built Dubai. 'Hang on to your seat, Major' Bill warned me. 'I hope you know what to do with all the cash, for if things go on like this, it may fill Alladin's Cave!'

The red telephone was indeed a remarkable instrument, scorched by the fire started deliberately by one of Hitler's aids in his bedroom directly after his suicide. Luckily, he had then shut the air tight door by mistake. But just before the sale, the press reported that an American museum had claimed that the telephone, because it had a British handset, was a fake. Frustratingly, I was unable reassure the auction house in time that Siemens had made similar handsets in their British factory during the 1930s, after which they had been kept in stock in Berlin before fitting one to Hitler's telephone. But by then all of the punters had scarpered!

So damning was the accusation that, because we had been advised that the telephone could not be be auctioned again for years, we reluctantly accepted the reserve price paid by someone not at the auction, although we were not permitted to know his name. However, when a German museum then waded in by stating that the telephone could not be genuine because Hitler would have insisted it was made in red bakelite, not painted red later, and the purchaser threatened to return it, I began to feel even more desperate.

Luckily I found the buyers email address somehow on the internet and immediately rang the man, who was a hedge fund tycoon from New Jersey. 'Thank heavens I have got hold of you' I said, then, having explained about the ridiculous accusations by both museums, I continued 'The reason that the telephone was painted red was that it was not ordered by Hitler, or his aides. For I have discovered that It was a standard black army issue telephone, which the Wehrmacht had presented to Hitler after they had arranged for it to be inscribed first and then painted red.' 'I believe you, Major' he replied. 'I am a Jew and why I have bought the telephone is to show it to the world, hoping that the holocaust never happens again.' My father would have been delighted.

Letter 92

The Curator. Dachau Concentration Camp Memorial
Alte Romerstrasse, Dachau, Germany

June 2016

Dear Sir

I understand that you are the curator of the Dachau memorial and keeper of the records of everything that happened in the concentration camp. But I am fully aware that some photographs of a more sensitive nature are withheld from public view and kept locked in your archives.

I refer, in particular, to a photograph of Adolf Hitler possibly visiting the camp on the invitation of Heinrich Himmler, during, I believe, March 1944, in order to see the porcelain works he had moved there at the outbreak of WWII. I would be grateful to know if you have any photographs of that event? Also do you have the precise date of Hitler visiting the camp?

Yours faithfully

RR British historian

Comment: Maybe I received no reply because I was delving too deeply. Adolf Hitler had always maintained that he had never visited a concentration camp so I was anxious to discover the truth.

My father with his Alsatian during the 1930s

It was said that he knew very little about concentration camps saying that he had ordered them to be set up. like Dachau, as holding camps for gypsies and other undesirables. I only needed the date of his visit to meet Heinrich Himmler in order to complete the Alsatian's provenance. My sister, Fleur, had asked me to include the porcelain Alsatian my father had brought back from the bunker with the red telephone, so they could be sold at the same auction.

The magnificent model, probably of Hitler's Alsatian Blondi, had been sitting on Hitler's desk when my father spied it on leaving the bunker. 'I too have an Alsatian' he said. So the Russians gave it to him as well.

Ever since that moment when my father had presented my sister with the porcelain Alsatian, it had sat on her piano until the day I arrived to take it away. But before placing it in a wooden box I turned it over. 'Heavens!' I exclaimed 'have you ever looked underneath it, Fleur?' She had not for there as plain as a pikestaff were the sinister runes of the Waffen-SS. So when I returned home I went straight to my computer and looked up Allach, the name inscribed above the logo.

Allach at the outset of WWII was probably the top porcelain factory in the world; but few people had ever heard of it. Within just a few months, Allach had begged, borrowed, or stolen leading craftsmen from all the great porcelain works in Europe such as Meissen, Nymphenburg and Rosenthal. This had come to the notice of Heinrich Himmler, who wished, he said, to educate the German people. Instead, however, he wanted to commandeer the Allach works in order to give most of the porcelain away as bribes, or presents, to his senior operatives.

As Himmler commanded the Wehrmacht, which included the Waffen-SS and the Gestapo, he had eyes on the entire production.

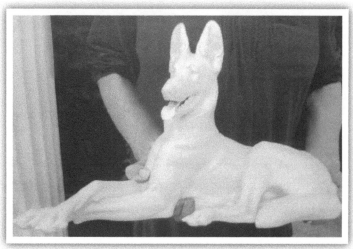

My sister's foot-long porcelain Alsatian

Hitler examining the porcelain with Heinrich Himmler early in 1944

So he moved the factory from the Bavarian Alps where it was, to a place where he would have total control over it, namely, the newly established Dachau concentration camp.

The camp, which was the prototype for all the concentration camps to follow, soon became notorious for its sadistic cruelty. However, more of its inmates were to die from brutal beatings than from execution, as Dachau was not an extermination camp. By the time it was liberated by the US Army, well over 30,000 deaths had been recorded at Dachau, including more than 1,000 rotting bodies they were to discover in a siding at the concentration camp, gassed earlier on a train. One of England's bravest SOE operatives, Noor Khan, was tortured and shot by the Gestapo at Dachau. When Hitler arrived early in 1944 to meet Heinrich Himmler, either there or nearby, there must have been many wretched inmates hanging on gallows and hundreds of corpses lying against the perimeter fence, waiting for the furnaces. They were, no doubt, the same furnaces as the one used for firing my sister's Alsatian.

The photograph I had found of Hitler meeting Himmler at the time, proved that he had lied through his teeth, but no historian has elaborated on this visit, and the date has never been established. So due to its macabre provenance, the porcelain Alsatian, which undoubtedly had been made by Jewish craftsmen imported from Auschwitz, was to create almost as much interest as the telephone.

Letter 93

The Right Honourable Theresa May MP
House of Commons, London SW1

July 2016

Dear Mrs May

With my son Giles, I am selling water sculptures all over the world, but such enterprises are still thin on the ground and export advice from the British government is always hard to come by.

Surely the time has come when we no longer need to be famous just as a nation of shopkeepers. MADE IN GREAT BRITAIN is our future.

After Brexit we hope that we will discover many new markets overseas and when you shortly become Prime Minister, why don't you appoint a senior minister to travel around the world and find out what the world wants?

Yours sincerely

RR

Comment: The Lady probably never read my letter while she was so busy preparing herself for battle. But as it was a subject close to my heart, I wanted to get my oar in fast before she became too embroiled in her new job. It must have been difficult for her to see the wood from the trees and certainly how much she was about to be bullied by Europe.

However busy and important a person is, it is still a pity not to receive an acknowledgement from an aide or a secretary. But such good manners no longer seem to be of any consequence.

It subsequently lifted many people's morale when one of Mrs May's first steps as PM was to appoint Dr Liam Fox as Secretary of State for International Trade with instructions to follow what I, a nobody, and probably many others had suggested to her. So we were all delighted to see that she was taking steps to establish trading with the rest of the world as an immediate priority.

Fox was to take his appointment by the horns and it was said that within just over two years he had travelled some 300,000 miles, or twelve times around the globe, looking for, and finding, more British business.

His Department of International Trade was soon taking on some outstanding new recruits eager to fight the British corner like bulldogs with a remit to develop, co-ordinate and deliver a new trade policy and then to negotiate future free trade deals with countries outside the European Union. But one huge stumbling block remained - the European Commission, backed by the European Council.

The European Customs Union, then known as the Common Market, had been started in 1968 by just six countries - France, Germany, Italy, Belgium, Luxembourg and the Netherlands - to remove all trade barriers between them but to keep to common tariffs when trading with the outside world. Now the commission were determined that Great Britain, which had joined later, but never adopted the Euro, was not going to wreck it all. Indeed they were going to make life as difficult as possible.

Some people, such as Young's seafood, have the right idea!

Many believe that problems within the EU stem from the financial straight jackets that were imposed through unnecessarily draconian European treaties, now clearly a design failure. The European parliament is much weaker than individual national parliaments and so the Maastricht Treaty, although for some was a step forward, for many others it was also a step backwards with inevitable consequences such as the Gilets Jaunes movement now rearing its head in France.

At first the idea of a common market had seemed to be attractive, so in 1973 Edward Heath, the British PM, arranged for Great Britain to join. However the euphoria of Europe trading as one important block with the rest of the world began to lose its shine as smaller countries signed up to the union and the butter became spread ever more thinly. By 2001, when Greece joined, the number of countries operating within the strict rules of the Eurozone had doubled to twelve. Then, however, largely due to the inflexible rules of the commission, particularly on the question of common interest rates, some countries like Greece, Spain and Italy started to regret their membership, none more so than Great Britain.

It was also because the commission, an independent body of non-elected representatives from each member country, set up much earlier and strengthened by the Treaty of Lisbon in 2008, was becoming far too political and autocratic. Thus, harassed by many of his MPs, David Cameron then Prime Minister, decided in 2016 to hold a referendum on leaving Europe, which once decided upon, became known as Brexit. That was fine if the commission, were ever going to let us go!

Letter 94

Managing Director. Brenton Engineering
Brentford, Essex

October 2016

Dear Sir

It is six years since my son Giles first travelled to Oman to talk to the Arabs about a water sculpture and over a year since we came to see you to discuss building 'Arches'. It proved to be such a complex design that although you were prepared to take it on, it would have been too time consuming and expensive. But I am writing to say how much we admired your stainless steel work and are not surprised that you look after so many top sculptors

I wrote recently to our Prime Minister about the necessity after Brexit to promote our skills to the rest of the world. Would your firm agree to participate in such a promotion scheme?

Yours faithfully

RR

Comment: I may not have received a reply, because the firm was busy enough already. How shortsighted, I thought; but determined not to let them off the hook I followed up my letter with another, which I sent for them to sign, knowing that such an approach would never work by email. It was addressed it to the Department of International Trade, which I now feel is so important to the future of our Country.

Knowing how many others, like James Dyson, were passionate about British engineering I wished I could have taken someone from the department with me when I travelled with Annette to see *Arches* being given a final polish in one of the largest sheds I had ever seen at Darwin, north of Manchester. 'Well its not going to shine like the stars' said a senior staff member 'for it is made of duplex, an ultra-hard grade of stainless steel, just developed by the Chinks.' Patting the metal, I added 'Yes and it was I who found it on the Internet being tested first for a railing leading down into the water in New York harbour.' Other engineers who had by then gathered round, intrigued that Giles's old father was still involved in such high technology; then told me how they were now often using the metal themselves and, including many export orders, were currently turning over £1 million every week!

Each side of *Arches* was not only 40-foot long but also twisted in such a shape that it was necessary to move it, plus the section which joined the two sides at the top, on two mammoth transporters before being stowed on the deck of a ship, as being too bulky to stow in the hold.

Arches photographed with Giles while under construction.

Unfortunately the ship was delayed, which caused the weather to hot up in Oman far too soon for us. Then once the sculpture arrived there, the whole procedure had to be repeated, until it reached its final destination in Muscat facing the Royal Opera House, where it had to be lifted vertically by cranes to stand on its reflective plinth in an oblong shaped lagoon. After that, some skilled engineers from Mtec, our fabricators in Darwin, were flown out free of charge from England to weld on the top and then thoroughly check the metalwork of the finished water sculpture.

We had gathered a number of friends to join us in Oman to inaugurate *Arches*, most of whom had invested in one or two of our sculptures previously. I had bought tickets for them to attend a night at the opera, where, after the impressive performance and a sumptuous dinner, we walked, all twenty of us, to watch the floodlit sculpture go through its sequence of dancing water jets designed to replicate the stringed instruments of the Opera House before dropping into the lagoon to form the S of *Sultanate*. That night we celebrated the tremendous efforts put in by our small team including some skilled Omanis, who had not only completed a magnificent formal garden designed especially for it, backed by a grove of newly planted palm trees, but also an astonishing underground pump room. From the computer activated pumps Giles had then managed to feed some 2 kilometres of piping into the metal fountain, while enduring more than forty degrees of unrelenting heat.

'The whole design is unbelievable' said an Omani while serving us breakfast. 'When I was a boy, I kicked a football where you have built that wonderful fountain. Those who come to Muscat cannot miss it!'

Arches with the Royal Opera House behind

The water effects had been a particular challenge as they are impossible to design in miniature. Because the jets were at different heights, they all had to be calibrated for different pressures.

Arches looks different from every angle

An early **design drawing** of the lagoon and gardens. The Opera House is on the left

Therefore in the early stages of building the water sculpture, it was necessary to erect a 50-foot high gantry with wooden platforms at every level so that the large number of jets employed could each be reached and adjusted individually.

While we were experimenting with the jets just outside London, it had to be remembered that the water temperature so near to the equator was very different. Then calculations had to be made on how quickly the lagoon, in which the sculpture was to be erected, would heat up every day of the year according to the total volume of water. The reflective plate incorporated in the design to light up the water effects, also added to the temperature, but apart from that the temperature of the water in each feed pipe also had to be calculated according to its individual length within the sculpture.

While we were there we grew to enjoy Oman and their people very quickly; always being careful to respect their religion and ancient traditions. The country was at peace, away from the problems effecting other parts of the Arab world, and we appreciated every place we visited, including the Grand Mosque and their new National Museum. I was particularly intrigued by the design of their famous dhows now only built, like all dying world traditions, in Sur a coastal town further south in Oman.

Oman had much to offer for His Majesty the Sultan, after taking over from his father in 1970, with the new found oil money had created a stable economy for its people and a welcoming country for visitors, with a growing number of attractions including, apart from trips into the interior, plenty of golf, scuba diving and swimming with Oman's famous turtles.

A team member installing the pipes.

Poster

The Grand Mosque

Everyone now hopes that as oil revenues drop in Oman, industry, shipping and tourism will take over, with the next in line of succession having the same vision and drive to keep the country prospering.

Our one regret was that we had no time while in Muscat to explore the interior of Oman with its mountains and remote villages, all so well photographed by Giles for the album we had first presented to Qaboos, the Sultan. But at least Annette and some more frisky members of our party were able to mount an expedition to the Wadi Shab and to swim through its crevices and deep caves while Giles carried some much needed refreshments. Before we left the country, our party were generously invited to a memorable dinner by a leading Omani who told us how the Sultan had been so clever about developing the city of Muscat with so many magnificent, but, thankfully, low rise buildings. Finally some of us were privileged to visit the royal stables, finding that the Sultan owned well over a thousand, well managed, Arabian horses. So later when asked about our most enduring impressions of Oman, they were of its beauty, its peacefulness and its welcoming people.

The work put into the sculpture's water effects at last seemed to have paid off, for while trying to perfect the accuracy of each jet, we had been almost overwhelmed. But on arrival in Oman, it was Sod's law that there had to be just one major disaster. Before replacing them after several weeks of worrying delay, Giles had found that all the individually calibrated jet nozzles had suddenly, and inexplicably, disappeared!

Letter 95

Patrizio Bertelli. Prada Group head office
Via Antonio Fogazzaro, Milan, ITALY

January 2017

Dear Mr Bertelli

Since writing my book The Story of The America's Cup, which is now published by Bateman in Auckland, it has been updated after every match. l look forward to including Prada and the new design of yacht for the 2021 match in the next edition, hopefully to also be printed in Italian

I am therefore writing to ask if Prada would be interested in sponsoring a branded version of the book. If so, I will send you my earlier draft for your comment. As Challenger of Record, you may also like to add some of your own valuable words. I would appreciate your thoughts?

Yours sincerely

RR Copy to Grant Dalton, Auckland New Zealand

Comment: Bertelli and his wife had once been ranked by *Forbes Magazine* as one of the most influential couples in the world, but perhaps they were also two of the busiest? The next America's Cup was still a long way ahead, so I decided to write again to Bertelli later, who I had only met briefly at the 2007 contest in Valencia. I had written at the same time to Grant Dalton, who was CEO of Emirates Team New Zealand, telling him of my letter to Bertelli and including another 2013 edition of my book. He had also not replied.

Patrizio Bertelli, a billionaire Italian businessman, had starting Prada in 1988. He was also a sportsman and such a keen yachtsman that, since 2000, he had challenged for the America's Cup with his yacht *Luna Rossa* all four times, until 2017, when he backed Emirates Team New Zealand to win instead. Prada's contribution was, subsequently, to play a major part in their success.

In 2017, when the New Zealand catamaran had arrived late in Bermuda, being determined not to give all their secrets away as they had done in 2013, it amazed all traditional yachtsmen when they saw bicyclists instead of the usual 'grinders', manning the winches.

The New Zealander's, always at the forefront of innovation, had stolen a march on the opposition by taking advantage of the new class of yacht's crazy 'powering up' system, by instead of using arm muscles, using the strength of leg muscles with significant eeffect. Now too late to copy!

 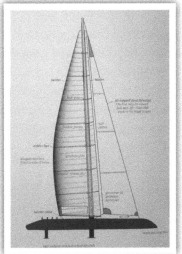

A design for a future America's Cup monohull yacht included in my book

The result had been a 7-1 whiteout against Larry Ellison's *Oracle*, enabling the Kiwis to defend in 2021 with their own design of yacht, which could no longer be a catamaran due to the winds and seas they might experience in the Southern Ocean. So they had decided on an innovative design of monohull with foils resembling adjustable outriggers, far more radical than the future design for an America's Cup yacht that I had drawn for my book.

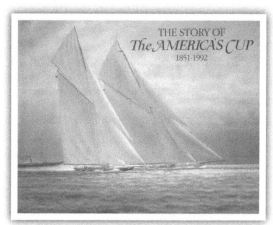

Draft jacket for an earlier edition of my book.

But just as I had suggested, it was agreed that they would be even faster and more challenging than the catamarans.

The problem was that just the development costs of these state-of-the-art 75-foot foiling monohulls were estimated to be so tear jerking that only three challengers - the British, who were first out on the water with a test boat, the Americans and the Italians, with their ever-faithful Prada, - were at the time of writing, yet to throw their hats into the ring. Meanwhile as they all started trying out the totally new way of sailing and balancing a monohull on skids, the Kiwis, largely funded by government money, decided, instead of sailing the opposition's scaled-down versions of the new yacht, to practise first by using only simulators.

I had long finished writing the tenth edition of my book but the publishers in New Zealand had agreed with me that it was best not to do so until shortly before the next event, by which time I hoped it would be possible to get the sponsorship I was trying for - but, perhaps, it was again unlikely from a billionaire!

Letter 96

HRH the Prince of Wales. Clarence House
London SW1

January 2018

Sir

I am arranging a West Country painting fair during June in aid of The Trinity Sailing Foundation, Brixham, a charity I support, which takes hundreds of disadvantaged young people to sea every year in their classic sailing trawlers. We would be most grateful if you could help us.

I am therefore writing to ask if it would be possible for your Royal Highness to provide us with one of your sketches, which we could either sell, or auction at the event, which will comprise a wide range of work by many leading West Country artists?

Yours sincerely

RR

Comment: I would not have expected a reply from Prince Charles who was always beavering away for other good causes. His secretary kindly responded.

My garden studio

Polar Bear painted in resins on aluminium

She said that the Prince thanked me for my letter and suggested that as an alternative to one of his sketches, which were in short supply, Trinity should apply for a £5,000 grant from his trust as he would like to contribute to our event.

I wrote back to Prince Charles thanking him for his contribution, saying that it would be put to good use by helping to finance a new engine for one of our four boats. The cost of maintaining them was considerable and getting worse with every year the old ladies took to the water. But as my Sea Picnic fund raising had been dashed by the Civil Aviation Authority and the resulting insurance hikes, the fair was my alternative.

I thought to myself how difficult and very ordinary it would be if letters were abandoned in favour of computers. Would an email written to our Royal Family ever become an alternative? I hoped not. I also doubt that painting will ever be taken over by computers although they sometimes achieve some remarkable results. As for my own innovative ideas of painting with transparent resins on reflective aluminum, no one seemed to know anything about it, a technique I had researched by looking up on the internet the only artist I could find using my unusual choice of materials. Having sent the artist an email I was amazed when she divulged more secrets than most artists would ever give to a stranger. When I thanked her for being so helpful, she replied 'No worries, I am replying from Brisbane in Australia'. Perhaps, for a moment, I had softened to the capabilities of those infernal machines! The exhibition was a success in raising money for the Trinity Sailing Trust but none of the thirty paintings I had completed for it sold!

Letter 97

Mr Christopher Loughlin. Chief Executive Officer
South West Water, Exeter

January 2018

Dear Sir

You will know from my previous letters that our water supply has been stopped countless times by power and pipe failures, which, despite constant protests, has not yet been rectified.

Since our reservoir was closed everyone and every animal in our village has been adversely effected, by clearly what is a cost cutting decision to the benefit of your shareholders.

We have dug a borehole here capable of supplying a small town, but unfortunately we do not have the resources to connect it to the farm water troughs, and many of the cottages. Could you now help us do that?

Yours Sincerely

RR Chairman. Dashcombe Parish Council

Comment: After trying to telephone the CEO, as no other form of communication was getting a response, I received the following email two months later from a junior employee:

Dear R (Bloody cheek!)

We are unable to agree to the customer request in this case. The water outage was recently due to a burst water main and therefore outside SWW's control. The customer should have alternative arrangements for the provision of water and we suggest that the customer attempts to claim via his insurance for these losses. Should you have any further questions regarding this then please do not hesitate to answer us.

Kind regards

In Columbia they say *'plata o plomo'* (a bribe or a bullet). But although I had tried bribing SWW with a new and copious supply of water, they could not be bothered to respond. It is sad that such services are now controlled by such large conglomerates that their executives don't care a fig about individual consumers any more. After that ridiculous reply SWW should have had the bullet.

When I asked SWW later why my letters had not been answered, an assistant haughtily informed me that both the chief executive and the managing director 'do not reply to customer's letters'.

Water, water everywhere   Have this as a present instead!

So this email, sent several months later by SWW Customer Services, was a pathetic and misinformed attempt to pacify an angry consumer trying to obtain a coherent answer to a problem effecting not only the health of his Devon village, but its important economy both in agriculture and tourism.

The situation has become so bad, in our overcrowded country, as more and more houses are built with insufficient services, that the government must step in and prevent us diving even faster into the third world, as clearly demonstrated by the arrogance of SWW. But, sadly, our case is the only one I know of that has recently been discussed in parliament, for most victims, resigned to what is becoming the norm, simply do not bother.

More serious is the fact that it is not just the services such as water that are being tested by the Government's headlong rush to build houses, half of which, in many areas, are unlikely to be filled. Also the existing sewage systems are often inadequate to cope with such a fast growing number of people. Rather than forcing developers to pay for the provision of such services when they are granted planning permission, local councils, determined not to be punished by the government for not meeting their housing targets, are often as weak as kittens about getting the ever more prosperous developers to do so. Great Britain is renowned for its plentiful supply of water while India and other countries with burgeoning populations, are losing theirs fast. But even our country's water supplies could be threatened, like ours at Dashcombe, unless there is sensible forward planning by the authorities and considerable investment in the future.

Letter 98

Andrew White. The Hamilton Princess Hotel
Pitts Bay Road, Hamilton, Bermuda

March 2018

Dear Mr White

You will not know me from Adam, but I amand the Giles's ancient father and the marketing director of his water sculpture business. I designed the proposed 'Wingsail' sculpture for Bermuda. As you know, the maquette was later presented to the winners of the Junior America's Cup.

Giles designed the 30ft high 'Blade', which you liked, to withstand the strong winds in Southern Ireland. Triangle' the bronze sculpture which Giles has suggested for your hotel, will now have a skeleton made of duplex, a particularly hard grade of non-corrosive stainless steel.

As Giles who is in Dubai has not heard from you, may I help?

Yours sincerely

RR

Comment: Perhaps there is a different code of conduct in Bermuda. But Giles had made a mistake by adding to his quotation, after finding out more about the salt saturated air and the occasional hurricanes that afflict the island. He had also been told that even marine grade stainless steel will degrade there. However we had been unable to contact White ever since.

'Never increase a quotation whatever the excuse' I advised Giles, who knew that already. 'Always over-quote but never underquote, and, if possible, get a second opinion first'. But I was angry that Giles had spent several days of his valuable time flying, by invitation, out to Bermuda to see the guy at the hotel and look at an appropriate site for his sculpture. I was also sad that White had not acknowledged the fact that I had designed the *Wingsail* sculpture and built its maquette, which he had then passed on to the organisers of the Junior America's Cup as their future challenge trophy, without a word of thanks.

Bermuda is a beautiful island, famous for its pink coral beaches and snow-white roofs. Bob Hope had once bragged when he first arrived there 'Its the only place I have ever visited where all the drinks are on the house!' It was true. Perhaps we should also collect more rainwater.

Other than 'dark and stormy', a mix of dark rum and ginger beer, Bermudans have not much other than their rainwater to drink. So the precipitation from every passing cloud was captured from their roofs in reservoirs built beneath every house or garden.

We came to the conclusion, despite the fact that Bermuda has the highest gross national product figure on the universe, that due to being islanders many of those we tried to deal with seemed to have unusually difficult temperaments.

But I also discovered over several visits, that although Bernudians manage to boost their economy with the rent from large offices mostly aligned to the British insurance industry, they do not welcome people such as nondescript looking British fountain builders like ourselves, when it means putting money into the pockets of foreigners!

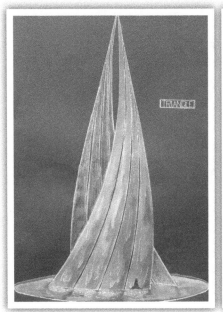

Triangle designed for the hotel   White roofs

Bermuda is classified as a British overseas territory; but in fact it is the oldest of all British colonies having been given limited self-governance by a royal proclamation in 1620, the year when the *Mayflower* sailed to America. After the American revolution, work started in 1811 on building a large naval dockyard on the island, still known today as Dockyard, which houses the National Museum of Bermuda and also its Maritime Museum. Bermuda, known for its famous Bermuda Triangle, is as far away from anywhere in the North Atlantic; and their sub tropical climate, when not humid, combined with their coral pink beaches, provide a wonderful place for a holiday. Although its government, controlled by blacks, is independent from Great Britain, it has a British governor. In 1973 Sir Richard Sharples, the governor, was shot dead by two assassins associated with a black power movement, who then became the last to be executed under British rule anywhere in the world.

Letter 99

The Editor. Letters to the Daily Telegraph
Buckingham Palace Road SW1

November 2018

Sir

Great Britain is suffering from the most feeble leadership in living memory and the lady responsible must go.

Get cracking MPs and elect a bright young whipper snapper to stand up to those smug Europeans for once and for all.

RR Dashcombe, Devon

Comment: There is a well known military confidential report stating 'Men will follow this officer - but only out of curiosity'.

The lady was not for turning while the European Commission waited to catch her!

Mrs May would have been followed if she had said what she was up to. Just as Europe may have followed her after the British referendum, if they had been told on what terms Great Britain was prepared to leave their treasured union. So when, on 29th March 2017, she signed Article 50, the set-in-stone withdrawal agreement, without any terms whatsoever, the Country despaired both for her lack of statesmanship and her inability to negotiate and tell us, if anything, what she had achieved. Even her closest advisors were unable to follow her drift, which clearly left Britain still joined by the hip to Europe but without being able to make decisions or trade internationally.

Although the two ministers she had appointed to negotiate 'terms', immediately resigned, many people, still believing that, like Margaret Thatcher, she was another Iron Lady, began to follow her not so much out of curiosity but more out of sympathy. However, her realistic electorate, saw her not as made of iron, but rather of putty, when confronted by any member of the European Commission.

Mrs May's ineptitude had already showed at her general election. By ignoring the young and the notice they took of the social media, she had only won enough votes to be kept in power by the Irish. But it was largely because of the reluctance of the Irish to accept a hard customs border for an unknown period of time under Article 50, that the PM's attempts to re-negotiate the deal, or to think up any alternative, failed.

As her confused electorate asked where the British Bulldog was hiding, and she did nothing to throw the dog a bone, while collaborating with the opposition, it looked increasingly likely that with teeth bared and hackles bristling, the dog was about to boil over and burst out of its kennel.

In every walk of life, particularly if you are running a country, leadership skills, even when putting out a fire in the kitchen, are paramount. Perhaps the old style of statesmanship no longer exists, but the essentials of being a good leader certainly do. So the British public were beginning to feel that the importance of listening to others and working as a team, was being ignored, while as the result of decisions being made by the PM without the knowledge of her cabinet, she had lost all her integrity. Mrs May also appeared to have no vision; for if so, why did she not stand up in front of the cameras and give her electorate some inspiration in order to ensure that the good ship *Britannia*, not that fast sinking ship the *Euro*, would once again rule the waves?

'Time was running out' Europeans who wanted a deal kept telling the UK. But it was only to be a deal on their terms, while Mrs May, after two years of trying, trapped by Article 50, still had nothing better in mind.

Looking back, the European Union, which Britain had joined in 1973 as the Common Market, was becoming so politicised that it no longer bore any resemblance to it. Indeed, when it was stated that the chains of European bureaucracy were to be tightened further, some other member states like Italy, Greece and Spain, also started fidgeting. Thus in order to prevent the EU from breaking up altogether, the European Commission, rather than look for a mutual advantage in future trading relationships, or peace with Northern Ireland, while hoping to dissuade others from leaving, were stupidly determined to make the British departure as difficult as possible. Meanwhile as Jean-Claude Juncker, president of the commission, was seen placing his hand reassuringly on Mrs May's shoulder, he and Donald Tusk, president of the European Council, were photographed congratulating each other on how clever they had been. But it was they who would end up as the losers.

Matters had come to a head when early in July 2018, Mrs May invited the members of her cabinet to Chequers, the prime minister's country residence, in order to inform her colleagues about the advantages of her Brexit deal. Not impressed, Boris Johnson, her foreign secretary, who then resigned, said that she had wrapped the nation up in a suicide vest.

As opinions swung from those preferring a no deal to those wanting to re-negotiate the deal, which the European Commission were no longer prepared to do, and from those who wanted to accept Mrs May's terms in order to settle the argument, to others who wanted a second referendum, the country began a period of uncertainty not experienced since the 1940s. So while businesses were unable to make future decisions, the economy leaked an ever increasing amount of money.

Like a bird without a nest, although the PM, showing too much leg, and not enough feather, had failed on three occasions to get her mysterious 'deal' through parliament, her impatient electorate still failed to get her to fly away. It was true that she had shown courage and determination, but when she extended the leaving date of 29th March, set by her in concrete, many from her faltering party hoped that she would walk the plank and be done with it. Instead, while offering to resign if her deal was passed, but knowing that it never would be, she failed to do so until the very last moment with the European Commission still attempting to catch her.

Winston Churchill once said 'The problem with committing political suicide is that you live to regret it'. Mrs May had finally done so but her many months as PM had been such mayhem that neither she, nor her electorate, had any idea of who, if anyone, was going to regret it!

Donald J Trump. President of The United States of America
The White House, Washington, USA

December 2018

Dear President

I write to offer you my oil painting of the dramatic moment in your history when
The Mayflower, two months after sailing from Plymouth, first sighted Cape Cod
during a violent storm at dawn on 9 November 1620.

Formerly High Sheriff of Devon, I am an amateur marine artist and author of the
book 'The Story of the America's Cup', which is the only pictorial account of the
race from 1851 through to the present day. 'The America's Cup Collection' of 36
paintings is held in Connecticut, New England.

During September 2020, Great Britain will be celebrating the 400th anniversary of
The Mayflower leaving for America. How special it would be if you could be with
us in Plymouth. Or shall I present it to your Ambassador?

Yours sincerely

RR (Major. British Army retired). Enclosed - my first water colour impression.

Comment: Love him or hate him, Donald Trump was more important to Great Britain than ever; and opposition to previously planned visits was, to many people, unthinking and unwarranted. Although Trump had said that Mrs May's withdrawal agreement would make trading with the USA more difficult, by refuting his statement, she had left people wondering on what grounds she had done so, for it all remained as clear as mud.

I had impressed on the *Mayflower 400 committee* in Plymouth, that the President of the United States should be the first to be invited to attend their ceremonies, but they had looked at me as though I was demented. 'OK then' I had said 'I will ask him myself'. I had absolutely no authority to do so, but at least in my letter I had encouraged him to come. Although it was unlikely that he would do so just before the American elections, If he then decided to be with us in Plymouth, it was necessary to plan in advance for him and his entourage to stay in Devon, where there are some outstanding hotels, complete with lodges, ideal for his visit.

What a boost it would be to the seafaring county of Devon, I thought, and because the mission would be solely historical and not involving our capital city, I believed that it would also be peaceful.

The *Mayflower* - a square rigger of about a hundred feet in length, with 'castles' at each end to protect those on board from the worst of the elements - was typical of the merchant ships of the early seventeenth century. Manned by some thirty crew members, her captain and owner Christopher Jones had found his boat difficult to sail against wind and sea, causing the *Mayflower* to take more than two months to complete the voyage, compared with the record crossing by a yacht from east to west, now of less than eight days!

Conditions for the 102 passengers were cramped and uncomfortable as their quarters were situated on the gun deck in a space of only about 25 x 50 feet, with a five-foot high ceiling where the cannons could be run out through five gun ports situated on each side of the ship. The only access to the open air was by lifting a heavy grating followed by climbing a wooden ladder, or a rope, to reach the upper deck, which was difficult for those suffering from seasickness. Then in order to reach their belongings passengers had to crawl down to the deck directly underneath. Being just a cargo ship there were also no lavatory or washing facilities. The passengers therefore had to use buckets lashed to the beams so that they would not slop over.

During July 1620 a party of about sixty-five of the eventual number of passengers boarded the ship while anchored on the River Thames.

My water colour impression of the oil painting to come.

She then sailed to Southampton, where she met up with another smaller boat, the *Speedwell*, which had sailed *over* from Holland bringing the rest of the ships complement.

This consisted of Brownist Puritans, who, on separating from the Church of England, had left Great Britain in 1607 and become members of the Leiden congregation in the Netherlands. Ten years later, wishing to leave Holland but intent on escaping from further religious persecution and the volatile political environment pervading at that time in England, they had subsequently arranged with some English investors to secure a 'land patent' so that they could establish their own new colony in North America. They were not to be the first, however because in 1607 the Virginia Company had established a small colony at Jamestown.

The two boats, having set sail for America early that August, had soon to return to Dartmouth when the *Speedwell* sprung a leak, where she was quickly patched up. But, when they both arrived back in Plymouth her repairs were not considered good enough for completing their mission. So the *Mayflower*, now obliged to find extra room for about thirty-five stranded separatists, some of them farmers originally bound for the earlier British colony in Virginia, did not set sail, after a further month's delay, until the sixth of September 1620. The unfortunate delay then caused added discomfort when *Mayflower* faced rapidly worsening sea conditions caused by the autumn weather.

Although the *Mayflower* had not been the first ship to take settlers to America, her passengers - initially known as the Old Corners, then as the Forefathers and not until two centuries later as the Pilgrim Fathers - were to set up the first permanent settlement in America. The voyage had been a miserable one. Most passengers retired seasick immediately and remained in their bunks for most of the voyage until, after 64 days at sea, while running desperately short of food due to the earlier delays, a lookout at last sighted Cape Cod at dawn during a raging storm, on the ninth of November. At first, they tried to sail south to join up with the small number of British settlers still surviving in Virginia; but after a few days, they had to abandon the idea and returned back up the coast to drop anchor within the hook of Cape Cod, where they eventually landed with their pigs, goats and poultry.

But unprepared for the harsher weather conditions they were to find there, as they tried to establish a permanent base, thirty-one of the settlers had already died before The Plymouth Colony, as they were to call it, was completed early the following February. Their leaders then drafted a 200-word document enacted to claim possession of this small corner of the vast lands much later to be known as The United States of America.

LONG LIVE GREAT BRITAIN. LONG LIVE THE
UNITED STATES OF AMERICA.

PEN TO PAPER

My hundred letters are a few of those I have chosen from many that have never been answered. Some were written on headed notepaper but as the copies do not show my address, it avoided the risk of being savaged by a mad objector, or by people who know far more than I do, or by those who say I am writing balderdash. Nor do I wish to be sued for defamation of character, which I am still hoping to avoid. But because I have kept dated copies of all my important letters, cuttings and photographs, I have been able to write accurately with supporting illustrations, and explain my reasons for writing them in the first place.

Many consider letter writing to be an art, although I was never taught to write well or complete decent letters at school. So I have always kept my letters as short as possible and should I require an answer, I ask the question last before signing it.

So what happens next? Does letter writing in the accelerating world of social media and other electronic wizardry, just die a slow death, or go out of fashion much faster?

Will letters continue to be read or even glanced at, or are they already outmoded and just more paper to be chucked into the bin?

Perhaps too many think most letters are written in anger as a result of unwanted information, misinformation, or accusation, and that they are too permanent and often dangerous. But soon people may no longer know how to write or to answer letters preferring to use an iPhone, iPad or a computer. Without putting pen to paper many important moments not just in our own short lives but also in history, will vanish into the ether, leaving us only with a deep sense of regret.

If I only remembered things better
than things which I wish to forget.
If I only had written that letter and
my memory was not in a sweat.
If I only had switched off the router
and got the clutter out of my head.
If I only had dumped the computer
- and put my pen to paper instead.

RR

Giles (GR@GRSculpture.com) is a celebrated British sculptor specialising in creating sculptures with remarkable water effects. He designs and implements his sculptures worldwide in a variety of modern and historic locations. Built in England with specialist methods of fabrication, mostly using non-ferrous metals such as bronze, copper and stainless steel, they are designed to be robust and timeless.

Public Buildings

Arches. Muscat, Oman

Open Spaces

Blade. Southern Ireland

Universities / Schools

Aspiration. Illinois, USA

Mansions / Hotels

Coriolis. Cambridge, UK

Parks / Gardens

Whirlpool. New York, USA

Walls/Terraces

Fire Wall. London, UK

Lightning Source UK Ltd.
Milton Keynes UK
UKHW012126021119
352746UK00003B/22/P